Cassell Business Companions

ITALY

Karsta Neuhaus and Margret Haltern

In association with
The British Chambers of Commerce

CASSELL

Cassell Publishers Limited
Villiers House, 41/47 Strand
London WC2N 5JE, England

387 Park Avenue South
New York, NY 10016-8810
USA

ILT Verlag are grateful to Margherita von
Spreti for her translation.

ɩ

First published 1992

British Library Cataloguing in Publication Data
Neuhaus, Karsta
  Cassell Business Companions: Italy
  I. Title   II. Haltern, M.
  458.3421

  ISBN 0-304-33045-0

Typeset by Litho Link Limited, Welshpool, Powys, Wales
Printed and bound in Great Britain by Biddles Ltd, Guildford and
King's Lynn

CONTENTS

PART II

INTRODUCTION

The realization of the Single European Market on 1 January 1993 will increase competition among British firms for foreign markets. This means contacting potential business partners abroad initially by phone, fax, and letter, and following up with talks and negotiations face to face. The ability to speak to business people in their own language will have a major role in determining the success or otherwise of these undertakings.

Conventional phrasebooks are not specifically designed to meet these complex needs. *Cassell Business Companions: Italy* meets this challenge by providing a wide range of practical information in an easily accessible format, creating a guide which is both an invaluable aid to learning and an indispensable reference source. *Cassell Business Companions* are specifically tailored to meet the needs of small and medium-sized companies.

Part I sets out the essential technical vocabulary and standard phrases for use in different aspects of business with Italian companies: advertising; buying and selling; insurance; accounting; personnel; contracts, etc.

This section is not intended as a substitute for technical dictionaries, but rather as a useful aide-mémoire for the practised negotiator. It will be especially useful for those companies which do not have access to translation services or trained interpreters. The vocabulary lists are complemented by formulation aids and model letters which enable the user to communicate in both the spoken and written word with accuracy and confidence.

A unique dimension to *Cassell Business Companions* is the provision of many useful addresses which are an invaluable source of information for those conducting business abroad. Contact details for official or institutional agencies are given alongside the relevant vocabulary (with translations where appropriate).

Part II sets out the general language requirements and information on customs, travel, hotels and banks, etc, for anyone intending to visit Italy. A special section on Small Talk lists those expressions which so often prove essential in establishing initial contact and in the successful fostering of a business relationship. Helpful tips on Italian customs are also provided.

Part III comprises a generous compendium of data, including a glossary of Italian job titles, common abbreviations, useful key addresses for further research, as well as information on the Single European Market.

The Appendix incorporates a bilingual glossary of technical terms with their phonetic transcriptions. A comprehensive index facilitates the use of this wide-ranging guide to the essentials of doing business in Italian.

The authors would like to point out that there is often no precise translation of technical terms and phrases, but that every effort has been made to provide translations which convey the closest meaning possible. Every care has also been taken to ensure the accuracy of the addresses and telephone numbers listed, but these are subject to change, particularly phone numbers.

Finally, good luck, and we hope that you will enjoy using this guide.

Karsta Neuhaus and Margret Haltern
Bochum

Notes on Signs, Symbols and Abbreviations Used in the Text

▼ Formulation aids for spoken and written contexts

✉ Model letters

■ Information on Italy and its inhabitants

▶ Possible reactions from listeners

→ Useful UK addresses

m masculine noun

f feminine noun

pl plural noun

PART I

INTERNATIONAL AIRPORTS

TORINO
MILANO
VENEZIA
GENOVA
BOLOGNA
PISA
ROMA
NAPOLI
PALERMO
CATANIA.

1

Markets	Il Mercato
common market	mercato comune
to compete	concorrere, competere
competition	concorrenza, competitività
competitor	concorrente
distribution network	rete di distribuzione
domestic market	mercato nazionale
highly competitive market	mercato altamente competitivo
market analysis	analisi di mercato
market research	ricerca di mercato
market situation	situazione del mercato
market survey	indagine del mercato
marketing	marketing, distribuzione, vendita
monopoly	posizione di monopolio
price maintenance	mantenimento del prezzo di vendita
questionnaire	questionario
sales potential	potenziale di vendita
sales territory	zona di vendita
single European market	mercato unico europeo
trend	trend

▼
Our products sell well.
I nostri prodotti si vendono facilmente.

We are putting our products on the market.
Stiamo lanciando i nostri prodotti sul mercato.

We are launching a new product.
Presentiamo un nuovo prodotto sul mercato.

Information on trade or organizations can be obtained from:

Ente Nazionale Assistenza Agenti e
Representanti di Commercio
(National Organization for Business
Representatives)
Via A. Usodimare 29
00154 Roma
Tel: (06) 5793

Associazione Nazionale Agenti Generale
Assitalia/ANAGINA
(National Association of Trade
Representatives)
Via XX Settembre 5
00187 Roma
Tel: (06) 461268

British Government Trade Office
Massimo D'Azelio 60
10126 Torino
Tel: (011) 687932

British Chamber of Commerce
Via Agnello 8
20121 Milano
Tel: (02) 876981/877798

The following are the most important sources of statistical data:

ISTAT
Istituto Centrale di Statistica
(Central Office for Statistics)
Piazza Repubblica 22
20124 Milano
Tel: (02) 6595133

Statistical Office of the European
Community
Bureau B 389
Bâtiment Jean Monnet
rue Alcide de Gasperi
L-2920 Luxembourg
Tel: 010 352 43011
Telex: 3423 comeur lu

→1 Useful UK addresses can be found in Part III, 10.

2

Advertising	Pubblicità
advertisement	inserzione, annunzio
advertising agent, adman	agente pubblicitario
advertising gimmick, free gift	omaggio di pubblicità
brochure, leaflet	opuscolo
business reply card	cartolina con risposta pagata
catalogue	catalogo
circular	circolare
commercial	pubblicità (radio/televisione), trasmissione pubblicitaria
demonstration	presentazione
display material	materiale da esposizione
follow-up letter	lettera pubblicitaria susseguente
free sample	campione pubblicitario
handbill	volantino
in-depth knowledge of the trade	profonda conoscenza del settore
instructions, leaflet	foglio di istruzioni, volantino
mail-shot	spedizione postale cumulativa
poster	cartellone, affisso, poster
promotional letter	lettera pubblicitaria
prospectus, catalogue	prospetto
public relations	pubbliche relazioni, public relations
publicity agency	agenzia pubblicitaria
publicity campaign	campagna pubblicitaria
publicity expenditure	spese pubblicitarie
sales promotion	promozione delle vendite
show room	sala d'esposizione
training courses for salespersons	formazione per addetti alla vendita
trial sample	campione di saggio/di prova

▼
We specialize in . . .
Siamo specializzati in . . .

5

We trade/deal in . . .
Commerciamo/vendiamo . . .

We are well-known distributors.
Siamo noti quali distributori di . . .

We are market leaders in the domestic market.
Abbiamo una posizione leader sul mercato nazionale.

We are manufacturers of . . .
Siamo produttori di . . .

The new technology which we sell is very reliable.
Vendiamo nuove tecnologie di alta fiducia.

We are retailers/wholesalers/importers/exporters in the . . . trade.
**Siamo commercianti al minuto/all'ingrosso/importatori/
esportatori di . . .**

We know the market well.
Conosciamo bene il mercato.

We are a small/medium-sized firm.
Siamo una piccola/media impresa.

We are an international company in the . . . sector with annual
sales of . . . and a range of well-established speciality products,
many of which are market leaders.
**Siamo una ditta internazionale sul settore . . . con un fatturato
annuo di . . . ed un'ampia gamma di prodotti speciali avviati sul
mercato, di cui molti sonno in posizione leader.**

I'm in advertising.
Lavoro nell'ambito di pubblicità.

For promotional purposes.
A scopo promozionale.

Information may be obtained from:

> **Associazione Utenti Pubblicità Assoziati
>   (UPA)
> (Amalgamated Society of Advertisers)
> Via Larga 13
> 20122 Milano
> Tel: (02) 861951
> Telex: 322570 UPA I**

Associazione Nazionale Agenti di
  Pubblicità (ANAP)
(National Association of Advertising
  Agents)
Via M. Gonzaga 4
20123 Milano

→2 Useful UK addresses can be found in Part III, 10.

3

Fairs, Exhibitions	Fiere, Mostre, Esposizioni
application	istanza
conditions of participation	condizioni di partecipazione
exhibit	oggetto d'esposizione
exhibition centre	salone da esposizione
exhibition regulations	regolamento della fiera
exhibitor	espositore/espositrice
fair management	direzione della fiera
fair pass	tessera d'espositore
floor plan	pianta, piano generale
floor space	area d'esposizione, area di posteggio
hall plan	pianta della sala
hostess	hostess della fiera
industrial fair	fiera industriale
list of exhibitors	elenco degli espositori
organizer (of a fair)	organizzatore (della fiera)
specialized fair	fiera specializzata
stand rental	noleggio dello stand
stand, stall, booth	stand della fiera
trade fair	fiera commerciale
visitor at a fair	visitatore della fiera
to book exhibition space	noleggiare un'area dell'esposizione

to dismantle a stand	**smontare lo stand**
to exhibit, to show	**esporre**
to open a fair	**inaugurare una fiera**
to organize a fair	**organizzare una fiera**
to participate in a fair	**partecipare ad una fiera**
to put up a stand	**montare lo stand**
to visit a fair	**visitare una fiera**

I work for . . .
Lavoro per . . .

We make . . . and are interested in . . .
Produciamo . . . e siamo interessati di . . .

This is our latest model.
Questo è il nostro ultimo modello.

We've got some of our latest models here on our stand.
Vi presentiamo qui allo stand alcuni dei nostri ultimi modelli.

We are launching our product at this exhibition.
Introduciamo il prodotto in occasione della fiera.

We are introducing our product.
Presentiamo il prodotto.

I'm sure there's a lot we can offer you.
Sono sicuro di poterVi accontentare con la nostra offerta.

Most customers appreciate the quality of our products.
La maggior parte dei clienti apprezza la qualità dei nostri prodotti.

Information about trade fairs can be obtained from:

> **Comitato Fiere Industria, CFI**
> **(Committee of Trade Fairs)**
> **Via Mascheroni 19**
> **20145 Milano**
> **Tel: (02) 4693428/633**
> **Telex: 332113 Cofind I**

 Model Letter 2

4

Conferences and Meetings	**Conferenze e Sedute**
agenda	ordine del giorno
chairperson	presidente (*m, f*)
unanimous(ly)	unanime
to attend a conference	partecipare ad una conferenza
to bring forward a motion	presentare una mozione
to carry a motion	adottare una mozione
to clarify a position	chiarire una posizione
to close the meeting	chiudere una seduta
to constitute a quorum	raggiungere il quorum
to decide on a motion	prendere una decisione, riguardo a una mozione
to go into details	entrare in dettagli
to keep the minutes	redigere il verbale
to open a meeting	aprire una seduta
to outline, summarize	dare un sommario
to reject a motion	rifiutare una mozione
to vote for/against	votare per/contro

Some useful phrases:

Frankly, . . .	Francamente . . .
I am convinced that . . .	Sono convinto che . . .
I don't think so	Non credo
I quite agree	Sono della stessa opinione
I think so	Credo/penso
I'm afraid I couldn't go along with that	Non condivido affatto questa opinione
I'm afraid I don't agree	Non condivido la Sua opinione
In my experience	Secondo la mia esperienza

9

May I bring up the question of . . .	**Vorrei discutere del problema . . .**
On the contrary	**Anzi/al contrario**
On the one hand . . . on the other hand	**Da un lato . . . dall'altro, dipende**
That's an important point	**Questo è un punto rilevante**
The main problem is . . .	**Il problema principale è . . .**
The pros and cons	**Il pro e il contro**
This sort of thing is in my line	**Questo fa parte del mio campo**
To start with . . .	**Per cominciare . . .**
To sum up, I can say that . . .	**Riassumendo si può dire . . .**
Well, it depends	**Dipende**
What do you think?	**Che cosa ne pensa?**
What's your opinion?	**Qual è la Sua opinione?**

Conference centres:

**Centro Congressi Milanofieri
(Congress Centre for Milan Fairs)
Palazzo Congressi
CAP 20094
Tel: (02) 284791/825976
Telex: 352009**

**Centro Congressi, Centro Traduzioni e
Servizi di Congresso
(Translation and Congress Services – at the
Congress Centre)
Via Sallustioni 23
00187 Roma
Tel: (06) 485990/465392**

**Centro Congressi Internazionale
(International Congress Centre)
Corso Tassoni 32
10143 Torino
Tel: (011) 740625/761870**

Information on Italian conferences can be obtained through:

> **ITALCONGRESSI**
> **Casella Postale 6254**
> **00195 Roma**
> **Tel: (06) 352558**

→3 Useful UK addresses can be found in Part III, 10.

5

Product Descriptions	Descrizione dei Prodotti
a limited number of	un numero limitato di
a wide range of	una grande scelta di
bulk goods	merci alla rinfusa
capital goods	beni strumentali
commodities, goods, merchandise	merci, merce, mercanzia
consumer goods	beni di consumo
finished products	prodotti finiti
item	voce, articolo
label	etichetta
mass production	produzione in serie
model, specimen, sample	modello, campione
one-off production	produzione singola
operating instructions	istruzioni per il funzionamento
pattern	stampo
product liability	responsabilità per il prodotto
quantity	quantità
raw materials	materie prime
sample	campione, provino
sample collection	campionario
sample of no commercial value	campione senza valore
semi-finished goods	prodotti semilavorati
shortage	quantità mancante
special design	produzione fuori serie

Some classifications:

blend (coffee, tea)	**miscela (caffè, tè)**
brand	**marchio**
grade	**qualità, classe, categoria, grado**
quality	**qualità**
– commercial quality	**– qualità d'uso commerciale**
– fair average quality (f.a.q.)	**– qualità buona media**
– first-class quality	**– di prima qualità**
– outstanding quality	**– di primissima qualità**
– poor quality	**– scadente qualità**
– second-rate quality	**– di seconda qualità**
– standard quality	**– qualità corrente**
registered trade mark	**marchio registrato**
size	**misura**

You inform your customer:

Our product . . .	**Il nostro prodotto . . .**
. . . conforms with the safety regulations	**. . . corrisponde alle norme di sicurezza**
. . . is made to the highest technical standards	**corrisponde al più alto standard tecnico**
. . . is carefully manufactured	**. . . viene confezionato con la massima cura**
. . . is maintenance-free	**. . . esente di manutenzione**
. . . is reliable	**. . . fidato**
. . . can be fully adapted to/is compatible with all XY systems	**. . . adattabile a tutti i sistemi XY**
. . . is easy and safe	**. . . semplice e sicuro**
. . . to handle, to operate	**. . . nell'uso**
. . . to assemble	**. . . nel montaggio**
. . . to repair	**. . . in caso di guasto**

This is what you might hear in Italian:

C'è un periodo di garanzia?
Does it come with a guarantee?

Assumiamo una garanzia per la durata di due anni.
The guarantee lasts for two years.

Il periodo di garanzia è passato.
The guarantee has run out.

È facile da usare?
Is it user-friendly?

Mi potreste spiegare come funziona?
Could you explain how it works, please?

6

Buying, Selling	Acquisti, Vendite
accepted in the trade	d'uso commerciale
buyer	acquirente, compratore
commission agent	commissionario, intermediario
customer	cliente
dealer, broker	commerciante su commissione
distribution network	rete di distribuzione
exporter	esportatore/trice
franchised dealer	concessionario
hire-purchase	acquisto a rate
importer	importatore
profit margin	margine degli utili
purchase	acquisto, compera, compra
purchasing power	potere d'acquisto
representative, agent	rappresentante, agente
retailer	commerciante al minuto
sales	vendite
sales on commission	vendita su base di commissione
seller	venditore
supplier	fornitore/trice

trade	commercio
trade custom	uso commerciale
trade mark-up	margine di commercio
trade relations	relazioni commerciali
trader, dealer, merchant	commerciante
turnover	giro d'affari, fatturato
wholesaler	grossista, commerciante all'ingrosso
to bargain	mercanteggiare
to buy, to purchase	acquistare, comprare
– to buy at best price	– alle migliori condizioni
– to buy secondhand	– di seconda mano
to find a ready market	vendere facilmente
to lease, to rent	prendere in affitto, dare in affitto
to sell	vendere
– to sell at a loss	– vendere in perdita
– to sell direct	– vendita diretta
– to sell off	–svendere (svuotare il magazzino)
to trade	commerciare
to trade in	dare in pagamento

▼
Sales are up by 10%.
La vendita è aumentata del 10%.

On a sale or return basis.
vendita con diritto di restituzione.

The goods are out of stock.
La merce è esaurita.

You may hear the following in Italian:

vendita sul mercato interno
domestic market

vendita per esportazione
export sales

aumento/regresso delle vendite
increase/decrease in sales

Istituto Nazionale per il Commercio Estero
– ICE
(National Institute for Foreign Trade)
Via Liszt 21
00100 Roma
Tel: (06) 59921
Telex: 610160/612282 ICERM 1

Associazioni delle Camere di Comercio
  Italiano all' Estero
(Association of Italian Chambers of
  Commerce Abroad)
Piazza Sallustio 21
00187 Roma
Tel: (06) 4743488/4750854
Telex: 622327 Unicam I

Ufficio Promozione Estera, Camera di
  Commercio Industria Artigianato e
  Agricultura di Milano
(Office for the Promotion of Foreign Trade
  at the Chamber of Industry, Crafts and
  Agriculture, Milan)
Via Asperto 5
20123 Milano
Tel: (02) 85155248
Telex: 312481 Comcam

Direzione Generale delle Importazioni e
  delle Esportazioni
(Central Office for Imports and Exports)
Viale America 341
00144 Roma
Tel: (06) 5993

Confederazione Italiana della Piccola e
  Media Industria, CONFAPI
(Italian Confederation of Small and
  Medium-Sized Industry)
Via della Colonna Antonina 52
00186 Roma
Tel: (06) 6782441 . . 2/6795406

Confederazione Generale dell'Industria
Italiana, Confindustria
(General Confederation of Italian Industry)
Viale dell'Astronomia 30
00144 Roma
Tel: (06) 59031
Telex: 613230 CONFIN 1

→**4** Useful UK addresses can be found in Part III, 10.

7

Inquiries, Offers, Prices	Richieste, Offerte, Prezzi
buying conditions	condizioni di acquisto
detailed information about	informazioni dettagliate su
latest catalogue	catalogo di data recentissima
list of products	elenco della merce
price list	listino dei prezzi
references	referenze
selection of samples	campionario
selling conditions	condizioni di vendita
specification	elenco dettagliato, specificazione
terms	condizioni
to be interested in	avere interesse in
to inform	informare
to refer to	rivolgersi a
estimate	preventivo di spesa, valutazione
offer, proposal	offerta
– bid	– offerta d'acquisto
– binding offer	– offerta vincolante
– offer subject to confirmation	– offerta senza impegno
– quote	– quotazione prezzo corrente

– written offer	– offerta scritta
pro-forma invoice	fattura proforma
tender	offerta d'appalto
to accept an offer	accettare un'offerta
to make a firm offer	offrire a prezzo e condizioni fissi
to offer subject to confirmation	offrire salvo approvazione
to revoke an offer	revocare un'offerta
to submit an offer	presentare un'offerta
all-in price	prezzo complessivo
at half price	a metà di prezzo
buying price	prezzo di acquisto
competitive price	prezzo competitivo
consumer price	prezzo al consumo
fair price	prezzo ragionevole
favourable price	prezzo favorevole
fixed price	prezzo fisso
list price	prezzo di listino
lump sum	somma forfettaria
manufacturer's/factory price	prezzo alla produzione
price reduction	riduzione di prezzo
price increase	aumento dei prezzi
retail price	prezzo al minuto
selling price	prezzo di vendita
special price	prezzo speciale
subscription cost	prezzo di sottoscrizione
surcharge	maggiorazione del prezzo
unit price	prezzo unitario
wholesale price	prezzo all'ingrosso
to adjust prices	equiparare i prezzi
to quote prices	quotare prezzi
to undercut	offrire a minor prezzi
cash discount	sconto per contanti, sconto di cassa
discount	sconto, ribasso
quantity discount	sconto di quantità
special discount	sconto speciale
trade discount	sconto commerciale

We see from your advertisement in . . . that you are producers of . . .
Apprendiamo dal Vs. annuncio che siete produttori di . . .

We have heard of your products.
Abbiamo sentito dei Vs. prodotti.

Your name was given to us by . . .
Abbiamo il Vs. nominativo da . . .

We saw your stand at the Hanover Fair.
Abbiamo visto il Vs. stand alla Fiera di Hannover.

We would like to have further details about . . .
Desideriamo ulteriori ragguagli su . . .

We require for immediate delivery . . .
Ci occorre una consegna immediata . . .

We are in the market for . . . / we require . . .
Abbiamo un fabbisogno di . . . /abbiamo bisogno di . . .

Would you please quote your best price and terms of payment.
Vi preghiamo comunicarci il Vs. miglior prezzo nonchè le condizioni di pagamento.

Full information regarding export prices and discounts for regular orders would be appreciated.
Vi preghiamo comunicarci dettagliate informazioni sui prezzi di esportazione e sui ribassi rispetto ordinazioni ripetute.

We are prepared to place a trial order.
Siamo pronti a passare un'ordinazione di prova.

Please find enclosed our price list, as requested.
Come richiesto trovate in allegato un listino prezzi.

We are sending you our illustrated catalogue under separate cover.
Separatamente Vi inviamo il nostro catalogo illustrato.

We can make a firm offer for . . .
Vi possiamo fare un'offerta ferma per . . .

Our offer is firm subject to acceptance by . . .
La nostra offerta è ferma se accettata entro . . .

We give a trade discount of 20% on our catalogue prices.
Vi facciamo uno sconto del 20% sui nostri prezzi di listino.

Packing included
Imballaggio incluso

The price quoted is fob . . .
Prezzo FOB da . . .

Recommended price
Prezzo indicativo senza impegno

No extra charge
Senza maggiorazione prezzo

Prices are subject to change without notice
Ci riserviamo il diritto di una modifica dei prezzi

Subject to prior sale
Offerta salvo venduto

Prices are subject to revision according to the following sliding scale:
I prezzi sono soggetti a modifica secondo clausola della scala mobile:

You have our assurance that your order will be carried out to your complete satisfaction.
Vi assicuriamo di eseguire l'ordinazione a Vs. piena soddisfazione.

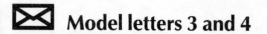 **Model letters 3 and 4**

8

Orders and Acknowledgement of the Order

Ordinazioni e Conferma dell'Ordine

acknowledgement of order	**conferma dell'ordine**
advance order	**ordine anticipato**
initial order	**prima ordinazione**
order	**ordine, ordinazione**
order book	**libro delle commissioni**
order form	**modulo d'ordinazione, cedola di commissione**
order number	**numero d'ordine**
orders on hand	**ordinazioni a disposizione**
repeat order	**ordine susseguente**
to enter/book an order	**prenotare un'ordinazione**
to carry out an order	**eseguire un'ordine**
to place an order	**dare un'ordinazione, commissionare**
as per your order/in accordance with your order	**come da Vs. ordinazione/in conformità a Vs. ordinazione**

▼
We thank you for your quote and have pleasure in placing our order for . . .
Vi ringraziamo dell'offerta e siamo felici poterVi passare il seguente ordine . . .

Kindly supply the following goods at your earliest convenience.
Vi preghiamo di provvedere ad una sollecita consegna della seguente merce.

The delivery dates stipulated in our order must be strictly adhered to.
Il termine di consegna indicato nella nosta ordinazione va rispettato rigorosamente.

Your careful attention to our instructions would be appreciated.
Vi preghiamo di voler gentilmente osservare le nostre direttive.

This order is subject to our General Terms and Conditions.
Quest'ordine è soggetto alle nostre Condizioni Generali.

Please confirm this order in due course.
Vi preghiamo di confermare il presente ordine in debito tempo.

We acknowledge receipt of your order for . . .
Confermiamo la ricevuta della Vs. ordinazione per . . .

The order will be carried out in accordance with your instructions.
Eseguiremo l'ordinazione secondo le Vs. istruzioni in merito.

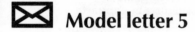 **Model letter 5**

9

Sales Contract	Contratto d'Acquisto
agreement	accordo
commercial settlement of a dispute	composizione d'una lite
contract clause	clausola contrattuale
contract of sale	contratto di vendita
contracting parties	parti contraenti
deadlines	limite determinato per prestazioni
dispute	lite, causa
fulfilment of contract	adempimento del contratto
guarantee, warrant	garanzia, mandato
hire-purchase	acquisto a rate
maturity date of contract	data di scadenza del contratto
penalties	pena convenzionale
period of contract	durata di un contratto
sale on trial	acquisto a prova

sale or return	**vendita con patto di riscatto**
terms of contract	**condizioni di contratto**
as per contract . . .	**conforme a contratto . . .**
the contract expires . . .	**il contratto scade . . .**
the contract is null and void	**il contratto è nullo e senza effetto**
to adhere to the terms of the contract	**obbligarsi per contratto**
to amend a contract	**modificare un contratto**
to cancel a contract	**stornare/disdire un contratto**
to certify a contract	**vidimare/legalizzare un contratto**
to contract/to enter into a contract	**stipulare un contratto**
to extend a contract	**prolungare un contratto**
to negotiate the conditions of a contract	**negoziare le condizioni di un contratto**

▼
We reserve title to the goods delivered, pending payment in full.
La merce rimane di nostra proprietà fino a pagamento effettuato.

In the event of litigation, the courts in London shall have exclusive jurisdiction.
Nel caso di processo, le corti di Londra avranno autorità esclusiva.

This is what you might read in Italian:

Vi offriamo il diritto di prelazione.
We will give you first option.

Lavoriamo al 10%.
We work on 10%.

Contacts with Italian solicitors and specialized lawyers can be made through:

Assoziazione Nazionale de Avocadi e
   Procuratori
(National Association of Lawyers and
   Public Prosecutors)
Piazza d'Horologio 12
00186 Roma
Tel: (06) 6869780

10

Production	Produzione
after-sales/customer service	assistenza post-vendita
assembly	montaggio
assembly instructions	istruzioni per il montaggio
assembly line	catena di montaggio
direct labour	manodopera diretta
engineering	progettazioni tecniche
industrial plant	impresa industriale
industrial production	produzione industriale
industrial standard	standard industriale
machine shop/workshop	officina meccanica
maintenance contract	contratto di manutenzione
mass production	produzione in serie
one-off production	produzione singola
operations programme	programma operativo
output	output, rendimento, produzione
production	produzione
production period	periodo di produzione
production programme	programma produttivo
production schedule	programma di fabbricazione
quality control	controllo della qualità
service	servizio
service manual	istruzioni di manutenzione
subcontractor	subappaltatore
tool	attrezzo, utensile
workshop	officina, officina meccanica

| to make, to produce, to manufacture | **produrre, fabbricare** |
| to streamline (production) | **rendere più efficiente** |

11

Storage | Magazzinaggio

stock	**scorte**
stock clerk, warehouseman	**magazziniere**
stock control	**controllo delle scorte**
stock rotation	**rotazione delle scorte**
warehouse	**magazzino**
– bonded warehouse	**– magazzino doganale**
warehouse company	**società magazzini generali**
to have in stock	**avere in magazzino**
to store, to stock	**immagazzinare**
to take stock	**fare l'inventario**

Our stock is running short.
Il nostro stock è quasi esaurito.

12

Packing and Marking | Imballaggio e Marcatura

export packing	**imballaggio per esportazione**
package	**collo**
packaging	**imballaggio**
packing	**imballaggio**

packing at cost price	**imballaggio al prezzo di costo**
packing list	**distinta pesi**
seaworthy packing	**imballaggio per trasporto marittimo**
special packing	**imballaggio speciale**
wrapping	**imballaggio**
gross weight	**peso lordo**
net weight	**peso netto**
tare	**tara**
barrel	**botte, barile**
can, metal container	**scatola**
cardboard box, carton	**cartone**
case	**scatola**
container	**container, contenitore**
crate	**cassa da imballaggio, crate**
pallet	**pallet**
returnable container	**recipienti a rendere**
sack, bag	**sacco**
skid (rollers)	**slittamento**

Shipping marks: ## Marcatura di spedizione:

made in . . . /country of origin	**paese d'origine**
marks	**breve distinzione destinatario**
order no.	**numero ordinazione**
package numbers	**colli contrassegnati con numeri**
port of destination	**porto destinazione**
weight and measurements	**peso e misure**

Caution marks: ## Marcatura per particolare precauzione:

Bottom	**Lato Inferiore**
Flammable	**Infiammabile**
Glass – Fragile	**Vetro – Fragile**
Handle with Care	**Attenzione**
Keep Dry	**Tenere al Secco**
Keep Cool	**Tenere al Fresco**
Lift Here	**Sollevare da Questo Lato**

Poison	**Veleno, Tossico**
Radioactive	**Radioattivo**
Store away from heat	**Evitare il calore**
Top	**Lato superiore/Sopra**
Use No Hooks	**Non Usare Ganci**

13

Transport and Delivery	**Trasporto e Consegna**
air cargo, air freight	carico aereo
Bill of Lading (B/L)	polizza di carico marittimo (not often used), **Bill of Lading**
– non-negotiable (n.n.) copy	– copia non negoziabile
bulk haulage	trasporto alla rinfusa
carriage	trasporto merci, carreggio, rimozione
Community Transport Procedure (CTP)	procedimento comune di spedizione (CTP)
consignee	destinatario/a, consegnatario/a
consignment, shipment	spedizione, consegna
consignor, shipper	mittente
country of destination	paese di destinazione
date of shipment	data di spedizione
deadline	termine ultimo
delivery note	bolla di consegna
dispatch department	reparto spedizione
dispatch note	avviso di spedizione
forwarder, carrier	spedizioniere
freight, cargo, carriage	trasporto
freight/forwarding charges	spese di nolo
freight rate	rata di nolo
– freight collect	– nolo assegno

– freight included	– nolo incluso
long haul	traffico merci a lunga distanza
lot	partita di merci
notifying address	indirizzo d'avviso
piggyback (combined road and rail service)	traffico combinato strada-rotaia
place of destination	luogo di destinazione
place of dispatch	luogo di spedizione
roll-on/roll-off service	servizio roll-on/roll-off
shipping documents	documenti di spedizione
– air waybill	– polizza di carico aereo (not often used), air waybill
– consignment note, waybill	– lettera di vettura
– duplicate consignment note	– duplicato lettera di vettura
– FIATA combined Transport Bill of Lading	– FIATA combined transport B/L (for container shipment)
– Forwarding Agent's Certificate of Receipt (FCR)	– certificato di accettazione dello spedizioniere (FCR)
– railway consignment note	– lettera di vettura ferroviaria
short haul load	traffico merci a breve distanza
suppliers, contractors	ditta fornitrice
supply contract	contratto di consegna
transport	trasporto
– air transport	– trasporto aereo
– rail transport	– trasporto ferroviario
– road transport	– trasporto su strada
water transport	– trasporto fluviale/marittimo
transshipment, reloading	trasbordo
to deliver	recapitare, consegnare
to deliver within the specified time	consegnare entro il termine previsto
to dispatch, to send off	inviare, spedire
to effect delivery	eseguire una consegna
to load, to unload	caricare, scaricare
to ship, to forward	inviare, spedire
to specify the delivery route	specificare la via di spedizione
to supply, to furnish a customer with goods	consegnare, fornire un cliente con merci
in transit	in transito
via (Dover)	via (Dover)

The delivery can be effected, e.g.:

free of charge	franco a domicilio
freight prepaid	franco di porto
freight forward	nolo pagato a destinazione
ex-warehouse	ex magazzino

Incoterms:

International Commercial Terms are a set of international rules for the interpretation of trade terms, published as ICC Publication Number 460, 1990 edition, by:

ICC Publishing SA
International Chamber of Commerce
38 cours Albert 1er
75008 Paris

Incoterms 1990

EXW	Ex works (. . . named place)	**EXW**	**Franco fabbrica (. . . luogo convenuto)**
FCA	Free Carrier (. . . named place)	**FCA**	**Franco vettore (. . . luogo convenuto)**
FAS	Free alongside ship (. . . named port of shipment)	**FAS**	**Franco lungo bordo (. . . porto di imbarco convenuto)**
FOB	Free on board (. . . named port of shipment	**FOB**	**Franco a Bordo (. . . porto di imbarco convenuto)**
CFR	Cost and freight (. . . named port of destination)	**CRF**	**Costo e nolo (. . . porto di destinazione convenuto)**
CIF	Cost, insurance and freight (. . . named port of destination)	**CIF**	**Costo, assicurazione e nolo (. . . porto di destinazione convenuto)**
CPT	Carriage paid to (. . . named place of destination)	**CPT**	**Trasporto pagato fino a (. . . luogo di destinazione convenuto)**

CIP	Carriage and insurance paid to	CIP	**Trasporto e assicurazione pagati fino a**
	(. . . named place of destination)		**(. . . luogo di destinazione convenuto)**
DAF	Delivered at frontier	DAF	**Reso frontiera**
	(. . . named place)		**(. . . luogo convenuto)**
DES	Delivered ex ship	DES	**Reso ex ship**
	(. . . named port of destination)		**(. . . porto di destinazione convenuto)**
DEQ	Delivered ex quay (duty paid)	DEQ	**Reso banchina (sdoganato)**
	(. . . named port of destination)		**(. . . porto di destinazione convenuto)**
DDU	Delivered duty unpaid	DDU	**Reso non sdoganato**
	(. . . named place of destination)		**(. . . luogo di destinazione convenuto)**
DDP	Delivered duty paid	DDP	**Reso sdoganato**
	(. . . named place of destination)		**(. . . luogo di destinazione convenuto)**

▼

Delivery can be effected at the earliest possible date.
La consegna potrà essere effettuata al più presto.

Delivery immediately after receipt of order.
La consegna verrà effettuata non appena ricevuta l'ordinazione.

We forwarded today by order and for account of . . .
Vi abbiamo spedito in data odierna per ordine e su fattura . . .

We inform you that the goods have been dispatched by rail today.
Vi comunichiamo che la merce è stata spedita oggi a mezzo ferrovia.

We hope that the consignment will reach you safely.
Speriamo che la consegna Vi giunga senza alcun danno.

Federazione Nationale Imprese Trasporti,
  FENIT
(National Association of Forwarding
  Agents)
Via in Lucina 17
00186 Roma
Tel. (06) 6871551

Confederazione Generale de Traffico e dei
  Trasporti
(General Association for Traffic and
  Transport)
Via Panama 62
00198 Roma
Tel. (06) 869151

→5 Useful UK addresses can be found in Part III, 10.

14

Complaints	Reclami
adjustment, to settle a claim	equiparazione, regolare il reclamo
circumstances beyond our control	circostanze imprevedibili
claim	domanda, diritto
compensation	risarcimento danni, indennizzo
complaint	reclamo
defect	difetto, guasto
defective goods	merce difettosa
delay	ritardo
fault	errore, sbaglio
faulty material	materiale difettoso
hidden defect	difetto nascosto
non-conformity with sample	non conformità al campione
poor quality	scadente qualità

replacement	fornitura di ricambio
substitute	consegna sostituita
well-founded complaint	reclamo fondato/giustificato
to allow a claim	riconoscere un reclamo
to compensate	risarcire, indennizzare
to complain about	lamentarsi di
to demand compensation, to claim damages	chiedere un indennizzo
to exchange the goods	cambiare la merce
to grant an allowance	concedere/fare uno sconto
to refund	rifondere, rimborsare
to refuse a claim	rifiutare un reclamo
to take the goods back	riprendere la merce

When dealing with this subject *orally*, you could begin as follows:

▼

I don't like to complain, but I have had a lot of trouble with . . .
Non mi lamento volentieri, ma ho avuto un sacco di grattacapi per via di . . .

I'm sorry, but I'm not at all satisfied with . . .
Purtroppo non sono affatto soddisfatto di . . .

I'm very annoyed about . . .
Sono assai seccato di . . .

I'm not the sort of person who normally complains, but . . .
Normalmente non mi lamento, ma in questo caso . . .

I'm disappointed with . . .
Sono deluso di . . .

I'm so sorry to hear . . .
Sono spiacente sentire . . .

I'm sorry about this, it's our fault.
Mi rincresce, è colpa nostra.

I'll look into the matter immediately.
Mi interesserò immediatemente della cosa.

I'll find out what happened.
Vedrò come sia potuto accadere.

Can I see the guarantee?
Posso vedere il certificato di garanzia?

The following phrases are used for written complaints.

▼

We are sorry to inform you . . .
Purtroppo dobbiamo comunicarVi che . . .

We are disappointed with the execution of our order.
La consegna ha deluso le nostre aspettative.

On checking the items we noticed . . .
Esaminando i singoli articoli ci siamo accorti che . . .

The quality of the goods does not correspond with that of the sample.
La qualità della Vs. merce non corrisponde ai campioni.

The goods were damaged in transit.
La merce ha subito danni durante il trasporto.

The damage seems to have been caused by inadequate packing.
Il danno è dovuto ovviamente ad un imballaggio non accurato.

We were promised delivery by the end of month.
La consegna ci è stata confermata per la fine del mese.

We are placing the defective goods at your disposal.
Vi mettiamo a disposizione la merce danneggiata.

Please send us replacements for the damaged goods.
Vi preghiamo di sostituirci la merce danneggiata.

We must apologize for not having dispatched the goods in time.
Ci scusiamo di non avere provveduto a spedire la merce in tempo debito.

We regret not having carried out your order properly.
Siamo spiacenti di non avere eseguito l'ordine a Vs. piena soddisfazione.

A new consignment has been sent off to you today.
Vi abbiamo spedito in data odierna della nuova merce.

Please return the goods at our expense.
Rinviate la merce a nostre spese.

We will take all possible steps to ensure that such a mistake does not occur again.
Faremo il possibile affinchè questo non succeda più.

Please accept our apologies for the trouble caused.
Ci scusiamo per gli inconvenienti causati.

We regret to inform you that we cannot assume any liability.
Ci rincresce comunicarVi che non possiamo assumerci nessuna responsabilità.

 Model letters 6, 7 and 8

15

Insurance	Assicurazione
beneficiary	**beneficario**
claim	**reclamo, indennizzo, sinistro**
cover	**copertura**
credit insurance	**assicurazione di crediti**
damage	**danno**
insurance	**assicurazione**
insurance certificate	**certificato d'assicurazione**
insurance company	**compagnia di assicurazioni**
insurance policy	**polizza di assicurazione**
insurance against loss on the exchange rate	**assicurazione contro le perdite sul cambio**
liability	**responsabilità**
policy holder	**titolare d'una polizza, assicurato**
premium	**premio**

transportation insurance	**assicurazione trasporto**
third-party insurance	**assicurazione di responsabilità civile**
underwriter	**assicuratore**
to cover a risk	**coprire un rischio**
to settle a claim	**regolare un reclamo**
to take out insurance	**stipulare un'assicurazione**
to underwrite a risk	**assicurare contro il rischio**

International insurance is frequently taken out under the terms of: Institute Cargo Clauses, e.g.:

Clause A	full cover/all risks
Clause B	stranding cover

> **Associazione Nazionale fra le Imprese Assicuratrici, ANIA**
> **(National Association of Insurance Companies)**
> **Via della Frezza 70**
> **00186 Roma**
> **Tel: (06) 6782941**
>
> **Piazza S. Babila 1**
> **20122 Milano**
> **Tel: (02) 77641**
> **Fax: (02) 780870**
> **Telex: 333288**

→6 Useful UK addresses can be found in Part III, 10.

16

Invoicing and Payment	**Fatture e Pagamento**
advance payment	**pagamento anticipato**
commercial invoice	**fattura commerciale**

consular invoice	**fattura consolare**
date of invoice	**data della fattura**
down-payment	**acconto**
invoice	**fattura**
invoice amount	**importo/somma della fattura**
invoice number	**numero della fattura**
item	**articolo, voce**
part payment	**pagamento parziale**
payment of the balance	**pagamento restante**
payment on account	**acconto**
payment, settlement	**pagamento**
remittance	**rimessa**
statement of account	**estratto conto**
terms of payment	**condizioni di pagamento**
total (sum) amounting to £/L	**somma totale per un ammontare di £/L**
as per invoice	**conforme a fattura**
brought forward (b/f)	**riporto**
E & OE (errors and omissions excepted)	**SE & O (salvo errori ed omissioni)**

Some usual terms of payment:

3% discount for cash	**in contanti 3% sconto**
3 months' credit	**netto a tre mesi**
2% discount for payment within 10 days (10 days, 2%)	**2% di sconto per pagamento entro 10 giorni**
30 days net	**netto per pagamento entro 30 giorni**
cash with order (CWO)	**pagamento all'ordinazione**
cash on delivery (COD)	**pagamento alla consegna**
cash against documents (CAD), documents against payment (D/P)	**pagamento contro documenti**
documents against acceptance (D/A)	**documenti contro accettazione**

payment against bank guarantee	**pagamento contro garanzia bancaria**
payment by acceptance	**pagamento a mezzo accettazione**
payment by cheque	**pagamento mediante assegno**
payment by irrevocable, confirmed documentary letter of credit (L/C)	**pagamento a mezzo credito documentario confermato e irrevocabile**
payment by sight draft	**pagamento a mezzo tratta a vista**
payment on receipt of goods (ROG)	**pagamento al recapito della merce**

The Credito Documentario (Documentary Letter of Credit) has an important role in exports: as a method of payment it protects both buyer and seller. Payment under a confirmed irrevocable L/C is the safest method of payment in foreign trade.

Normally the following shipping documents have to be presented under the terms of the credit:

freight/consignment note	**lettera di vettura**
commercial invoice	**fattura commerciale**
bill of lading	**polizza di carico (B/L)**
air waybill	**lettera di trasporto aereo**
certificate of origin	**certificato d'origine**
insurance certificate	**certificato d'assicurazione**

The International Chamber of Commerce, Paris, has published sets of rules governing documentary credits. The guidelines, *Uniform Customs and Practice for Documentary Credits, 1983 Revision*, are used by the banks and banking associations of virtually every country and territory in the world.

to balance an account	**pareggiare un conto**
to charge	**fatturare, addebitare**
to credit	**accreditare**
to draw a cheque	**emettere un assegno**
to invoice, to bill	**emettere una fattura, fatturare**

to pay, to make payment, to effect payment	**pagare**
to pay on the due date	**pagare a scadenza**
to pay cash	**pagare in contanti**
to pay in advance	**pagare in anticipo**
to pay under reserve	**pagare con diritto di riserva**
to remit	**inviare, rimettere**
to transfer	**trasferire**
without charge	**senza addebitamento**

▼

Please remit the sum of £ . . .
Vi preghiamo di versare l'ammontare di £ . . .

I have an account with XY Bank.
Ho il mio conto presso la banca XY.

We transferred £ . . . to your account yesterday.
Abbiamo versato ieri sul Vs. conto £ . . .

The amount of £ . . . will be paid to your account with XY Bank.
L'importo di . . . verrà versato sul Vs. conto presso la Banca XY.

We have drawn a cheque for L . . . on XY Bank.
Abbiamo emesso un assegno per l'ammontare di L . . . intestato alla Banca XY.

We have accepted your draft and will honour it at maturity/when it is due.
Abbiamo accettato la Vs. tratta che riscuoteremo al momento della scadenza.

Please credit this amount to our account.
Vi preghiamo di accreditarci detto importo.

We enclose a cheque covering your invoice no . . .
Per pareggiare la Vs. fattura No . . . Via accludiamo un assegno.

Please send us an official receipt.
Vi preghiamo di confermarci ricevuta.

Classification of Italy's credit institutions:

THE CENTRAL BANK
— Banca d'Italia
— Ufficio Italiano dei Cambi (UIC) (Italian Exchange Control Office)

THE BANKING SYSTEM
— Banks (Short-term Credit Institutions)

> — Public charter banks:
> (Banca Nazionale del Lavoro, Banco di
> Napoli, Banco di Sardegna, Banco di
> Sicilia, Istituto Bancario S. Paolo di
> Torino, Banca Nazionale delle
> Comunicazioni and Monte dei Paschi di
> Siena)
>
> — Banks of national interest:
> (Banca Commerciale Italiana, Banco di
> Roma and Credito Italiano)
>
> — Ordinary banks
> — Branches of foreign banks
> — Co-operative banks
> — Savings and pledge banks
> — Rural and artisan banks
> — Central credit institutions

— Special Credit Institutions

> — Industrial credit institutions and
> departments
> — Public works credit departments
> — Housing credit institutions and
> departments
> — Agricultural credit institutions and
> departments

The banks carry out short-term business, while the special credit institutions' activities are in the medium- to long-term sector.

Banking association:

> **Associazione Bancaria Italiana**
> **(Association of Italian Banks)**
> **Piazza del Gesù**
> **00186 Roma**
> **Tel: (06) 67671**

 Model letters 9 and 10

17

Outstanding Accounts	**Crediti in Pendenza**
additional period of time	**periodo addizionale**
amount overdue	**importo in sofferenza**
arrears	**arretrati**
assignment of a debt	**cessione di crediti**
bill overdue	**cambiale in sofferenza**
collection agency	**ufficio di incasso**
debt	**credito, debitto**
– bad debt	**– credito inesigibile**
– doubtful debt	**– credito di dubbia esazione**
default interest	**interesse di mora**
due date	**scadenza, data di rimborso**
dunning/reminder letter	**lettera di sollecitazione**
extension	**proroga**
factoring	**factoring**
outstanding accounts	**crediti pendenti**
overdue/unpaid	**in sofferenza, scaduto**
payee	**beneficiario/a**
period of limitation	**prescrizione contrattuale**
prolongation (cheque)	**proroga**

recourse	**regresso**
reminder	**lettera di sollecitazione**
security	**sicurezza**
to bounce (cheque)	**essere respinto al beneficiario**
to control, check	**controllare**
to demand payment	**invitare al pagamento,**
	ingiungere il pagamento
to fall due	**scadere**
to grant an extension	**accordare una proroga**
to object to something	**opporsi a**
to overdraw an account	**trarre allo scoperto**
to prolong, to extend	**prolungare**
to remind somebody of something	**ricordare a**
business reputation	**reputazione sul campo affari**
credit inquiry	**richiesta di informazioni**
	commerciali
credit rating	**credito**
estimated annual turnover	**movimento annuo stimato**
financial standing	**stato patrimoniale**
honest	**onesto/a**
reliability	**fidatezza**
solvency	**solvenza**
strictly confidential	**strettamente confidenziale**
without obligation	**senza impegno**

▼

Looking through our books we note that a balance of . . . is still outstanding.
Abbiamo registrato nella nostra contabilità un saldo scoperto di . . .

Our statement of account has probably been overlooked.
Molto probabilmente non avete notato il nostro estratto conto.

May we remind you that your payment has been overdue since 31 July?
Ci permettiamo di ricordarVi che il limite di pagamento è scaduto il 31 luglio?

Our invoice of . . . is still unpaid.
La nostra fattura del . . . non è stata ancora saldata.

Your account is overdrawn/in the red.
Il Vs. conto è scoperto/aperto.

Please send your remittance by . . .
Vi preghiamo di inviare un assegno entro il . . .

Messrs. . . . have given us your name as a trade reference.
La ditta . . . ci ha fatto il Vs. nominativo quale referenza commerciale.

Do you think it would be justifiable to grant them a credit of up to . . .?
Possiamo concedere un credito fino ad una somma di . .?

They have always met their financial obligations promptly.
La ditta ha sempre adempito puntualmente a tutti gli impegni di pagamento.

This information is given in strictest confidence and without any obligation on our part.
Le presenti informazioni sono strettamente confidenziali e senza alcun impegno da parte nostra.

 Model letters 11, 12, 13 and 14

18

Bankruptcy, Liquidation	Fallimento, Liquidazione
affidavit	**affidavit**
attachment (seizure, distraint)	**pignoramento**
bankruptcy, liquidation	**fallimento, liquidazione**
composition, bankrupt's certificate	**composizione, concordato**
compulsory sale	**vendita forzata**

creditor	**creditore**
debtor	**debitore**
dispute	**lite, causa**
insolvency	**insolvenza**
lawsuit, litigation	**processo, causa**
lawyer	**legale, avvocato**
official receiver (OR)	**curatore fallimentare**
receiving order	**sentenza iniziale di fallimento**
reservation of title	**riserva di proprietà**
solicitor	**avvocato**
trustee	**curatore fallimentare**
to bring an action against . . .	**iniziare un'azione legale contro . . .**
to file for bankruptcy	**presentare istanza di fallimento**
to go bankrupt	**fare fallimento, fallire**

Contacts with Italian solicitors can be made through:

> **Associazione Nazionale de Avvocadi e Procuratori**
> **(National Association of Lawyers and Public Prosecutors)**
> **Piazza d'Horologio 12**
> **00186 Roma**
> **Tel: (06) 6869780**

→7 Useful UK addresses can be found in Part III, 10.

19

Accounting Contabilità

account	**conto**
accountant, bookkeeper	**contabile, ragioniere**
accounting, bookkeeping	**contabilità**
amortization rate	**tasso d'ammortamento**
annual financial statement	**documenti contabili annuali/ bilancio annuale**
auditing	**revisione**

balance	saldo, bilanco
book value	valore contabile
call-money	denaro rimborsabile a richiesta
cash flow	cash flow
credit note	nota d'accredito
debit note	nota d'addebito
entry	registrazione
expenditure	spese
inventory	inventario
ledger	mastro/libro mastro
liquidity	liquidità
mortgage	ipoteca
order book	libro delle commissioni
overdraft credit	credito in conto corrente
percentage	percentuale
profitability	redditività
receipts	entrate, proventi
(trading) result	risultato
short-term/medium-term/ long term credit	credito a breve/medio/ lungo termine
statistics	statistica
valuation	valutazione
voucher	buono, documento giustificativo
yield	redditiva, rendita
to book, to enter a booking	registrare
to book in conformity	registrare in conformità
to calculate	calcolare
to cancel	stornare
to carry forward (the balance)	riportare
to certify	attestare, certificare
to close an account	chiudere un conto
to open an account	aprire un conto

Associazione Italiane Revisori Contabili, ASSIREVI
(Italian Association of Auditors)
Via V. Monti 16
20123 Milano
Tel: (02) 436950
Fax: (02) 437326

20

The Balance Sheet Il Bilancio

accruals	**spese da pagare**
assets	**attivo**
balance sheet	**bilancio**
borrowed capital	**capitale prestito**
chartered accountant	**revisore dei conti, ragioniere professionista**
current assets	**attivo realizzabile, attiva correnti**
equity capital	**patrimonio netto**
finished products/goods	**prodotti finiti**
fixed assets	**attivo fisso**
inventories	**stocks, provviste, scorte**
legal reserves	**riserve legali**
liabilities	**passivo**
liquid funds	**attivo liquido**
loan	**prestito**
notes payable	**cambiali passive**
raw materials	**materie prime**
receivables	**titoli esigibili**
share	**azione**
work in progress	**prodotti in corso di lavorazione**

See the Appendix for a layout of the balance sheet according to the Legge di Attuazione delle Direttive CEE in Materia di Bilancio (Accounting and Reporting Legislation, Adoption of the 4th, 7th, 8th EC Directives).

If you have any queries about the preparation of accounts or a balance sheet you can contact:

**Istituto Nazionale Revisori Uffiziale di Conti
(National Office of Public Auditors)
Viale Premuda 23
20129 Milano
Tel: (02) 784165**

21

Statement of Earnings	Conto Proffiti e Perdite
administration expenses	spese di amministrazione
after-tax profit	utile tasse detratte
compound interest	interesse composto
depreciations	ammortamenti
dividend	dividendo
gross profit	proffito lordo
interests	interesse
operating expenses and income	spese e proventi di gestione
pre-tax profit	utile tassabile
profit and loss account	conto profitti e perdite
rate of interest	tasso d'interesse
sales	vendite
to write off	ammortare

See the Appendix for a layout of the Profit and Loss Account according to the Legge di Attuazione delle Direttive CEE in Materio di Bilancio (Accounting and Reporting Legislation, Adoption of the 4th, 7th and 8th EC Directives).

22

The Annual Report	Documenti Annuali
annual general meeting of the shareholders	assemblea generale annuale
annual report	relazione annuale del bilancio
bookings	ordini pervenuti, acquisizioni di ordini
business development, growth	sviluppo commerciale
capital structure	struttura finanziaria
development (of a product)	attività di sviluppo
economic position	situazione economica

expected growth	**sviluppo previsto**
indebtedness	**indebitamento**
investment	**investimento**
production	**produzione**
research	**attività di ricerca scientifica**
return, yield	**redditività, rendita**
revenues	**ricavati, ricavi**
subsidy	**sovvenzione**
trading result	**risultato di gestione**
year under review	**anno in esame**

23

Costs and their Calculation

Spese e Calcoli

all-in costs	**spese totali**
at cost	**a prezzo di costo**
at your/our expense	**a Vostre (Vs.)/nostre (ns.) spese**
calculation	**calcoli**
capital gains tax	**imposta sulla plus-valenza**
corporation tax	**imposta sulla società**
cost effective	**costo efficace**
cost-free/free of charge	**franco di spese, gratis, gratuito**
cost price	**prezzo di costo**
cost-covering	**che copre i costi**
costs	**costi**
direct labour	**manodopera diretta**
direct material	**materiale diretto**
excise tax	**imposta sul consumo**
expenditure, expenses	**spese**
extras	**spesa extra**
fixed costs	**spese fisse**
income tax	**imposta sul reddito**
inheritance tax	**imposta di successione**
liable for tax	**soggetto a tasse**
marginal costs	**costi marginali**
overhead charges	**imputazione dei costi comuni**
overhead (indirect) costs	**costi indiretti**

production costs	**costi di produzione**
profit mark-up	**aumento degli utili**
property tax	**imposta patrimoniale**
refund on costs	**rimborso di spese**
royalties	**diritti di licenza, royalties**
selling expenses	**spese di vendita**
surtax	**tassa supplementare, soprattassa**
tax	**imposta, tassa**
tax allowance	**detrazione fiscale**
tax consultant	**consulente fiscale**
tax exemption	**esenzione fiscale**
tax-favoured	**con agevolazione fiscale**
tax on profits	**imposta sul profitti**
tax-free	**esente da tasse, da imposte**
turnover tax	**imposta sulla cifra d'affari**
unit cost	**costo unitario**
VAT (value-added tax)	**imposta sul valore aggiunto (IVA)**
variable costs	**costi variabli**
wealth tax	**imposta sul patrimonio**
zero-rated	**IVA non compresa**

Value-Added Tax in EC countries

	Lower %	*Standard* %	*Higher* %
Belgium	6 and 17	19	25 and 33
Denmark	—	22	—
France	5.5 and 7	18.6	33.3
Germany	7	14	—
Great Britain	0	17.5	—
Greece	6	18	36
Ireland	0 and 10	23	—
Italy	2 and 9	18	38
Luxembourg	3 and 6	12	—
The Netherlands	5	19	—
Portugal	0 and 8	17	30
Spain	6	12	33

24

Personnel Matters   Personale

application (for a job)	**domanda d'impiego**
apprentice, trainee	**apprendista** (*m/f*)
boss	**capo**
chairman	**presidente**
clerk	**impiegato/a (commerciale)**
contract of employment	**contratto d'impiego**
curriculum vitae	**curriculum vitae**
dismissal	**licenziamento**
education, training	**istruzione, formazione professionale**
employee	**impiegato** (*m/f*), **dipendente**
employer	**datore di lavoro**
executive	**dirigente**
expert	**esperto/a, perito**
financial controller	**controllore finanzario**
flexible working hours, flexi time	**orario di lavoro flessibile**
foreign language secretary	**segretaria di lingue**
foreman	**capo**
fringe benefits	**indennità accessoria/addizionali**
full-time worker	**chi lavora a tempo pieno**
interview (person)	**colloquio per un impiego**
job, position	**posto di lavoro, posizione**
management	**management, direttivo**
manager(ess)	**gerente, dirigente, direttore/ direttrice**
managing director	**amministratore delegato**
master	**mastro**
on-the-job training	**istruzione professionale**
part-time workers	**chi lavora part-time/a tempo parziale**
payroll	**conteggio del salario, elenco del personale**
pension fund, superannuation fund	**fondo pensioni**
personal data sheet	**curriculum vitae breve**

personal secretary, PA	**segretario/a (del capo)**
personnel manager	**capo del personale**
plant manager	**direttore di stabilimento**
probation period	**periodo di prova**
professional experience	**esperienza professionale**
profit sharing	**compartecipazione agli utili**
promotion (person)	**promozione**
proxy	**procuratore**
purchasing manager/chief buyer	**responsabile degli acquisti**
qualification	**qualificazione, qualifica**
questionnaire	**questionario**
references	**referenze**
rise (person)	**aumento di stipendio**
salary	**stipendio, salario**
sales manager	**sales manager**
school leaving certificate	**licenza scolastica**
secretary (to . . .)	**segretario/a (di . . .)**
shift work	**lavoro a turno**
skilled worker	**operaio/a, specializzato/a**
superior	**superiore** (*m/f*)
temporary staff	**avventizi** (*m pl*)
testimonial	**attestato del datore di lavoro**
trade union	**sindacato**
typist	**dattilografa/o**
unemployment	**disoccupazione**
unskilled worker	**operaio/a non qualificato/a**
vacancy, opening	**posto vacante**
vocational training	**formazione professionale**
wage(s)	**paga**
worker participation (in decision-making)	**cogestione**
workforce, staff, personnel	**forza di lavoro personale**
working hours	**orario lavorativo**
works council member	**membro consiglio di gestione**
to apply for	**applicarsi**
to attend an evening course	**frequentare un corso serale**
to employ, to engage, to take on	**assumere**
to give notice	**dare il preavviso a**

to manage	**dirigere, amministrare**
to serve an apprenticeship	**fare un tirocinio**
to train, to instruct	**formare professionalmente, istruire**
to work overtime	**fare le ore straordinarie**

In an interview you may be asked:

Potrebbe raccontarmi qualcosa sull'istruzione ricevuta, nonché qualcosa sulla Sua persona?
Could you tell me something about yourself and your educational background?

Quali lingue straniere conosce/ha studiato?
What foreign languages have you learned/studied?

Sa usare il computer?
Are you computer-literate?

Perché vuole cambiare lavoro?
Why do you want to leave your present job?

Quando può cominciare da noi?
When can you start working for us?

Qual è il Suo attuale lavoro?
What does your current job entail?

amministratore, delegato	managing director
direttore, dirigente	manager/head of . . .
capo reparto	head of department
segretario/a	secretary
assistente	assistant
capo contabile	accounting manager

signatures:		
(holder of procuration):	ppa	by proxy
(other clerks):	p	by order of

▼

With reference to your advertisement in yesterday's . . ., I would like to apply for the position of . . . in your company.

Riferendomi al Vs. annuncio di ieri nel . . ., vorrei applicarmi quale . . . per il posto vacante nella Vs. ditta.

I am familiar with export and import procedures.
Ho esperienza sul settore export import.

I am extremely interested in working in Italy because . . .
Desidero vivamente lavorare in Italia perché . . .

I have a good working knowledge of Italian.
Ho una buona conoscenza dell'italiano.

I enclose a CV with details of my practical training and experience.
Accludo un dettagliato curriculum vitae che Vi darà le informazioni necessarie sulla mia formazione ed esperienza professionali.

Please find enclosed copies of testimonials by . . .
Trovate in allegato i certificati attestati delle ditte . . .

My present position is subject to three months' notice.
Ho un periodo di preavviso di licenziamento di tre mesi.

Book tip:

Contratti di Formazione e Lavoro: Una guida per le imprese
(*Contracts for vocational training and employment: a guide for companies*)
SIPI Srl, Roma

 **Model letter 15**

25

Data Processing	Elaborazione Dati
blank, space	**spazio**
cable connection	**allacciamento via cavo**
calculator (pocket)	**calcolatore (calcolatrice)**

central processing unit (CPU)	**CPU, unità centrale**
communication line	**linea di comunicazione**
daisy wheel	**margherita di stampa**
database	**database, base di dati**
data transfer	**trasferimento dati**
density	**densità**
direct memory access	**accesso diretto alla memoria**
disk	**dischetto**
disk operating system (DOS)	**sistema operativo (DOS)**
disk storage	**memoria a massa**
display, screen	**video, schermo**
drive	**drive, unità a (disco, nastro)**
EDP	**EDP**
E-mail, electronic mail	**posta elettronica**
– fax	**– telefax, fax**
– teletex	**– teletex**
– telex	**– telex**
erase	**cancellare**
file	**filo, archivio**
floating point	**virgola mobile**
flowchart	**diagramma di flusso dei dati**
hard disk	**disco rigido, disco fisso**
input	**input, immissione dati**
interface	**interfaccia**
keyboard	**tastiera**
magnetic head	**testina magnetica**
magnetic tape	**nastro magnetico**
manual	**manuale**
mask, picture	**maschera**
master file	**archivio principale**
memory	**memoria**
memory protection	**protezione della memoria**
office automation	**automazione d'ufficio**
operating system	**sistema operativo**
output	**output**
paper feed	**alimentazione carta**
password	**password, parola d'ordine**
plotter	**plotter**
power supply	**alimentatore**
programming language	**linguaggio di programmazione**

random-access memory (RAM)	memoria ad accesso casuale (RAM)
read-only memory (ROM)	memoria a sola lettura (ROM)
scanner	scanner
screen, monitor	schermo, monitor
service	manutenzione
shift key	tasto
slot	slot
software	software
source program	programma sorgente
spreadsheet	modulo multiplo 'spreadsheet'
tape drive unit	unità a nastro
teleprocessing	elaborazione dati a distanza
transmission channels	canali di trasmissione
update	aggiornamento
user identification	identificativo (id) utente
utility	utilità
word processing	elaborazione testi
working storage	memoria di lavoro
write head	testina di stampa
write-lock, file protection	protezione da scrittura/del file

▼

Is the computer IBM compatible?
Il computer gira con software IBM compatibile?

Can I use 3½" or 5¼" disks?
Posso utilizzare dischetti da 3½ o da 5¼ pollici?

Can I run colour and graphics software on the PC?
Posso utilizzare software grafico e a colori sul PC?

Are there single or twin disk drives?
È a floppy singolo o doppio?

Can I use any IBM compatible monochrome or colour monitor?
Posso utilizzare qualsiasi monitor monocromatico o a colori IBM compatibile?

Can I choose foreground or background colours?
Posso scegliere i colori dello sfondo e del testo?

53

Can I use any type of PC monitor provided it has a standard 9-pin 'D' connector?
Posso utilizzare qualsiasi tipo di monitor per PC, ammesso che sia provvisto del connettore 'D' standard a 9-pin?

Can I use the modem for commercial information services?
Posso utilizzare il modem per servizi informativi commerciali?

Does the computer include a built-in modem?
Il computer monta di serie un modem?

Does the keyboard have all the special function keys?
La tastiera è provvista di tutti i tasti funzione speciali?

Does the price include manual, word processor and software?
Il prezzo comprende anche il manuale, word processor e dischi di software?

26

Co-operation and Business Partnerships	Collaborazione e Partecipazioni Commerciali
acquisition	**acquisto, acquisizione**
agent, representative	**agente, rappresentante**
branch	**filiale**
commission	**provvigione**
commission agent	**commissionario, intermediario**
consortium	**consorzio**
franchise	**concessione, franchise**
general agency	**rappresentanza generale**
group, concern	**gruppo**
head office, headquarters	**sede principale/centrale**
joint venture	**associazione in partecipazione**
legally protected	**legalmente protetto**
letter of intent	**lettera d'intenti**
merger	**fusione**
parent/holding company	**società madre, holding**
patented	**brevettato**

registered office	**sede legale**
royalties	**diritti di licenza, royalties**
sole proprietorship	**impresa individuale, unico proprietario**
subject to payment on royalties	**sottomesso a diritti di licenza**
subsidiary	**società affiliata/sussidiaria**
take-over	**take-over, acquisizione di una partecipazione societaria prevalente**
under patent law	**secondo diritto di brevetto**
venture capital	**venture capital, capitale di rischio**
to acquire a licence	**acquisire una licenza**
to apply for a patent	**depositare domanda di brevetto**
to do business	**fare affari**
to entrust a firm with the agency	**affidare la rappresentanza**
to establish, to found	**fondare**
to exploit a patent	**utilizzare un brevetto**
to grant sole selling rights	**dare diritto esclusività di vendita**
to join a firm	**entrare in una ditta**
to manufacture under licence	**fabbricare su licenza**
to merge	**fondere, fondersi**
to run a business	**gestire un'impresa**
to sell as sole agent	**vendere come rappresentante esclusivo**
to sell goods on commission	**vendere merce in commissione**
to set up a business	**mettersi in proprio**

▼

We are looking for representatives to sell our products.
Cerchiamo rappresentanti commerciali per la vendita dei nostri prodotti.

Please state the terms on which you are willing to act as your representative.
La preghiamo di comunicarci a quali condizioni è disposto a lavorare come nostro rappresentante.

You will be paid a 3% commission on all sales.
Vi diamo il 3% su tutte le vendite.

Forms of companies in Italy:

Sole proprietorship
The sole trader is fully liable for all debts.
There are also partnerships:

Partnerships

Società in nome collettivo SNC (Partnership)
The name of at least one partner must appear in the name of the firm. It is the simplest form of company without any stipulations concerning minimum capital. Individual and collective liability is unlimited. The firm is run jointly by the partners.

Società in accomandita semplice SAS (Limited partnership)
A more developed form of partnership (SNC), where the name of at least one partner ('Soci Accomandatari') must appear in the name of the firm. Two types of partner are possible: 'soci accomandanti' and 'soci accomandatari'. The liability of the 'soci accomandanti' is limited to the amount of capital they have invested; the liability of the 'soci accomandatari' is individually and jointly unlimited. The firm is run jointly by the 'soci accomandatari'. There are no minimum capital requirements.

Joint stock companies

Società per azioni SPA (Public company)
The liability of the shareholders is limited to the amount of capital they have invested. There is a prescribed minimum nominal capital of 200,000,000 Lire. Shareholders' meetings, ordinary and extraordinary must be held, and an executive committee appointed. Accounts must be audited.

Società a responsabilità limitata SRL (Italian equivalent of a private company)
Liability of the members is limited to the capital they have invested, the minimum nominal capital being 20,000,000 Lire. All directors must be shareholders in the firm. Decisions are taken at shareholders' meetings.

If you are planning to enter the Italian market and need help you can refer to:

> **Unione Italiana delle Camere die Commercio Industria Artigianato e Agricoltura**
> **(Italian Association of Chambers of Commerce, Industry, Crafts and Agriculture)**
> **Piazza Sallustio 21**
> **00187 Roma**
> **Tel: (06) 465188-465 772**
>
> **British Chamber of Commerce in Italy**
> **Via Agnello 8**
> **20121 Milano**
> **Tel: (02) 876981/ 877798**

Further information on the Single European Market can be found in Part III, 7.

Book tips:

Company formation:
Le Società Personali
(*Partnerships*)
Adriano Propesi
Pirola Editore, Milan, 1989

Franchising:
Il Sistema Franchising
(*Franchising*)
Etas Libri, Milan, 1990

Il Franchising: Aspetti giuridici, finanziari e fiscali prospettive di sviluppo in Italia
(*Franchising: legal, financial and tax aspects of development prospectus in Italy*)
Giorgio Fossati
Pirola Editore, Milan, 1988

Venture Capital: Capitale di rischio per lo sviluppo
(*Risk capital for development*)

(With analyses and statistics of individual European countries)
Il Sole 24 Ore Libri, Milan, 1990

→**8** Useful UK addresses can be found in Part III, 10.

27

Business Letters	**Lettere d'affari**
address	indirizzo
care of (c/o)	presso, c/o
date	data
enclosure(s)	allegato/i
for the attention of:	all'attenzione di:
(our/your) letter	(ns/Vs) lettera
letterhead	intestazione
signature	firma
(subject line)	oggetto, riguarda, argomento

See the Appendix for a standard layout of an Italian business letter.

 **Model letter 1**

PART II

1

First Contacts

1.1 Greeting someone and saying goodbye

Good morning	**Buongiorno**
Good afternoon	**Buongiorno**
Good evening	**Buona sera**
Good night	**Buona notte**
Hello	**Ciao**
Are you Signora Rossi by any chance?	**Scusi, Lei è mica la signora Rossi?**
▶ Yes, that's me	▶ **Si sono io**
Nice to meet you/ How nice to see you	**Piacere vederLa**
Did you have a good journey/ trip?	**Ha fatto buon viaggio?**
How was your flight?	**Com'è stato il volo?**
How long as you planning to stay?	**Quanto tempo ha intenzione di fermarsi?**
Are you enjoying your stay?	**Si trova bene qui?**
How are you?	**Come sta?**
▶ Fine, thanks and you?	▶ **Bene, grazie, e Lei?**
▶ Not too bad, thanks	▶ **Abbastanza bene**

If you are not feeling well, you can respond to the question, **'Come sta?'** by saying: **'Mi dispiace, ma non sto affatto bene.'**

Goodbye/bye-bye	**Arrivederci/ArrivederLa** (very formal)
Cheerio	**Ciao**
Have a good trip/safe journey	**Buon viaggio**

Take care	**Sta bene**
See you soon	**A presto**
I'll see you later	**A più tardi**
See you tomorrow	**A domani**
All the best ▶ The same to you	**Ogni bene/Tante belle cose!** ▶ **Altrettanto**
Have a nice time	**Buon divertimento**
I'm afraid I must go now	**Purtroppo devo andarmene**
Thank you very much for . . .	**Grazie di/per . . .**
Thank you very much for making my stay so pleasant	**Grazie per il piacevole soggiorno**
It was very nice	**È stato bellissimo**
I've enjoyed talking to you	**È stato molto bello parlare con Lei**
It's been a useful meeting	**È stato un incontro interessante**
Pleased to have met you	**È stato un piacere fare la Sua conoscenza**
I'll give you a ring soon	**Telefonerò presto**
I'll be in touch	**Mi farò sentire al più presto**
Please give my regards to your wife	**Mi saluti Sua moglie**

1.2 Communication

Do you speak English?	**Parla inglese?**
I don't speak much Italian	**Io parlo un pochino l'italiano**
I'm afraid my Italian isn't very good	**Il mio italiano non è molto buono**
I'm English	**Sono ingles(a)**
I don't understand	**Non capisco**
Don't speak so fast, please	**Non parli così presto, per favore**

Could you speak more slowly, please?	**Parli più lentamente, per favore**
Could you repeat that, please?	**Può ripetere, per piacere?**
I'm afraid I didn't quite understand	**Mi dispiace, ma non ho capito bene**
I'm sorry, I can't follow you. Could you write it down, please?	**Scusi, non capisco. Potrebbe scrivere quello che ha detto?**
Could you spell it, please?	**Me lo può sillabare?**
Could you translate that for me, please?	**Potrebbe tradurmelo?**
What does it mean? ▶ Oh, I see	**Che cosa significa?** ▶ **Capisco**
How do you pronounce this word?	**Come si pronuncia questa parola?**
How do you say . . . in Italian?	**Come si dice . . . in italiano?**

If you do not know the exact Italian equivalent of an English word and wish to paraphrase something, you can say:

It's a kind of . . .	**È una specie di . . .**

1.3 Introductions

My name's . . .	**Mi chiamo/sono**
May I introduce . . .	**Posso presentarLe . . .**
This is my wife	**Questa è mia moglie**
– my husband	**– questo è mio marito**
– my son/daughter	**– questo è mio figlio/questa è mia figlia**
– my (boy)friend/(girl)friend	**– questo è il mio amico/questa è la mia amica**
– my colleague	**– questo è il mio collega**

– a colleague of mine	**– un(a) mio/a collega**
– our chief engineer	**– il nostro ingegnere in capo**

■ Please note:

When you introduce yourself in Italy you shake hands. It is not customary to address one another by first names. You should leave this to your business partner. Just give your first and second names; your partner should do the same, and you can also add 'piacere' (pleased to meet you).

'You' can be either 'tu' or 'Lei' in Italian. 'Tu' is used when speaking to children or friends; 'Lei' is used when speaking to acquaintances and business contacts. You say 'ciao' only if you say 'tu'.

Remember, titles are important in Italy.

If you introduce someone else you say:

Le presento Mario Verdi/Ti presento Mario Verdi	May I introduce Mario Verdi to you/Meet Mario Verdi
▶ **Piacere**	Pleased to meet you

1.4 Appointments and arranging to meet someone

I'm . . . /I'm from . . .	**Sono . . . /sono di . . .** (if a name of a city follows), **vengo da . . .**
I work for . . .	**Lavoro presso . . .**
May I speak to . . .?	**Posso parlare con . . .?**
I've got an appointment with . . .	**Ho un appuntamento con . . .**
Nice to meet you/Pleased to meet you	**Sono lieto di fare la Sua conoscenza**
When?/At what time?	**Per quando?/Per che ora?**
At two o'clock	**Alle due**
From two to three	**Dalle due alle tre**

Between two and three	**Tra le due e le tre**
In an hour's time	**Fra un'ora**
Not before seven	**Non prima delle sette**
Not after nine	**Non dopo le nove**
It's (too) late	**È troppo tardi**
It's (too) early	**È troppo presto**
I'm sorry I'm late	**Mi dispiace essere in ritardo**
Have you been waiting long?	**Aspetta da tando?**

What you might hear in Italian:

Avanti!	Come in, please
Il signor Maniago L'aspetta	Signor Maniago is expecting you
Che piacere verderLa!	How nice to see you
Sono felice che abbia potuto venire	I'm glad you could come
Posso aiutarLa a togliersi il mantello?	Let me take your coat
Si accomodi	Won't you take a seat?
Posso offrirLe qualcosa da bere?	Can I get you a drink?
Prende una tazza di caffè?	Would you like a cup of coffee?
Fuma?	Do you smoke?
▶ **No, grazie, non fumo**	▶ No, thank you, I don't smoke
La disturba se fumo?	Do you mind if I smoke?
▶ **No, prego**	▶ No, go ahead
▶ **Preferirei se non fumasse**	▶ I'd rather you didn't
Ha un accendino?	Have you got a light?
▶ **Prego**	▶ Here you are
Ha fatto buon viaggio?	Did you have a good journey?

Da quanto è già qui?	How long have you been here?
▶ **Da due giorni**	▶ For two days
E il Suo primo viaggio a Milano?	Is this your first trip to Milan?
▶ **Ci siamo già stati due anni fa**	▶ We came here two years ago
Si trova bene qui?	Do you like it here?
▶ **Si, molto**	▶ Yes, I do
Dove abita?	Where are you staying?
▶ **Sto all'hotel . . .**	▶ I'm staying at the . . . Hotel
Spero che sia contento dell'albergo	I hope everything is all right at your hotel
Possiamo forse pranzare/ cenare insieme?	Perhaps we can have lunch/ dinner together
Ha tempo domani?	Are you free tomorrow?
▶ **Volentieri**	▶ Yes, that's fine, I'm free then
▶ **Accetto con piacere**	▶ Yes, I'd love to come
Preferisce la settimana prossima?	Would next week be more convenient for you?
▶ **Si, sarebbe meglio**	▶ Yes, that would be better
Vorrei farLe vedere il nostro reparto	I'd like to show you round the department
▶ **Molto gentile da parte Sua**	▶ That's very kind of you
Le potrei fare da cicerone	I could show you something of the town
Per esempio lunedì?	What about Monday?
▶ **D'accordo/volentieri**	▶ That's fine
▶ **Vediamo un po' . . .**	▶ Let me see . . .
▶ **Le darò conferma scritta per l'appuntamento**	▶ I'll confirm that date in writing
▶ **Cercherò di organizzarmi**	▶ I'll try and make it
▶ **Mi dispiace, ma non posso**	▶ Sorry, I can't
▶ **Mi dispiace, ho già un altro impegno**	▶ I'm sorry, I can't make it, I have another engagement
A più tardi/a domenica	See you later/on Sunday

È libero domani?
▶ **È un vero peccato, ma purtroppo non va**

Are you free tomorrow?
▶ I'm really sorry but I'm not

There are several ways of answering in the affirmative and in the negative:

Yes, of course	**Ma certo**
With pleasure	**Molto volentieri**
Perhaps	**Forse**
I'm afraid not	**Temo che non vada**
Certainly not	**Proprio impossibile**

1.5 Asking and telling the time

What's the time, please?	**Che ora è?/Che ore sono?**
It's about/exactly . . .	**Sono circa le . . . /Sono le . . . in punto**
two o'clock	**sono le due**
a quarter past twelve	**è mezzogiorno e un quarto**
ten past twelve	**è mezzogiorno e dieci**
half past twelve	**è la mezza**
twenty to one	**è l'una meno venti**
a quarter to one	**è l'una meno un quarto/è mezzogiorno e tre quarti**

General expressions of time:

during the day	**di giorno, durante il giorno**
in the morning	**di mattina, in mattinata**
at noon	**a mezzogiorno, il pomeriggio**
in the evening	**di sera, la sera**

at night	**di notte, la notte**
at midnight	**a mezzanotte**
today/yesterday/tomorrow	**oggi/ieri/domani**
the day before yesterday	**ieri l'altro, avantieri, l'altro ieri**
the day after tomorrow	**dopo domani**
daily	**quotidianamente/ogni giorno**
hourly	**ogni ora**
at any time	**sempre**
this morning/tonight	**questa mattina, stamattina, stamane/questa sera, stasera**
last week	**la settimana passata, scorsa**
every week	**ogni settimana**
two weeks ago/two years ago	**due settimane fa/due anni fa**
in two days' time	**fra due giorni**
in two weeks/in a fortnight	**fra due settimane/fra quindici giorni**
for two days	**da due giorni**
8 o'clock onwards	**dalle otto**
1992	**millenovecentonovantadue**

See Part III, 5 for a list of days of the week, months and public holidays.

The date:

What's the date today?	**Che giorno è oggi? I quanti ne abbiamo?**
Today's January the 26th	**Oggi è il ventisei gennaio**
On July the 6th	**Il sei luglio**
of this year/last year/the next year	**di quest'anno/dell'anno passato/dell'anno prossimo**

Until the 1st of January	**Fino al primo gennaio**
In your letter of May the 5th	**Nella Vs lettera del cinque maggio**
The letter was posted on the 30th of March	**La lettera è stata spedita il trenta marzo**
The 10th of this month	**il 10 c.m.**
The 10th of last month	**il 10 u.s.**

■ Please note:

There are a number of ways of writing the date in Italian:

15th April 1990	**15 aprile 1990 / 15/4/1990 / 15-4-1990**

Only for the first day in the month do you use an ordinal number: il primo maggio; for the other days you use cardinal numbers: il due marzo.

Remember that months are written without an initial capital letter.

Part III, 3 contains a list of ordinal numbers which will be useful when stating the date.

The Time:

sono le tre

è mezzogiorno e venti
sono le dodici e venti

sono le tre e trentacinque

è l'una meno un quarto
è mezzogiorno e tre quarti

sono le dieci e un quarto

sono le nove e mezzo/a

2

Everyday Topics

2.1 The weather

The weather is as popular a topic of conversation as it is in Britain. You may hear the following in Italian:

It's a beautiful day	**Che bella giornata oggi/Bel tempo oggi!**
Nice day today, isn't it?	**Un tempo splendido oggi, vero?**
It's an awful day, isn't it?	**Un tempaccio, no?**
It's going to rain	**Pioverà**
It's going to stay fine	**Resterà bello**

69

What's the weather like in England?	**Cosa fa il tempo in Inghilterra?**
What's the weather going to be like tomorrow?	**Quali sono le previsioni per domani?**
It's rather foggy	**È piuttosto nebbioso**
The temperature is above/ below freezing point	**Abbiamo . . . gradi sopra/ sotto zero**

Make sure you don't talk about this topic too much: you'll risk being regarded as a boring conversationalist.

In Part III, 4 you will find a conversion table for Fahrenheit and Celsius (centigrade) temperatures.

2.2 General questions

Where is . . . /where are . . .?	**Dov'è . . .?/Dove sono . . .?**
▶ It is . . . /they are . . .	▶ **Là c'è . . . /là ci sono . . .**
Is there . . . /are there . . .?	**C'è . . . /ci sono . . . ?**
Who?	**Chi?**
What?	**Che cosa?**
Which/what kind of . .?	**Quale?**
Whose?	**Di chi?**
Where?	**Dove?**
Where from?	**Da dove?**
Where (to)?	**Dove?**
When?	**Quando?**
Since when?/How long?	**Da quando?**
Why?	**Perché?**
How?	**Come?**
Pardon?/I beg your pardon?	**Scusi?**
What would you like?	**Che cosa desidera?**

How much does it cost?	**Quanto costa?**
Have you got . .?	**Avete . .?**
What does that mean?	**Che cosa significa?**
What's that?	**Che cos'è questo?**
Who's that?	**Chi è questa persona?**
When do you open/close?	**Quando aprite?/chiudete?**
How do I get to . . .?	**Mi può indicare la strada per . . .?**
Excuse me, can you tell me where I can find . . .	**Scusi, mi sa dire dove trovo . . .**

a department store?	**un grande magazzino?**
a tourist information office?	**un'agenzia di turismo?**
a toilet?	**un gabinetto, una toletta, una toilette?**

Excuse me, can I park here?	**Scusi, posso parcheggiare qui?**
Excuse me, do you happen to know if there's a bank around here?	**Senta, scusi, c'è una banca qui vicino?**
How do I get to . .?	**Come posso raggiungere . .?**
Where's the British Embassy?	**Dov'è l'ambasciata Britannica?**

**Embassy of the United Kingdom of
  Great Britain and Northern Ireland
Ambasciata Britannica
Via XX Settembre 80A
00187 Roma
Tel: (06) 4825441
Telex: 626119**

There are UK Consulates in the following towns: Cagliari, Florence, Genoa, Milan, Naples, Rome, Trieste, Venice.

2.3 Apologizing

I'm (so) sorry/Sorry	**Scusi/Mi dispiace**
I'm very sorry (about it)	**Mi dispiace molto**
▶ It's all right	▶ **Non fa niente/di niente/non c'è di che**
▶ It was my fault	▶ **È stata colpa mia**
I'm afraid it's not possible, I must apologize	**No, non è possibile, sono io che devo scusarmi**
I'm sorry to hear that	**Mi dispiace**
I'm sorry, I didn't notice	**Mi scusi della svista**
My apologies for being late	**Mi scusi del ritardo**
Excuse my saying so, but . . .	**Mi dispiace doverLe dire che . . .**

2.4 Requesting and thanking

Can you do me a favour, please?	**Mi potrebbe fare un piacere?**
▶ Certainly	▶ **Ma certo**
Excuse me, I wonder if you could help me?	**Potrebbe aiutarmi, per favore?**
I'm sorry to trouble you, but could you . . .?	**Scusi il disturbo, ma potrebbe . . .?**
May I?	**Permette?**
▶ Yes, by all means	▶ **Certo**
Do you mind if I open the window?	**Posso aprire la finestra?**
May I ask you a question?	**Posso farLe una domanda?**
Can I help you?	**Posso aiutarLa? Desidera?**
▶ Can you tell me . . ., please?	▶ **Sa dirmi . . .?**
▶ Can you show me . . ., please?	▶ **Potrebbe farmi vedere . . . ?**
▶ I need . . .	▶ **Ho bisogno di . . .**

▶ I'd rather . . . /I'd prefer . . .	▶ **Preferirei . . .**
Please hurry up, it's urgent	**Si affretti, per favore, è molto urgente**
Pardon?/I beg your pardon	**Scusi?**
There/here you are	**Prego**
Thank you	**Grazie**
Thank you very much (indeed)	**Tante grazie/molte grazie/ grazie mille**
Thank you for your trouble	**La ringrazio dell'aiuto suo**
Thank you for showing me round the factory/shop	**Grazie di avermi mostrato la fabbrica/l'officina**
It's been a useful meeting, thank you	**È stato un colloquio utile ed interessante, grazie**
That's very kind of you, thank you	**La ringrazio della Sua gentilezza**
You've been very helpful	**Lei è stato/a di grande aiuto**
Thank you for all your help	**Grazie del Suo aiuto**
▶ Don't mention it	▶ **Non c'è di che**
▶ My pleasure	▶ **L'ho fatto volentieri**

See the Appendix for the format of a thank-you letter.

 Model letters 16–19

2.5 Personal data

What's your name, please?	**Come si chiama, per favore?**
▶ My name is . . .	▶ **Mi chiamo . . .**
When were you born?	**La Sua data di nascita?/Quando è nato?**
▶ I was born on . . .	▶ **Sono nato il . . .**
How old are you?	**Quanti anni ha?**

▶ I'm . . . years old
▶ I'm over . . ./under . . .

▶ **Ho . . . anni**
▶ **Ho oltre . . . anni/
meno di . . . anni**

Are you married?
▶ I'm married
▶ single

È sposato?
▶ **Sono sposato/a**
▶ **celibe, scapolo** (man)
nubile (woman)

▶ divorced
▶ a widow/widower

▶ **divorziato/a**
▶ **vedovo/a**

Do you have any children?

Ha figli?

Are you here on business?
▶ Yes, I am

È qui per lavoro?
▶ **Sì**

Where do you come from?

Di dov'è?

Which part of Italy do you come
from?

Di quale parte d'Italia è?

Where do you live?

Dove abita?

Please fill in this form

**La prego di compilare questo
modulo**

What do you do for a living?

Qual è Sua professione?

May I ask you what you do?
▶ I work in an office
▶ I'm a businesswoman/
businessman
▶ I'm responsible for/in charge
of the export department
▶ I'm head of research
▶ I'm a sales manager

Posso chiederLe che cosa fa?
▶ **Sono impiegato**
▶ **Sono una donna d'affari/un
uomo d'affari**
▶ **Sono responsabile del
reparto export**
▶ **Dirigo il reparto ricerca**
▶ **Sono il capo reparto vendite**

What's your line of business?
▶ I'm in computers

Per quale settore lavora?
▶ **Lavoro sul settore computer**

Who do you work for?
▶ I work for . . .

Chi è Suo datore di lavoro?
▶ **Lavoro per la . . .**

I'm over here for the trade fair

Sono venuto per la fiera

How are you getting on?

Procede tutto bene?

What are your hobbies?

**Quali sono i Suoi passatempi/i
Suoi hobby?**

74

Do you do any sport?	**Pratica uno sport?**
Do you like football?	**Le piace il calcio?**
Do you speak any foreign languages?	**Conosce qualche lingua straniera?**

See the Appendix for a standard layout of a curriculum vitae.

 **Model letter 15**

3

Travel

3.1 Customs and Immigration

import/export duty	**dazio importazione/ esportazione**
entry	**entrata**
border	**frontiera**
customs/customs officer	**dogana/doganiere**
duty/duty-free/dutiable	**dazio/esente da dazio/soggetto a dazio**
customs clearance	**sdoganamento**
customs declaration	**dichiarazione doganale**
customs declaration form	**modulo dichiarazione doganale**
customs control	**controllo doganale**
I'm travelling with my family	**Viaggio con la famiglia**
I'm here on business	**Sono qui per affari**
I'm here on holiday	**Sono qui privatamente**
I'm staying for three weeks	**Mi fermo tre settimane**
I've been here before	**Sono già stato qui**

I'm not going to work in Italy	**Non ho intenzione di lavorare in Italia**
These are only personal belongings	**Sono solamente oggetti personali**
These are samples	**Questi sono campioni**
These are presents	**Questi sono regali**
This is my suitcase	**Questa è la mia valigia**
This is not mine	**Questa non è la mia**
I've nothing to declare	**Non ho niente da dichiarare**
I'm declaring these bottles of wine	**Ho da dichiarare queste bottiglie di vino**

At the border you might hear or read the following sentences in Italian:

Cittadini della CEE	Citizens of EC Countries
Merce da dichiarare	Goods to declare
Merce esente da dazio	Nothing to declare
Posso vedere il Suo passaporto, per favore?	Can I see your passport, please?
I documenti, per favore	Your travel documents, please
Ha compilato i moduli di sbarco?	Have you filled in your landing card?
Qual è lo scopo della Sua visita?	What's the purpose of your visit?
▶ **Sono qui per affari**	▶ I'm here on business
Quanto tempo si ferma?	How long are you going to stay?
È il Suo primo soggiorno in Italia?	Is this your first visit to Italy?
Può passare	You can go through, then

Ha qualcosa da dichiarare?	Have you got anything to declare?
È questo il Suo bagaglio?	Is this your suitcase?
Apra il portabagagli, per favore	Open the boot, please
Che cosa c'è qui?	What's in here?
Fino a duecento sigarette non paga dazio	You're allowed 200 cigarettes
Per questo deve pagare dazio	You'll have to pay duty on this

■ Please note:

Customs regulations are beyond the scope of this language guide, but if you have any questions on customs matters you can obtain information by writing to:

> **HM Customs and Excise**
> **Dorset House**
> **Stamford Street**
> **London SE1 9PS**

You can also make inquiries at the London Chamber of Commerce and Industry:

> **London Chamber of Commerce and**
> **Industry**
> **69 Cannon Street**
> **London EC4N 5AB**
> **Tel: 071-248 4444**
> **extension: 3008/9/10**

The 'Customs and Trade Procedures' department provides helpful information on the following: customs procedures/documents/clearance/import controls/UK/foreign exports/temporary movements, as well as:

> **Italian Chamber of Commerce** (in the UK)
> **Walmar House**
> **296 Regent Street**
> **London W1R 6AE**
> **Tel: 071-637 3153**

**Ministero delle Finanze
(Ministry of Finance)
Viale America
00144 Roma
Tel: (06) 59971**

**Ministero dell'Industria, del Commercio e
dell'Artigianato
(Ministry for Industry, Commerce and
Crafts)
Via Vittorio Veneto 33
00187 Roma
Tel: (06) 4705**

3.2 Planes

Can you help me, please?	**Mi può aiutare, per favore?**
Where's the office of Alitalia/ British Airways?	**Dov'è l'ufficio dell'Alitalia/della British Airways?**
I'd like to book a flight to London, please	**Vorrei prenotare un volo per Londra**
A single/return flight	**Solo andata/andata e ritorno**
When's the next plane to . .?	**Quando parte il prossimo aereo per . . .?**
I'd like to fly to . . .	**Vorrei andare a . . .**
Can I fly directly from here?	**C'è un volo diretto?**
Do I have to change planes?	**Devo cambiare?**
Is there a connection to . .?	**C'è subito un volo di coincidenza?**
Is there a stop-over?	**C'è uno stop?**
Are there any seats available?	**Ci sono ancora posti liberi?**
Where can I confirm the return flight?	**Dove mi confermano il volo di ritorno?**

I'd like a seat by the window	**Vorrei un posto al finestrino**
Non-smoking section	**reparto non-fumatori**
What is the flight number?	**Qual è il numero del volo?**
When does the plane take off?	**Quando decolla?**
Will we arrive on time?	**Arriveremo puntuali?**
How long will the flight be delayed?	**Di quanto ritarderà il volo?**
Has the plane already landed?	**L'aereo è gia atterrato?**
Will a meal be served during the flight?	**Verrà servito un pasto durante il volo?**
How much does my suitcase weigh?	**Quanto pesa la mia valigia?**
What's the charge for excess luggage?	**Quando si paga per l'eccedenza di peso?**
I'll take this hand luggage with me	**Questo lo tengo come bagaglio a mano**
I feel sick. Could you bring me something for airsickness?	**Mi sento male. Ha qualcosa contro il mal d'aria?**
My suitcase has got lost	**La mia valigia è andata persa**
My suitcase has been damaged	**La mia valigia è rovinata**
Could you send this suitcase to the following address, please?	**Spedite la valigia al seguente indirizzo**

You might read and hear the following at Italian airports:

Accettazione Bagagli	Baggage Check-in
Aeroporto	Airport
Arrivi/Partenze	Arrivals/Departures
Bagaglio Ingombrante	Bulky Luggage
Biglietto di bordo	Boarding Card

Classe Business	Business Class
Classe Turistica	Economy Class
Compagnia Aerea	Airline
Dichiarazione di Esportazione	Export declaration
Gate	Gate
Merce Esente da Dazio	Duty-free
Noleggio Macchine	Car Hire
Ora Locale	Local Time
Pregasi Allacciare le Cinture	Fasten your Seatbelts, Please
Prenotazioni	Reservations
Prima Classe	First Class
Punto di Partenza	Take-Off
Ricerca Bagagli	Baggage Tracing/Lost Luggage
Ritiro Bagagli	Baggage Reclaim
Scalo Intermedio	Stop-over
Sportello Informazioni	Information Desk
Ultima Chiamata	Last Call
Uscita di Emergenza	Emergency Exit
Valido	Valid
Voli in Arrivo	Incoming Flights
Volo in Orario	Scheduled Flight
Attenzione, Prego	Attention Please
Tutti i passeggeri di transito della . . . vengono pregati di recarsi subito al gate cinquanta sette	All transit passengers from . . . continuing their flight to . . . are now requested to proceed immediately/urgently to gate 57
Ultima chiamata per il volo 123 della Alitalia a Londra, Gate B 53	Last call for Alitalia Flight 123 to London, Gate B 53

Può consegnare i bagagli un'ora prima del decollo	Check-in is one hour before take-off
Ha bagagli a mano?	Have you got any hand luggage?
Posso metterLa sulla lista d'attesa	I can put you on the waiting list
Il volo è rimandato	The flight is delayed
Abbiamo un ritardo di 40 minuti	We're 40 minutes late
Il volo è stato cancellato	The flight has been cancelled

■ Please note:

There are direct flights by Alitalia or British Airways between London and Milan, Turin, Venice, Genoa, Bologna, Pisa/Florence, Rome, Naples; between Birmingham and Milan; and between Manchester and Milan. (There is a map of main airports on p. 2.) Inland flights connect various towns as well as the mainland and the islands.

For 24-hour information on flights dial 116 or (06) 5456.

Alitalia in the UK:
(London)
27 Piccadilly
W1V 9PF
Tel: 071-602 7111

British Airways Linkline:
Customers anywhere in the UK may contact BA reservations via the 'linkline' number; calls will be charged at local call rate.
General reservations: (0345) 222111

British Airways in Italy:
(Milan)
Corso Italia 8
Tel: (02) 809041

(Rome)
Via Bissolatti 54
Tel: (06) 479991

3.3 Trains

Where's the main station?	**Dov'è la stazione centrale, per favore?**
Which bus goes to the station?	**Quale linea porta alla stazione?**
Take me to the station, please	**Mi porti alla stazione, per piacere**
At which counter can I get international tickets, please?	**A quale sportello si fanno i biglietti internazionali?**
What's the fare to . .?	**Quanto costa il biglietto per . .?**
Are there any reductions?	**Ci sono delle riduzioni?**
I'd like a ticket to . . .	**Vorrei un biglietto per . . .**
Two singles to Bologna, please	**Due volte solo andata per Bologna per favore**
Do I need a reservation?	**Ci vuole la prenotazione?**
Do I have to pay a supplement/ excess fare?	**Pago un supplemento/fare un biglietto in viaggio?**
How long is the return ticket valid?	**Quanto è valido il biglietto di ritorno?**
When's the next train to . .?	**Quando parte il prossimo treno per . .?**
When does the train arrive at . . .?	**Quando arriva a . . .?**
When does the last train leave?	**Quando parte l'ultimo treno?**
Which platform does the train leave from?	**De quale binario parte?**
Where do I have to change?	**Dove devo cambiare?**
Is this the train for . . .?	**Scusi, è questo il treno per . . .?**
Does the train stop at . . .?	**Il treno ferma a . . .?**
I've just missed my train, will there be another one?	**Ho appena perso il treno, ce n'è un altro per . . .?**

Where will I find a porter?	**Dove trovo un facchino?**
Can you help me with my luggage, please?	**Potrebbe aiutarmi con i bagagli, per favore?**
Where can I check-in my luggage?	**Dove posso depositare i bagagli?**
Excuse me, please	**Permesso!**
Is this seat free/taken?	**È libero/occupato questo posto?**
Is anybody sitting here?	**È già seduto qualcuno qui?**
I'm afraid this is my seat	**È il mio posto, mi dispiace**
Are there any free compartments in the sleeping car?	**Ci sono compartimenti letto ancora liberi?**
Is this a non-smoking compartment?	**Questo compartimento è fumatori o non?**
Whose suitcase is this?	**Di chi è questa valigia?**
▶ It's mine	**▶ È la mia**
Do you mind if I open/shut the window?	**Posso aprire/chiudere il finestrino?**
Would you mind keeping an eye on my luggage, please?	**Potrebbe dare un occhio al bagaglio, per favore?**
Where do I have to get off?	**Dove devo scendere?**
Could you tell me when we're there, please?	**Mi può dire, per favore, quando siamo arrivati?**
Where can I get a taxi, please?	**Dove soni i taxi?**

At railway stations and on trains you may hear or read the following:

Solo andata o andata e ritorno?	Single or return?
Prima o seconda?	First or second class?
Quando parte?	When do you go?
Deve cambiare a . . .	You have to change at . . .

Il treno parte dal binario uno	The train leaves from platform 1
C'è un treno ogni ora	There's a train every hour
Il treno viaggia con un ritardo di dieci minuti	The train will be delayed by ten minutes
Il prossimo treno per . . . viaggia con un ritardo	The next train for . . . is late
per causa di uno sciopero	. . . because of industrial action
biglietto, per favore	Tickets please
È salito qualcuno?	Any more tickets, please?
Salite, per favore	All aboard!
Cambiare a Pisa	Change at Pisa
I passeggeri per Milano devono cambiare qui	Change here for Milano
Il treno ferma qui. La coincidenza è . . .	All change please. The connection is . . .
qui/là, laggiù	Here/over there
Deve pagare un supplemento	You'll have to pay a supplement
Rapido 713 Udine–Venezia–Bologna è in partenza dal binario due	The express train 713 Udine–Venice–Bologna will leave from platform 2
Rapido 713 Udine–Venezia–Bologna viaggia con venti minuti di ritardo	The express train 713 Udine–Venice–Bologna will be 20 minutes late
Rapido 713 Udine–Venezia–Bologna è in partenza dal binario due	The express train 713 Udine–Venice–Bologna will leave from platform 2
Il treno appena giunto al binario 18 prosegue alle ore 5.53 per . . .	The train arriving at platform 18 is the 5.53 to . . .

If you do not understand announcements made over a public address system such as these, you can ask:

Non ho capito, potrebbe dirmi che cosa hanno detto all'altoparlante?	Can you tell me what was just announced on the PA?
Ai Treni	To the Trains
Arrivi/Partenze	Arrivals/Departures
Bagagli	Luggage
Bibite	Light Refreshments
Bigliettaio/Controllore	Guard/Ticket Collector
Binario/Marciapiede	Platform
Capostazione	Station Master
Carrello Bagagli	Luggage Trolley
Cartellone Indicatore	Platform Indicator
Cuccetta	Couchette
Deposito Bagagli	Left Luggage Lockers
Donne	Ladies
Entrata	Entrance
Ferrovie dello Stato (FFSS/FS)	Italian Railways
Fumatori/Non-fumatori	Smoker/Non-smoker
Le prime vetture/le vetture in testa	Front Coaches
Le ultime vetture/Le vetture in coda	Rear Coaches
Libero	Vacant
Occupato	Engaged
Orario Treni	Timetable
Sala d'Aspetto/d'Attesa	Waiting Room
Sportello Biglietti	Ticket Office
Sportello Informazioni	Information Desk
Tolette/Gabinetti	Lavatories/Toilets

Ufficio Viaggi	Travel Agency
Uomini	Gentlemen
Uscita	Exit
Vagone Letto	Sleeping Car
Vagone Ristorante	Restaurant Car

■ Please note:

The various kinds of trains in Italy are as follows:

EC	EuroCity – fast train, connecting European cities. Subject to payment of a supplement. The supplement includes seat reservation.
IC	InterCity – fast train, connecting major Italian cities: Milano–Roma, Venezia–Roma, Firenze–Roma, Roma–Palermo. Supplement required.
Expr	Treno espresso: Express trains
Dir	Treno diretto: Through trains
R	Treno con prenotazione obbligatoria del posti: Trains with obligatory seat reservation
PG	Treno a prenotazione facoltative con assegnazione gratuita del posto: Trains with optional seat reservation, free of charge
Z	Treno con pagamento di supplemento: Trains where surcharge is payable

If you need to arrive punctually, you should travel by EuroCity or InterCity.

There are several EuroCity trains which connect European centres, for example:

Daytime	Night-time
Dortmund–Sestri	Paris–Venice
Hamburg–Milan	Paris–Rome
Geneva–Milan	Cologne–Milan
Zurich–Milan	
Vienna–Rome	
Geneva–Venice	

Reservations (Riservazioni):

You are strongly advised to reserve a seat even if travelling first class as the trains are always overcrowded. The seat reservations for InterCity or EuroCity also include the supplement. During peak hours you can also use special trains (treni straordinari).

Seats can be reserved for normal, InterCity and EuroCity trains for journeys within Italy by dialling 110. Authorised travel agencies can also obtain tickets and make reservations for you.

It is also essential to reserve couchettes (posti cuccette) and sleeping car berths (posti letti) in advance. You can do this either through a travel agent (agenzie autorizzate) or directly through Compagnia Internazionale delle Carrozze letti del Turism.

There are porter services at stations. When buying train tickets in Italy ask about possible fare reductions.

Reductions (Riduzioni):

One of the cheapest tickets is the tourist ticket, 'biglietto turistico di libera circolazione', which can be bought abroad or at authorized travel agents in Italy. The ticket is valid for 8/15/21/30 days and can be used for an unlimited number of kilometres and journeys without any additional charges.

If you buy your ticket on the train, expect to pay a surcharge of 20%.

At 44 ticket offices of Italian State Railways you can buy a ticket using a credit card instead of cash.

You can obtain information about Italian State Railways at some of the larger stations at the 'Agenzie Viaggi' FS:

Bologna Centrale, Firenze S. Maria Novella, Genova Porta Principe, Livorno Centrale, Milano Centrale, Roma Termini, Napoli Centrale, Palermo Centrale, Pisa Centrale.

For telephone information about rail services you will find the number under 'Ferrovie dello Stato' in the telephone directory.

If you want to make enquiries about train services in Italy from abroad, contact travel agencies authorized to sell Italian train tickets. Unfortunately there are no FS representatives in the UK.

If you want to send luggage outside Italy you will have to fill in a Customs Declaration form ('dichiarazione verde').

For inquiries on freight you can contact:

Direzione Centrale Merchi
Piazza della Croce Rossa 1
00161 Roma
Tel: (06) 8419265

3.4 Ships, boats, ferries

When does the boat for . . . leave?	**Quando parte il prossimo traghetto per . .?**
Where can I get tickets?	**Dove si fanno i biglietti?**
I'd like a single/double cabin	**Vorrei una cabina singola/una cabina doppia**
How long does the crossing take?	**Quanto dura la traversata?**
When do we land at . . .?	**Quando siamo a . . .?**
Is the sea rough?	**Il mare è mosso?**
Where's the purser's office?	**Dove di trova l'ufficio del commissario?**
I feel sick, have you got anything for seasickness?	**Mi sento male, avete qualcosa contro il mal di mare?**

■ Please note:

Many ferries travel between the Italian mainland and the numerous island. These are operated by Italian State Railway (Ferrovie dello Stato), Tirrenia Navigazione, Grandi Traghetti and Sardinia Ferries. You can make enquiries about connections at shipping companies, travel agencies and local tourist information offices.

You can also reach the islands by car ferry. Phone (06) 4212 or contact the shipping companies for information about the following boat journeys:

Genoa–Bastia
Genoa–Porto Torres–Olbia–Cagliari–Arbatax
Genoa–Palermo
Livorno–Palermo
Cagliari–Palermo
Napoli–Cagliari
Napoli–Palermo

You can also write to the following:

**Assessorato al Turismo
Via Emanuele Notarbartolo 9
Palermo 90141
Tel: (091) 291777**

**Assessorato al Turismo
Viale Trento 69
Cagliari 09100
Tel: (070) 654393**

3.5 Cars

Which is the best road to . .?	**Qual è la strada migliore per . .?**
How many kilometres is it to . .?	**Quanti chilometri sono fino a . .?**
Have you got a road map?	**Ha una mappa stradale?**
Where does this road go to?	**Dove porta questa strada?**
Where's the nearest garage?	**Dov'è il prossimo distributore di benzina?**

Travel

Fill it up, please,	Il pieno, per favore,
. . . Lire worth, please	Per . . . Lire
Pleae check the oil/tyres/battery/water	Controlli l'olio/le gomme/la batteria/l'acqua, per favore
Wash and wax, please	Lavare e lubrificare, per favore
Where can I park?	Dove posso parcheggiare?
I've had an accident	Ho avuto un incidente
My car has broken down	Ho un guasto

See Part II, 7.5 for Accidents and Breakdowns.

You may hear or read the following words in Italian:

scorciatoia	short cut
targa	registration number
noleggio autoveicoli	car hire service
senza piombo/benzina verde	lead-free, unleaded
diesel	diesel
patente di guida	driving licence
macchine usate/di seconda mano	second hand cars
limite di velocità	speed limit
autocarro	lorry/truck
garage/parking	multi-storey car park
parking	car park
stazione servizio	petrol station/garage
garage sotterraneo	underground car park
numero dell'assicurazione	insurance number

■ Please note:

In Italy you drive on the right and overtake on the left. Those coming from the right have right of way.

It is obligatory to carry a hazard triangle with you for display in case of an accident. Seat belts are compulsory for the driver and front seat passenger.

Speed limits depend on the cubic-centimetre capacity of your engine:

	Roads	*Motorways*
up to 1100 cc	90 km/h (56 mph)	110 km/h (69 mph)
over 1100 cc	90 km/h	130 km/h
Lorries above 8 tonnes	60 km/h	80 km/h (50 mph)

In residential areas the speed limit is 50 km/h unless otherwise indicated.

Petrol is sold in litres. The types of fuel are:

Standard	Normale	91 octane
Standard unleaded	Normale senza piombo, Normale verde	91 octane
Four-star unleaded	Super senza piombo, Super verde	98 octane
Diesel	Diesel	

Some conversions for litres and gallons:

Gallons	1.1	2.2	4.4
Litres	5	10	20

Distances are measured in kilometres: 1 km is 0.622 mile; 1 mile is 1.609 km.

1.

3.

2.

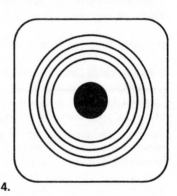

4.

Road and location signs

Blue background	**Località extraurbana**	Locality outside town
Yellow background	**Indicazioni turistiche**	Tourist information
Grey/white	**Strada importante**	Main road
White background	**Destinazioni urbane**	Destinations in the town centre

| Grey/yellow | **Indicazioni industriali** | Industrial estate |
| Green | **Indicazioni autostradali** | Motorways |

Motorways:

To use the motorways in Italy you will need small change to pay the tolls. If you pay in foreign currency you will receive change in lire. You can buy a special credit card for the motorway called a 'Viacard', obtainable from ACI, TCI, Autogrills and tobacconists'.

Emergency telephones for calling medical assistance or breakdown services are located every 2 km on the motorway. Alternatively, dial 116 for help.

ITALIAN TRAFFIC SIGNS

1. La sosta è vietata nei giorni dispari dal lato della ciffra I e nei giorni pari dal lato della ciffra II.
I giorni sono pari o dispari secondo la data 2, 4, 6, . . . ovvero 1, 3, 5, . . .)
Parking is forbidden on odd (uneven) dates at the side of the street of the number I and on even dates at the side of the street of number II.
Odd or even dates are the 1st, 3rd, 5th . . . of a given month or the 2nd, 4th, 6th of a month respectively.

2. Obbligo d'arresto all'incrocio su strade di montagna con autobus di linea
Obligation to stop when encountering a bus ('di linea') on mountainous road

3. Indica un tratto di strada adiacente un luogo di cura, per si cui sono da evitare il più possible i rumori.
Hospital nearby – avoid unnecessary noise.

4. CENTRO
Symbol for town centre

Radio traffic information:

Along the motorway are signs advertising RAI (Radio informazioni stradali) with the appropriate wavelengths. Information about road conditions is given daily to foreign motorists on the radio.

In addition to the ACI offices and the telephone emergency service, 24-hour information in foreign languages is available by dialling (06) 4212.

As the Italian Automobile Clubs work together with their European counterparts you can obtain much of this information before leaving home.

Petrol vouchers:

Petrol coupons can be obtained at a reduced price by motorists in their own countries or at offices at the frontier. Foreign currencies are accepted. At the same time you will also be given motorway vouchers. You will need to show these when purchasing petrol.

These vouchers also entitle you to use the ACI breakdown service, free of charge, and you can claim the use of a car while your own is being repaired after a breakdown or an accident.

Unused vouchers can be returned up to two years after issue and the money will be refunded.

Petrol vouchers can be bought at frontier offices, for example at Ventimiglia, Brennero Strada, Brogeda Autostrada, Ponte Chiasso Strada, Autoporto Val d'Aosta.

In Italy many petrol stations close at lunchtime during the week, and at weekends (except on motorways).

Parking:

Many Italian town centres are for pedestrians only. Car parks are located on the outskirts from where you travel into the centre by bus.

Supervised open-air parking areas are indicated by a sign showing a white P on a blue background. Parking fees are charged by the hour.

Areas in which parking is restricted are indicated by the following signs: zona a traffico limitato (ZTL); escluso veicoli autorizzati (area with limited access except for authorized vehicles).

This sign shows a car being towed away ('rimozione forzata'). Cars parked in the wrong place will certainly be towed away and taken to a pound. They can be recovered on payment of a fine of between 60,000 and 100,000 lire (about £120 to £200).

If you experience difficulties parking the city police (vigili urbani) will help you. They direct traffic and give information, which they can often do in foreign languages, at least in tourist centres.

Make sure that your car is securely locked and don't leave any valuables inside as thefts from cars are relatively common.

Parking is not allowed on black and yellow lines.

In blue areas you need a parking disc (disco di sosta), which you can obtain from the ACI.

What you may read on parking ticket vending machines:

Pagamento Parcometro	Payment by meter (Pay and Display)
9–18.00 dal lunedì al venerdì	between 9 a.m. and 6 p.m. Monday to Friday
Esporre il biglietto visibilmente	Parking ticket must be clearly visible
1 Selezionare la tariffa	Select the charge
2 Introdurre la moneta o la tessera	Insert coins or card
3 Esporre il biglietto sul cruscotto	Place parking ticket on the dashboard
Annullo	Cancellation
Fuori servizio	Out of order

The British and Italian automobile associations can give you information about traffic regulations and parking facilities:

ACI	**TCI**
Automobil Club Italiano	**Italian Touring Club**
Via Marsala 8	**Corso Italia 10**
00185 Roma	**20122 Milano**
Tel: (06) 4998	**Tel: (02) 85261**
AA: Automobile Association	**RAC: Royal Automobile Club**
Tel: 081-954 7373	**Tel: 081-686 2525**

Insurance numbers:

Insurance discs are fixed onto the windscreens of Italian cars. If you have an accident it is essential to make a note of the insurance number (controassegno di assicurazione) of the other car involved, the name of the car owner, how the accident occurred and details of any witnesses and the police station involved.

3.6 Car hire

Is there a car hire service nearby?	**C'è un autonoleggio qui vicino?**
I'd like to hire a car	**Vorrei noleggiare una macchina**
I need a big/small car for one week	**Mi occorre una macchina grande/piccola per una settimana**
How much does it cost per week/per day/per weekend?	**Qual è il prezzo per una settimana/al giorno/per un fine settimana?**
What do you charge per kilometre?	**Qual è il prezzo per il chilometro?**
What type of petrol does it run on?	**Con quale tipo di benzina va?**
Is the mileage unlimited?	**Il numero di chilometri è illimitato?**
How much is the insurance?	**Quanto viene l'assicurazione?**
Do I have to pay a deposit?	**Devo versare un deposito?**

Here's my driving licence/my identity card	**Ecco la mia patente/la mia carta d'identità?**
Do you accept credit cards?	**Accettate carte di credito?**
What documents do I need?	**Di quali documenti ho bisogno?**
Exclusion of liability	**Esonero da responsabilità**
Passenger insurance	**Assicurazione persone trasportate**

If you hire a car you may read or hear the following sentences in Italian:

Posso vedere la patente?	May I see your driving licence?
Compili il presente modulo, per favore	Fill in this form, please
L'assicurazione è di rigore	Insurance is required
È attualmente in possesso di un assicurazione autoveicoli?	Are you currently insured?
Desidera l'assicurazione supplementare?	Would you like the extra insurance?
Dove desidera restituire la macchina?	Where would you like to leave the car?
La vuole riportare qui?	Would you like to return it here?
Legge l'altro lato per informarVi delle condizioni generali	Please read other side for conditions
Dichiaro che tutte le indicazioni suddette rispondono a verità	I hereby declare that the above statements are true
Contrassegnate con le iniziali per favore	Your initials, please

General conditions (condizioni generali):

To hire a car in Italy you must produce a valid driving licence and a passport or identity card. You must be a minimum of 21 years of age – some companies stipulate a minimum of 25 years of age – and you must have had your driving licence for at least a year.

If you pay in cash a deposit of at least L250,000 is required. If you pay by credit card no deposit is necessary. The exact details of the hire-contract can be found on the back of the agreement. Sometimes insurance is included in the price, but at other times insurance and other services are additional costs.

comprehensive insurance	**assicurazione CASCO**
insurance cover against third party liability	**copertura assicurativa RCA con i seguenti massimali**
personal accident insurance for driver and passengers	**assicurazione per infortunio il conducente ed i passeggeri**
fire and theft insurance	**assicurazione incendio e furto auto**
Rental charge is subject to 19% Value-Added Tax	**IVA 19% sull'importo totale del noleggio**

Cars can be hired at stations and airports; hotels will also be able to give you the names of rental services.

Some names and addresses of car hire services (centri prenotazioni) in Italy are as follows:

Budget Rent-a-Car
  Milano, Via Vittor Pisano 7
  Tel: (02) 6709228/6694499
  Fax: (02) 6702469
  Firenze, Via Borgo Ognissanti 134 R
  Tel: (055) 293021
  Fax: (055) 293021
  Roma, Via Boncompagni 14/c
  Tel: (06) 4870010/4825726
  Fax: (06) 4870010

Autorent
  Head Office
  Via F. 11i Bandiera, 25
  Marghera–Venezia
  Tel: (041) 929272/ 921111
  Fax: (041) 5204880

Hertz
  Roma Tel: (06) 547991
  Milano Tel: (02) 20483
  Numero Verde 1678 22099

Europcar
  Head Office
  Via Fiume Giallo 196
  00144 Roma
  Tel: (06) 5732577
  Fax: (06) 5732317

Avis
  Roma Tel: (06) 4701400
  Telex: 610372
  Milano Tel: (02) 6888933
  Numero Verde: 1678 63063

4

Hotels and Restaurants

4.1 Hotels

Have you got a room free?	**C'è una camera libera?**
Can I have a quiet room, please?	**Posso avere una camera tranquilla, per favore?**
– not facing the street	**– che non dia sulla strada**
– a single room	**– una singola**
– a double room	**– una doppia**
– with a double bed	**– con letto matrimoniale**
– with twin beds	**– a due letti**
– with/without a bath/shower	**– con/senza bagno/doccia**
– with breakfast	**– con prima colazione**
– with half board	**– mezza pensione**
– with full board	**– pensione completa**
I made a reservation by phone	**Ho prenotato telefonicamente**
Can I see the room please?	**Posso vedere la camera?**
I'll take it	**La prendo**
I'm sorry, it's too small/too noisy	**Mi dispiace, ma è troppo piccola/ troppo rumorosa**
Can you show me another room, please?	**Potrebbe mostrarmi un altra camera?**
Have you got rooms with conference facilities?	**Avete delle sale per riunioni di affari?**

Requests:

Can you wake me at 7 o'clock, please?	**Può svegliarmi alle sette?**
Can you call a taxi, please?	**Può chiamarmi un taxi, per favore?**
Where can I leave my luggage?	**Dove posso lasciare il bagaglio?**

Where can I deposit our valuables?	**Dove posso depositare i valori?**
Where can I post a letter?	**Dove posso imbucare una lettera?**
Could you forward my post to . . ., please?	**Potrebbe inoltrare la mia posta a . . .?**
Could you bring me . . ., please? – some coathangers – a blanket – a pillowcase – an ash-tray	**Può portarmi . . ., per favore?** **– qualche attaccapanni** **– una coperta** **– un cuscino** **– un portacenere**
What's the voltage here? (In Italy, 220 volts, 50 Hz)	**Il voltaggio com'è?**
The lights are not working	**La luce non funziona**
Can you repair this?	**Può farla riparare?**
The TV needs repairing	**Il televisore dev'essere riparato**
switch/socket/plug	**interruttore/presa/spina**

Plugs normally used in Britain are not suitable for most Italian hotels. You should take a multiple adapter with you.

Can I have the bill, please?	**Posso avere il conto, per favore?**
Are tax and service included?	**Tassa e servizio sono inclusi?**
We're leaving tomorrow	**Partiamo domani**
Thank you for everything, we enjoyed ourselves very much	**Grazie di tutto, ci siamo sentiti a nostro agio**

Services:

I'd like to have my shoes cleaned, please	**Vorrei far lucidare le scarpe**
Can you wash these clothes, please?	**Potrei dar da lavare questi capi di vestiario?**
Can you dryclean and press my suit, please?	**Potete far pulire a secco e stirare l'abito?**

Can I have it back as soon as possible?	**Posso riaverlo al più presto?**
Can you repair these shoes, please?	**Potete far riparare queste scarpe?**
How much do I owe you?	**Quanto Vi devo?/Quanto Le devo**
Is there a hairdresser's in the hotel?	**C'è un parrucchiere in albergo?**
I'd like a haircut, please	**Vorrei farmi tagliare i capelli**
Is service included?	**Il servizio è compreso?**

General questions:

Has anyone asked for me?	**Qualcuno ha chiesto di me?**
Are there any messages for me?	**È stato lasciato detto qualcosa per me?**
Can you post these letters for me, please?	**Potrebbe imbucare queste lettere per favore?**
Do any tours leave from this hotel?	**Ci sono dei giri della città guidati che partono dall'albergo?**
Is there a good restaurant nearby?	**Mi può indicare un buon ristorante qui vicino?**
I need an interpreter who speaks English	**Avrei bisogno di un interprete che conosca l'inglese**

What you may hear or read in Italian in your hotel:

La posso aiutare?/Desidera?	Can I help you?
Ha prenotato una camera? **– con bagno/doccia** **– senza bagno/doccia**	Have you booked a room? – with bath/shower – without . . .
Quanto tempo intende rimanere?	How long do you want to stay?
Per una notte?	Just for one night?

101

Per quante notti?	For how many nights, please?
Per quando, per favore?	For what time, please?
Mi dispiace, siamo al completo	I'm sorry, we're fully booked
Siamo completi	Sorry, we're full
Desidera vedere la camera?	Would you like to see the room?
La camera costa . . .	The room costs . . .
La prima colazione (non) è compresa	Breakfast is (not) included
La prima colazione si serve delle . . . alle . . .	Breakfast is served from . . . to . . .
Lì c'è l'ascensore/il lift	There's a lift over there
Il ragazzo Le porterà il bagaglio in camera	The porter will take your luggage up
La prego di iscriversi	Will you sign the register, please?
Posso avere il passaporto?	May I see your passport, please?
Ha dei documenti d'identità?	Do you have some means of identification?
La prego di compilare questo modulo?	Would you fill in this form, please?
Firmi qui, per favore	Please sign here
Qual è la Sua professione?	What's your occupation, please?
L'indirizzo di dov'è domiciliato	Your home address, please
Come desidera pagare, in contanti o con carta credito?	How would you like to pay, in cash or by credit card?
Potrei avere un recapito, per favore?	Can I have a receipt, please

reception/portiere	receptionist
portabagagli/ragazzo	porter
telefonista	switchboard operator
cameriera	chambermaid

servizio camere	room service
I sigg. ospiti sono pregati di liberare la camera entro le ore 12,00 il giorno della partenza	Guests are requested to vacate their rooms before 12.00 noon on the day of departure
Non disturbare	Please do not disturb
Compilare in stampatello	Please complete in block letters

On the registration form you will find:

Cognome	Surname
Nomi	First names
Nazionalità	Nationality
Professione	Occupation
Data di nascita	Date of birth
Luogo di nascita	Place of birth
Domicilio	Home address
Numero . . .	Passport number
Rilasciato il . . .	Issued at
Prossima destinazione	Next destination
Data di arrivo	Date of arrival
Data di partenza	Date of departure
Firma	Signature

Breakfast:

During breakfast you might hear or read the following in Italian:

What's your room number, please?	**Che numero di camera ha?**
Are you ready to order?	**Desidera ordinare?**
What would you like for breakfast?	**Che cosa desidera come prima colazione?**

103

bread/toast/rolls	**pane/toast/panini**
with butter/jam	**con burro/marmellata**
coffee/tea	**caffè/tè**
hot chocolate	**cioccolata**
orange/grapefruit/tomato juice	**succo d'arancia/ di pompelmo/di pomodoro**
milk	**latte**
with cream/sugar/lemon	**crema/zucchero/limone**

■ Please note:

If you don't want to have breakfast in a bar, but in a hotel, you should ask if breakfast is included in the price. Breakfast normally consists of coffee or tea, bread and butter and jam.

The various types of accommodation:

Hotel/Albergho:	There are five different types of hotels in Italy: luxury, and first, second, third and fourth class.
Pensione:	Private hotels; these are divided into three classes. You can choose between half board (mezza pensione) and full board (pensione completa).
Locanda:	Inns. Simple accommodation, sometimes comprising only a restaurant.
Motels:	For information about motels you can contact: ACI, the Italian Automobile Club in Rome.
Albergo diurno:	These are often found at stations. A practical facility where you can rest and relax for a couple of hours during the day and where you will find the following services:
servizio bar	bar service

camere da riposo	rest room
deposito bagagli	left luggage
parrucchiere uomo e signora	ladies and gentlemen's hairdressers
manicure pedicure	manicure and pedicure
lavanderia	laundry
stireria	copying service
bagni/docce	baths/showers
toilettes/gabinetti	toilets
aperto tutti i giorni dalle 7 alle 20 festivi compresi	open daily from 7 am to 8 pm, including public holidays

There are several international hotel chains in Italy:

Best Western Italia
Via Cechov 48
Centro Bonola
20151 Milano
Tel: (02) 33 40 34 20
Fax: 33 40 39 34

Concorde Hotels Italy s.r.l.
Via Clerice 97
21040 Gerinzano
Tel: (02) 9682317

Space Hotels
(50 Hotels in Italy)
Via Marche 54
00187 Roma
Tel: 1678-13013

Ata Hotels SpA
Via Lampedusa 11a
20141 Milano
Tel: (02) 8467541/2/3/4
Telex: 326895 ATAHOT

Cigahotels SpA
(Luxury class)
San Marco Calle del Teatro 2245 A
30100 Venezia
Tel: (041) 782011
Fax: 52 11184

Jolly Hotels
Valdaguo 36078
Tel: (0445) 410000
Telex: 480077

Best Tours
Tour Operator
Via Aurora 39
00187 Roma
Tel: (06) 4817028

There are also numerous private hotels.

Finding a hotel:

You will be able to obtain addresses and reserve a room at airports, railway stations and local tourist information offices (Ente di Turismo).

ENIT, the Italian Tourist Board, publishes a comprehensive hotel guide every year.

When you book a room ask if the cost of breakfast is included and whether any taxes and service charges will be added to the price quoted, e.g. Value-Added Tax (IVA).

Hotel/tourist guides:

Italy 90/91: The Best Guide
Berti Renato, 1990

Guida agli Alberghi d'Italia
Giorgio Lindo and Mario Ghirardi
Editoriale l'Espresso, 1991

Guida Turistica d'Italia
Touring Club Italiano, Milan, 1987

4.2 Food and drink

Can you reserve a table for two, please, for 8 o'clock?	**Può riservarci un tavolo per due persone per le otto?**
Could we have a table by the window, please?	**Si potrebbe avere un tavolo vicino alla finestra?**
Is this seat taken?	**È occupato questo posto?**
Waiter/waitress	**Cameriere/Signorina**

We'd like something to drink, please	**Desideriamo qualcosa da bere, per favore**
May I see the menu, please?	**Posso avere la lista del giorno/il menu?**
May I see the wine list, please?	**Mi può dare la lista dei vini, per favore?**
What would you recommend?	**Che cosa ci raccomanda?**
hors d'œuvres/starters	**antipasto**
main course	**secondo**
dessert	**dessert/dolce**
a set meal	**menu turistico**
soup	**minestra**
meat	**carne**
poultry	**pollo**
fish	**pesce**
vegetables	**verdura**
salad	**insalata**
fruit	**frutta**
pie	**soufflé**
baked/grilled	**fritto/alla griglia**
boiled/stewed	**bollito/cucinato a vapore**
roasted	**arrosto**
What's today's special?	**Qual è il piatto del giorno?**
I'm hungry/thirsty	**Ho fame/sete**
I only want a snack, please	**Vorrei una piccolezza**
For starters I'll have . . .	**Prendo come antipasto . . .**
I'm in a hurry, can I have the bill, please?	**Ho molta fretta, se mi da il conto**
We'd like to pay separately	**Paghiamo separatamente**
Altogether, please	**Un conto unico, per favore**
Is everything included?	**È tutto compreso?**
Is service included?	**Il servizio è compreso?**
How much is it?	**Quanto fa?**

I'm afraid you have made a mistake	**Temo che ci sia un errore**
Do you accept traveller's cheques/credit cards?	**Accettate anche traveller's cheques/carta di credito?**
Thank you, that's for you	**Grazie, è per Lei**
Keep the change	**Va bene così**
Where are the toilets?	**Dove sono i gabinetti/le tolette?**
It tastes very good/nice	**È tutto molto buono**
I've enjoyed the meal	**Mi è piaciuto molto**
I'm afraid that's not what I ordered	**Guardi che ho ordinato un'altra cosa**
It's too cold/tough/salty	**È troppo freddo/duro(a)/ salato(a)**

At a restaurant you might hear or read in Italian:

Mi segua, per favore	Come this way, please
Che cosa desidera da bere?	What would you like to drink?
Le posso raccomandare . . .	I can recommend . . .
Quale antipasto desidera?	What would you like to start with?
Che cosa prende? **– di secondo** **– dolce**	What would you like? – as a main course – as a dessert?
Come vuole la bistecca?	How would you like your steak done?
– cotta/media/al sangue	– well-done/medium/rare
Purtroppo non abbiamo . . .	Sorry, we don't have any . . .
Purtroppo il lunedì abbiamo giorno di riposo, siamo chiusi	I'm sorry, we don't open on Mondays
dish of the day	**piatto del giorno**
set menu	**lista del giorno**

home-made	**fatto in casa**
recommended by the chef	**raccomandata dallo chef**
cold buffet	**buffet freddo**

There are various types of eating places in Italy:

Ristorante	Restaurant
Trattoria	Simple local cooking, highly recommended
Pizzeria	not only pizzas; other dishes served too
Taverna	simple cooking, drinks served
Locanda	very simple food
Rosticceria	grill-snacks, usually eaten standing up
Creperia	sells all kinds of pancakes
caffé	see below
Bar	see below
Paninoteca	serves tasty sandwiches, cold or toasted
Osteria	normally very simple food, where you can drink wine and have a snack, but can also be very smart and expensive
Pasticceria	confectioner
Gelateria	ice-cream parlour

Bars:

Bars are open from 7 am until 10 pm and serve snacks like sandwiches, cake and rolls, as well as alcoholic and non-alcoholic drinks. It is cheaper to have your snack standing at the bar or around the small tables than sitting down. There are bars in almost every street and they are very popular. You can eat breakfast or a light lunch and meet friends here after work for a drink or an aperitif before dinner.

At most bars it is customary to pay at the cash desk before presenting the receipt (scontrino) and ordering.

Aperitifs (aperitivi)

Campari (soda/bitter)
Martini
Grappa
Analcolico
Aperitivo della casa

A choice of savouries, biscuits and olives is often served with aperitifs.

Cafés (caffè):

In cafés you will normally be served hot and cold drinks, buttered rolls with cheese or meat, and cake. Very often a set breakfast is offered.

Various kinds of coffee are served in Italy:

espresso   black, very strong, served in small cups

cappucino   coffee with milk (froth) and a dusting of cocoa powder

caffelatte   half coffee, half milk (like café au lait in France).

lungo   quite weak coffee served in a tall glass

Restaurants (ristoranti):

In restaurants you can ask for the tourist menu (menu turistico) comprising three to four courses at a fixed price, if you are in a hurry, or the dish of the day (piatto del giorno).

You should always keep the bill because random checks may be made by the police outside the restaurant to find out if the customer has paid 'properly'. Restaurants have to present these bills ('ricevuta fiscale') to the tax office.

Usually the dish ('coperta') and the bread ('pane') have to be paid for separately. Even though service charges are usually included in the price – 'menu tutto compreso' – you should still leave a tip.

■ Meals in Italy:

Italian cuisine does not only mean spaghetti and pizzas: you should ask for local specialities (specialità locali) and local wines. A good Italian meal consists of:

hors d'œuvres (antipasti), soup/risotto (primo piatto di minestre/risotto), main course (secondo piatto), dessert (dolce), cheese (formaggio).

First course (Antipasti)

All pasta dishes are recommended for the first course, but do not be surprised if the portions are small. It is unusual to have only pasta.

For those who like a soup, Zuppa Pavese, clear soup with toasted cheese, is very good. Risotto can be very tasty as well. This is a rice dish with various regional differences – for example, 'risotto ai frutti di mare' (rice with seafood) or 'risotto nero', a Venetian speciality of rice and squid, the ink of the fish giving the dish its characteristic black colour.

Second course (Carne)

There are many typical Italian meat dishes which are worth trying:

saltimbocca alla Romana (veal cutlet with ham and sage), scaloppine al Marsala (veal cutlet cooked in Marsala), bistecca alla Fiorentina (a huge rib steak like a T-bone), scaloppa alla Milanese (fillet of veal cooked in breadcrumbs).

Second course (Pesce)

Fish can be highly recommended; very good fresh fish dishes are served almost everywhere in Italy.

Vegetables (Contorni)

Vegetables are ordered separately.

finocchi al gratin, al forno (fennel with a lightly browned crust of breadcrumbs and cheese), peperonata (steamed vegetables, including red peppers, aubergine, courgettes and tomatoes).

111

Desserts (Dolci)

zuppa inglese (a kind of trifle with biscuits, vanilla sauce, and fruit marinated in alcohol, which is covered and baked with meringue), firami sù (a combination of Boudoir biscuits, Mascarpone cream, coffee and alcohol), crostata di frutta (a kind of Linz gateau), frutta (fruit), macedonia (fruit salad).

Book tips:

Hotels and Restaurants in Italy
Michelin

Guide to Italy (*Restaurants*)
(GMG Publishing)

Guida ai Ristorante
Editoriale l'Espresso, 1991

Ristorante di Veronelli
Luigi Veronelli
Jaca Book, Milan, 1990

Drinks:

I'd like . . .	Vorrei . . .
a black coffee	**un caffè**
with cream	**con panna/crema**
without sugar	**senza zucchero**
a tea	**un tè**
with lemon/milk	**con limone/latte**
a glass of milk	**un bicchiere di latte**
a hot chocolate	**una cioccolata calda**
a glass of mineral water	**un bicchiere di minerale**
lemonade	**limonata**
orange juice	**succo di arancia**
a beer/lager	**una birra**
a pint	**un mezzo litro**
a cognac/brandy	**un cognac**
a gin and tonic	**un gin tonic**
a red/white wine	**del vino rosso/bianco**

champagne	**spumante**
sherry	**sherry**
. . . dry/medium-dry/sweet	**. . . secco/medio/dolce**
a whisky with/without ice	**whisky con/senza ghiaccio**
a glass of tap water	**un bicchiere d'acqua**
waiter/waitress	**cameriere/signorina**
the bill, please	**il conto, per favore**
Is service included?	**Il servizio è compreso?**

■ Italian wines:

Italy is famous for its wines, which come from all parts of the country. Listed below are the names of some of the best-known wines and wine districts.

Piemonte:	Barolo	(red)
	Barbaresco	(red)
	Barbera	(dry red)
	Asti Spumante	(sparkling white wine)
Verona:	Valpolicella	(red)
	Bardolino	(light dry red wine)
	Soave	(dry white wine)
Tuscany:	Chianti	(red wine)
	. . . classico	(quality Chianti)
	. . . riserva	(superior quality)
Rome:	Frascati	(dry white wine)

You will find the following labels:

| DOC | **Denominazione di Origine Controllata** | wine that has been tested in a registered district of origin |
| DOCG | **Denominazione di Origine Controllata e Garantita** | top-quality wine that has been tested and grown in a specific area |

You can also ask for 'vino aperto' (wine that has been opened), 'vino della casa' (house wine).

113

Book tips:

Conoscere i Vini
Il Castello, Milan, 1969

Vini d'Italia 1990
Gambero Rosso Editore, 1989

Grandi Vini Italiani
La Spiga, Milan, 1990

Everybody's Wine Guide
Anthony Hogg
Quiller Press, London, 1985

Pocket Wine Book 1990
Hugh Johnson
Mitchell Beazley, London

What you may read or hear in an Italian bar:

Vendita vini e alcolici	Off-Licence
Ancora una birra?	Another beer?
Grande o piccola?	Large or small?
Di nuovo la stessa cosa?	The same again?
Che cosa prende, offro io	What are you drinking, it's my round
Che cosa prende/beve?	What will you have?
▶ Vorrei un quartino di vino rosso/bianco	▶ I'd like a half litre of red/white wine
▶ una bibita non-alcolica, per favore	▶ A soft drink/non-alcoholic drink, please
Desidera qualcos'altro?	Anything else?
▶ No, grazie, per il momento va bene così	▶ No, thank you, not just at the moment
Salute/Cincin	Cheers
Offro io	Let me pay
▶ Grazie, molto gentile	▶ That's very nice of you, thank you

114

5

In Town

5.1 Asking the way

Can you help me, please? I've lost my way

Può aiutarmi, ho sbagliato strada

How do I get to . . .?

Vorrei andare a . . .?

I'm looking for . . .

Cerco . . .

I wonder if you can tell me the way to . . .?

Sa dirmi per caso dov'è . . .?

Where's the nearest bank?

Dove trovo una banca qui vicino?

▶ straight on at the traffic lights
▶ (to the) right
▶ (to the) left
▶ straight ahead
▶ first left
▶ second right
▶ at the roundabout
▶ you'll see it opposite
▶ you'll see it on your right
▶ I'm afraid you're going in the wrong direction
▶ I'm afraid I don't know
▶ I couldn't tell you, you'd better ask again

▶ **dopo il semaforo continua sempre dritto**
▶ **a destra**
▶ **a sinistra**
▶ **diritto**
▶ **la prima a sinistra**
▶ **la seconda a destra**
▶ **alla circolazione rotatoria**
▶ **proprio qui di fronte**
▶ **lo/a vede a destra**
▶ **Tempo che stia andando nella direzione sbagliata**
▶ **Mi dispiace non lo so**
▶ **Non glielo so dire, mi dispiace, chieda di nuovo**

Is it far/nearby?
▶ it's five minutes' walk
▶ ten minutes by car
▶ take the bus/train/tram

▶ You can't miss it

È lontano/vicino?
▶ **cinque minuti a piedi**
▶ **dieci minuti con la macchina**
▶ **prenda l'autobus/il treno/il tram**
▶ **non può non vederlo**

5.2 Public transport: buses, trams, Underground, taxis

Tickets for public transport can be bought at tobacconists', bars, and newspaper stands which display the sign 'vendita biglietti'. The tickets are usually valid for a limited period, and you must cancel them in the bus or tram. Instructions on how to do this are given as:

Solo obliterazione   Please cancel tickets yourself

Tickets for the little boats (vaporetti) which operate as public transport in Venice must be bought before boarding.

Buses, trams:

How often do the buses run?	**Ogni quanti minuti passano gli autobus?**
Do you go near . .?	**Va verso . .?**
Do you go to . .?	**Va in via . . ./in piazza . . .?**
Whereabouts in . . . Street?	**È dove ferma precisamente in via . . .?**
Please let me know when we get to . . .	**Mi può dire quando siamo a . . .?**
Would you let me off, please?	**Mi lascia scendere, per piacere?**
Are you getting off at the next stop?	**Scende alla prossima fermata?**

What you might hear or read in Italian in this context:

distributore automatico biglietti	automatic ticket machine
uscita di emergenza	emergency exit
salita solo davanti	entry at the front
salita soli dietro	entry at the rear
pagare con denaro contato	exact fare please

deve prendere la linea 25	you want a number 25
Le dirò quando siamo arrivati	I'll tell you when we get there
Attenzione	Attention/mind your step
Tutte le fermate sono a richiesta	request stops only
È pertanto necessario segnalare per tempo al guidatore l'intenzione di salire alla fermata	It is important to indicate to the driver in good time that you want to board
Per scendere, premere, per tempo, gli appositi pulsanti a lato delle portiere	To alight, please press the button near the exit in good time
dal lunedì al venerdì	from Monday to Friday
sabato	Saturdays
festivo	Bank holidays
primi passaggi	first journeys
ultimi passaggi	last journeys

■ Please note:

When buying tickets for trams, buses, trolley buses (filovia) or the Underground, you should ask for daycards (biglietto valido per la giornata) or booklets of tickets (libretto per più corse).

Underground

Where's the nearest Underground station, please?	**Dov'è la fermata della metropolitana, per piacere?**
Where can I buy tickets?	**Dove posso fare i biglietti?**
▶ at the counter	▶ **allo sportello**
▶ at the automatic ticket machine	▶ **al distributore automatico**
How much is it to . . .?	**Quanto costa il biglietto per . . .?**
Do I have to change?	**Devo cambiare?**

Where do I change for . .?	**Dovo devo cambiare per . .?**
Is the next station . .?	**La prossima fermata è . .?**
Where do I have to get off?	**Dove devo scendere?**
Are you getting off at the next station?	**Scende alla prossima fermata?**
Could you tell me when we get there, please?	**Mi può dire quando devo scendere, per favore?**

There are Underground systems in Milan and Rome. Tickets can be bought from vending machines, tobacconists and newsagents.

The instructions for use of these machines ('distributore biglietti') are given in several languages. Details of the lines, stations and connections are displayed.

Taxis:

Where can I find a taxi?	**Dove trovo un taxi?**
Will you get me a taxi, please?	**Mi chiami un taxi, per favore**
Is there a taxi-rank nearby?	**C'è qui vicino un parcheggio taxi?**
Is there any chance of getting a taxi at this time of day?	**Si trova a quest'ora un taxi libero?**
To the . . . Hotel, please	**All'hotel . . ., per favore**
Can you take me to . . .?	**Mi porti in . . ., per favore**
What's the fare to . . .?	**Quanto costa la corsa per . . .?**
I'm in a hurry, will you take the shortest route, please?	**Ho molta fretta, prenda la via più breve, per favore**
Can you stop on the corner please?	**Si fermi all'angolo**
Can you wait, please?	**Può attendere, per favore?**
Could you put my bags into the taxi, please?	**Porti il mio bagaglio nel taxi, per piacere**
Can you give me change, please?	**Mi può dare il cambio?**

Keep the change | **Va bene così. Tenga, è per Lei**

■ Please note:

The colours of Italian taxis vary from town to town. You will find taxis at cab-ranks or you can phone for them (the numbers can be found in the telephone directory or in your hotel). You can also hail a passing taxi.

The fare is shown on the taximeter, and there are additional charges for luggage and night journeys.

At airports be sure to ask beforehand what the fare is likely to be.

5.3 Shopping

antique shop	**negozio di antiquariato**
baker's	**panetteria, panificio**
bookshop	**libreria**
chemist's	**farmacia/drogheria**
china shop	**negozio di porcellane**
confectioner's	**pasticceria**
currency exchange/bureau de change	**cambio/ufficio cambio**
dairy	**latteria**
department store	**grande magazzino**
dry cleaner's	**tintoria**
electrical supplies shop	**negozio di elettrodomestici**
boutique/clothes shop	**negozio di moda**
flea market	**mercato delle pulci**
florist's	**fiorista/negozio di fiori**
furniture shop	**negozio di mobili**
furrier's	**pellicceria**
greengrocer's	**erbivendolo**
grocer's	**alimentari**
haberdasher's	**merceria**
hairdresser's	**parrucchiere** (women), **barbiere** (men)
health food shop	**negozio di prodotti dietetici**
ironmonger's	**negozio di ferramenta**
jeweller's	**gioielliere**

laundry/laundrette	**lavanderia**
leather shop	**pelletteria**
market	**mercato**
newsagent	**giornalaio**
off-licence	**negozio di bevande alcoliche**
optician	**ottico**
perfumery	**profumeria**
photographer's	**negozio di fabbisogno fotografico/fotografo**
record shop	**negozio di dischi**
self-service	**self-service**
shoe shop	**negozio di scarpe/calzature**
souvenir shop	**negozio di souvenir**
sports shop	**articoli da sport**
stationer's	**cartoleria**
sweet shop	**confettureria**
supermarket	**supermercato**
tailor's/dressmaker's	**sarto**
toyshop	**negozio di giocattoli**
tourist information centre	**centro informazioni turistiche**
travel agency	**ufficio viaggi**
watchmaker's	**orologiaio**
wine merchant's	**fiaschetteria**

Where are the biggest department stores?	**Dove si trovano i grandi magazzini?**
Can you tell me where I can find a good bookshop?	**Mi sa dire dov'è una grande libreria?**
Where can I buy/get . . .?	**Dove posso comprare . . .?**
Is it far/nearby?	**È lontano/vicino?**
How do I get there?	**Che strada prendo?**
Which floor is the gift department on, please?	**Dove trovo il reparto regali, a quale piano?**
Can you help me, please?	**Mi può esser di aiuto?**
I'd like an electrical adapter, please	**Avrei bisogno di un adapter elettrico**
Can you show me . . ., please?	**Mi può far vedere . . .?**

Can you show me some other . . . please?	**Me ne può mostrare anche altri, per favore?**
May I try it on?	**Posso provare?**
How much is this?	**Quanto viene?**
Please write it down for me	**Me lo scriva, per favore**
It's too expensive/small	**È troppo caro/piccolo**
Have you got anything cheaper?	**Ha qualcosa a più buon mercato?**
It's fine, I'll take it	**Va bene, lo(a) prendo**
No, thank you, I don't like it	**Grazie, ma non è di mio gusto**
I think I'll leave it, thanks	**Grazie, ma non credo lo(a) prenderò**
I'll come back later	**Ritorno più tardi**
I'm just looking	**Vorrei dare un'occhiata**
I'm being served, thank you	**Grazie, mi stanno già servendo**
Can I pay by traveller's cheques?	**Posso pagare con traveller's cheques?**
Do you accept credit cards?	**Accettate carte di credito?**
Has VAT been deducted?	**L'IVA viene detratta?**
Can I have a receipt, please?	**Posso avere una ricevuta/uno scontrino?**
Can I have a carrier-bag, please?	**Mi dà un sacchetto/una sportina, per favore?**
Can you wrap it up for me, please?	**Le dispiace impacchettare tutto per me?**
Would you send it to this address, please?	**Sarebbe da mandare a questo indirizzo**
Can I change this, please?	**Posso cambiare questo?**

See Part II, 7.6 for phrases to use when returning goods.

When shopping you might hear the following:

Posso aiutarLa?　　　　　　　　Can I help you?

Che cosa desidera?　　　　　　　What would you like?

Qual è Sua taglia/qual è il　　　What colour/size would you like?
colore che desidera?

Che taglia porta?　　　　　　　What size are you?

Si trova al piano terra/al primo/　It's on the ground floor/first/
al secondo piano　　　　　　　second floor

Temo che non l'abbiamo più　　I'm afraid we are out of stock

Non abbiamo . . .　　　　　　　We haven't any . . .

Questo è tutto quello che Le　　I'm sorry that's all we have
posso mostrare

Si accomodi alla cassa, prego　　The cash desk is over there

Come desidera pagare? In　　　How are you paying? Cash?
contanti?

Con assegno/con carta di　　　By cheque/by credit card?
credito?

Questa è la Sua copia/ricevuta　This is your copy/receipt

Firmi qui, per favore　　　　　Sign here, please

Mi dispiace, ma non accettiamo　I'm sorry, we don't accept
traveller's cheques　　　　　　traveller's cheques

Non ho da darLe cambio　　　I can't change that note

IVA (Imposta sul valore　　　　VAT (Value Added Tax)
aggiunto)

Le posso dare un buono　　　　I can give you a credit note

Altro?　　　　　　　　　　　　Anything else?

Orario chiusura negozi　　　　Closing time

Commesso(a)　　　　　　　　Shop assistant

Che colore desidera?　　　　　Which colour would you like?

chiaro/scuro　　　　　　　　light/dark

bianco/nero	white/black
rosso	red
azzurro/blù	blue/navy blue
giallo/verde	yellow/green
marrone/beige	brown/beige
lilla	lilac
viola	violet
color porpora	purple
rosa	pink
grigio	grey
oro/argento	gold/silver

Clothing sizes

Women's clothing:

Continental	36	38	40	42	44
Great Britain	10	12	14	16	18

Menswear

Continental	46	48	50	52	54	56
Great Britain	36	38	40	42	44	46

Men's shirts

Continental	36	37	38	39	40	42
Great Britain	14	14½	15	15½	16	17

Shoes

Continental	38	39	41	42	43	44	45
Great Britain	5	6	7	8	9	10	11

■ Please note:

Many shops in Italy are closed on Monday mornings; food shops on Wednesdays or Thursday afternoons. Shops are usually open at the following times:

Monday till Friday: 9.30 am – 12.30 pm and 3.30 pm – 7.30 pm
Food shops: 8.30 am – 1.00 pm and 4.00 pm – 7.30 pm
Saturdays: 9.00 am – 4.00 pm

Times may vary from shop to shop.

Book tip:

Guida Capital d'Italia
(A guide to shopping across Italy)
Rizzoli

■ Tabacchi

'Tabacchi' (tobacconists) also function as bars. They usually open between 7 am and 8 pm. Tabacchi can be recognized by a black sign on which there is a white T.

If you smoke be sure to get your supply during these hours as it may be difficult to buy cigarettes in the evenings or on Sundays. There are no cigarette vending machines in Italy: cigarettes can only be sold by shops and bars specially authorized for this purpose.

5.4 At the bank

Where's the nearest bank, please?	**C'è una banca qui vicino, per favore?**
. . . a bureau de change	**. . . un ufficio cambio?**
I'd like to change £100	**Vorrei cambiare 100 libre sterline/pounds**
What's the exchange rate, please?	**A quanto quota il pound?**
Where can I buy Italian currency?	**Dove posso comprare valuta italiana?**

I'd like to cash traveller's cheques, please	**Vorrei riscuotere dei traveller's cheques**
What commission do you charge?	**Quant'è la tassa?**
I've got a credit card/letter of credit	**Ho una carta di credito/ credenziale**
I'd like . . . notes	**Vorrei avere banconote da . . .**
. . . in small notes, please	**. . . in piccole banconote**
Some small change, please	**Qualcosa in spiccioli, per favore**
Can foreigners open an account here?	**È possibile per uno straniero aprire un conto presso la Vs. banca?**
I'd like to open a current/ deposit account	**Vorrei aprire un conto corrente/ conto di risparmio**
I'd like to pay money into my account	**Vorrei versare del denaro sul mio conto**
. . . to draw money from my account	**. . . prelevare una somma**

You might read or hear the following at a bank:

Ha il passaporto, per favore?	May I see your passport, please?
Firmi qui, prego	Sign here, please
La Sua carta assegni, per favore	Your banker's card, please
Si accomodi alla cassa	Go to the cash desk, please
Come desidera il denaro?	How would you like your money?
valuta estera	foreign currency
codice bancario	bank sort code
spese amministrative	handling charge/bank charge
ordine permanente	standing order
reparto divise	foreign exchange department
conto corrente	current account

carta di credito	credit card
conto di risparmio	deposit account, savings account
versamento	remittance/transfer
officio cambio	foreign exchange
mandato di pagamento	money order
ricorrere a un credito/prendere	to raise a loan/to borrow money
un prestito	from the bank

■ Please note:

Banks usually close for lunch. They are open from Monday to Friday at the following times: 8.35 am – 12.35 pm and 3.00 pm – 4.00 pm.

At some of the larger railway stations are branches of the Banca Nazionale delle Comunicazioni, which are open from 8.30 am to 7.30 pm (on public holidays from 8.00 am to 2.15 pm).

There are bureaux de change at the major airports; these are open longer than the banks.

Italian lire are available in the following denominations:

Coins: 500, 200, 100, 50, 20, 10, 5
Banknotes: 100,000; 50,000; 10,000; 2,000; and 1,000

Using a Eurocard and your personal identification number you can withdraw up to 300,000 lire from a cashpoint (bancomat). Instructions for use are given in English, French, German and Italian.

Eurocheques are accepted at all banks, although not without a passport or some other means of identification. These cheques are not, however, accepted in all shops.

International credit cards are accepted in many shops, restaurants and hotels, facsimiles of which are usually displayed on doors or windows as a guide.

There is no limit on the amount of Italian money that can be brought into the country, but only a limited amount can be taken out. For larger sums of money a Customs Certificate (V2) is necessary. You should ask your bank for further details.

Addresses of some Italian banks:

Banca d'Italia
Via Nazionale 91
00184 Roma
Tel: (06) 47921

Banca d'Italia
39 King Street
London EC2V 8JJ
Tel: 071-606 4201

Banca Commerciale Italiana
P. della Scala 6
20121 Milano
Tel: (02) 88501

Banca Commerciale Italiana
42 Gresham Street
London EC2V 7LA
Tel: 071-600 8651

Banca Nazionale
    dell'Agricoltura
Via Salaria 231
00199 Roma
Tel: (06) 85881

Banca Nazionale
    dell'Agricoltura
85 Gracechurch Street
London EC3V 0AR
Tel: 071-623 2773

Banca Popolare di Milano
P. Meda 4
20121 Milano
Tel: (02) 77001

Banca Popolare di Milano
51 Moorgate
London EC2R 6AE
Tel: 071-628 4210

Banco di Napoli
Via Toledo 177
80132 Napoli
Tel: (081) 7911111

Banco di Napoli
1 Moorgate
London EC2R 6JH
Tel: 071-726 4131

Banco di Roma
Via Tupini 180
00144 Roma
Tel: (06) 54451

Banco di Roma
87 Gresham Street
London EC2V 7NQ
Tel: 071-726 4106

Istituto Bancario S. Paolo di
    Torino
P. San Carlo 156
10121 Torino
Tel: (011) 5551

Istituto Bancario S. Paolo di
    Torino
9 St Paul's Churchyard
London EC4M 8AB
Tel: 071-822 7800

5.5 At the post office

Where's the nearest post office?	**C'è un ufficio postale qui vicino?**
What time does it close?	**A che ora chiude?**
At which counter can I get stamps, please?	**A quale sportello posso comprare dei francobolli?**
A stamp for a postcard to England, please	**Un francobollo per cartolina per l'Inghilterra, per favore**
How much is a letter to . . .?	**Quanto va per una lettera in . . .?**
Two 500-lire stamps, please	**Due bolli da cinquecento, per favore**
Do you have any special editions?	**Avete francobolli commemorativi?**
I'd like to send a telegram	**Vorrei spedire un telegramma**
How long will this letter take to get to England?	**Quanto metterà questa lettera per l'Inghilterra?**
By airmail	**Per via aerea**
By surface mail	**Per posta normale**
How much is the postage?	**Quant'è l'affrancatura?/Quanto ci va di bollo?**

You might read or hear the following at an Italian post office:

Strettamente confidenziale	Private and confidential
Accettazione meccanizzata	Circulars by mail
Aerogrammi	Airmail letters
Altre destinazioni	Other destinations
Assegno	Postal order
Buca delle lettere	Letterbox
CAP (Codice Avviamento Postale)	Postcode

Carte valori	Stamps
Cartoline illustrate/Cartoline postali	Postcards
Chiuso	Closed
Con preghiera di far seguire	To be forwarded
Conti di credito	Credit account
Corrispondenze	Letter rate
Destinatario	Addressee
Distribuzione racommandate casellisti	Distribution of registered letters for boxholders
Espresso	Express letter
Fermo Posta	Poste restante
Filatelia	Special stamps
Lettere espresso	Express delivery
Lettere raccomandatea	Registered letters
Lettere	Letters
Levata	Collection
Mittente	Sender
Orario apertura	Opening hours
Paccetti postali	Small parcels
Pacchi	Parcels
Pagine gialle	Yellow Pages
Per l'estero	Abroad
Raccomandate per l'estero	Registered letter abroad
Raccomandate per l'intero	Registered letter inland
Raccomandazione	Registered matter
Stampe	Printed matter
Tasse	Charges

129

Ufficio postale/poste	Post office
Vaglia postale	Postal orders
Vendita francobolli	Sale of stamps
Compensi diversi	Various fees

■ Please note:

There are over 14,000 post offices in Italy. Smaller post offices are very often open until mid-day on Saturdays, and from about 8.30 am until 1.50 pm weekdays.

Main post offices are open until 6.15 pm to 7.50 pm, and on Saturdays to 6.40 pm, especially for individual deliveries, telegrams/fax and payments by postal order.

A yellow sign on which there is a blue PT indicates the location of a post office.

The Italian Post Office provides three services: Delivery (letters, telegrams, parcels), money service (telegraphic and normal postal orders, money transfer, etc.), express service national (PI) and international (CAI post).

There is a special express service for deliveries weighing up to 20 kg which need to be delivered quickly and safely to major cities in Italy: Servizio posta celere interna (PI). The offices which offer this service are located in several large towns: Bologna, Florence, Genova, Livorno, Milan, Naples, Palermo, Rome, Turin, Verona and Padua. The opening hours, from Monday to Friday, are between 8.30 am and 7.30 pm and on Saturdays, between 8.30 am and noon.

CAI is an express service that is similar to Datapost. It operates between Italy and most European countries. Should you have any queries about Italian postal services you can dial 160 daily from 8.00 am to 8.00 pm.

5.6 Telephones

Where's a public telephone (call) box?	**C'è un telefono pubblico qui vicino?**

I'd like to make an international phone call	**Vorrei telefonare all'estero**
What's the cost of the call?	**Quanto costa la chiamata?**
May I use your telephone, please?	**Posso usare il telefono?**
Have you got a phone book?	**Ha un elenco telefonico?**
Information, please	**Le informazioni, per favore**
Directory enquiries	**Informazioni telefoniche**
I'd like the number . . . please	**Vorrei avere il numero . . .**
Can I dial direct?	**Posso formare il numero direttamente!**
Can you put me through to . . .?	**Mi può collegare con . . .?**
I'd like extension 123, please	**Vorrei il numero interno 123, per favore**
Can I call abroad from here?	**Posso chiamare all'estero da questo apparecchio**
I'd like to reverse the charges, please	**Vorrei fare una chiamata con risposta pagata**
Miller speaking	**Parla il signor/la signora Miller**
Can I speak to . . ., please?	**Posso parlare con . . .?**
▶ Speaking	**▶ Sono io**
▶ Sorry, he isn't in	**▶ Mi dispiace, è fuori**
When will he be back?	**Quando sarà di ritorno?**
Could you take a message, please?	**Potrebbe lasciargli un messaggio?**
Please tell him I called	**Gli dica, per favore, che ho telefonato**
Please ask him to call back	**Lo preghi di richiamarmi non appena possibile**
I'll give you a ring	**Richiamerò**
I'm ringing about . . .	**Telefono per via di . . .**

131

You might hear the following Italian words and sentences on the telephone and see them written in telephone boxes:

Pronto	Hallo
Una chiamata/telefonata per Lei	There's a telephone call for you
Chiamate urbane/interurbane	A local/national call
Telefonata all'estero	An international call
Chiamata con risposta pagata	A reverse charge call
Chi parla?/Qui parla	Who's calling, please?
Sono Smith	Smith speaking
Purtroppo non è qui	Sorry, she's out at the moment
È a una seduta	He's at a meeting
Può richiamarLa?	Can he call you back?
Mi da il Suo numero, per favore?	Can I take your number?
Chi devo dire ha telefonato/ha chiamato?	Who shall I say called?
Vuole lasciare un messaggio?	Would you like to leave a message?
Non risponde nessuno	I'm sorry there's no answer
La linea è occupata, vuole attendere un momento?	The line's engaged, will you hold?
Non riagganci	Hold the line, please
Tutte le linee sono occupate	All the lines are engaged
Le passo	I'll put you through
Mi dispiace, ho sbagliato numero	Sorry, wrong number
Il numero chiamato non esiste più	Number unobtainable

Un tale numero non esiste	There's no such number
Non si sente bene/chiaramente	Sorry, the line's not very clear
L'apparecchio non funzione	The phone is out of order
Ci hanno interrotti	I'm afraid we were cut off
Per chiamare un abbonato estero in teleselezione e necessario formare di seguito il prefisso internazionale (00) seguito dall'indicativo dello Stato, dall'indicativo interurbano della località di destinazione e dal numero dell'abbonato desiderato.	To make a call outside Italy dial the international code of the country, then the code of the town and then the number of the individual required.

■ Please note:

The rather inconspicuous public telephone boxes can be recognized by a sign with a red telephone on a white background. You may also see a dialling disc on a yellow background. Public telephones can also be found at stations and in public buildings, as well as in most bars.

If you want to make a long-distance call it is best to go to one of the offices of the SIP (Società Italiana per l'Esercizio delle Telecomunicazioni), which are separate from general post offices. SIP Offices are open from 7.00 am to 11.00 pm.

In Italy you can telephone using 100, 200, 500 lire coins, tokens (gettoni) and cards. You can buy cards at post offices, tobacconists, from vending machines and in most bars; telephone cards can be bought in tobacconists and from SIP.

In about a quarter of call boxes you can use a special telephone credit card which deducts the charge directly from your account.

Notices on the doors of the telephone kiosks will tell you what kind of card you can use.

When answering the phone in Italy you say 'pronto'. It is not customary to give the names of the family or the firm.

133

Codes for dialling abroad from Italy:
the UK (0044), Ireland (00353), the USA (001).

If you have any further queries about telephone services dial 160 or 116.

Dialling tones:

tu-tuu at repeated intervals shows that the number is ringing.
tu-tu-tu (continuous) shows the number is engaged.
tuuuuuuu (continuous signal) shows that the line is free.

Telephone books:

Tutta Città
This series of telephone books of the various Italian towns, apart from telephone numbers, provides a great deal of information on local public transport, hospitals, post offices, church services, opening times of museums and street maps.

Pagine Gialle (Yellow Pages)
Like its British equivalent, this is a telephone trade directory listing trades and services in the towns and the adjacent postal areas. It is the quickest and and most economical way of finding business addresses and telephone numbers.

Important Telephone Numbers

Ambulances, Police, Red Cross	113	**Soccorso publico di emergenza**
(ACI) Breakdown service	116	**Soccorso stradale**
Police	112	**Carabinieri**
First Aid		**Pronto intervento**
Information on postal and telecommunication services	160	**Poste e telecomunicazioni**
Fire Brigade	115	**Vigili del fuoco**
International information	176	**Informazioni internazionali**

Inland and foreign telegrams	186	**Dettatura telegrammi nazionali e esteri**
Operator assisted service	115	**Servizio tramite operatore**
Free information	176	**Informazioni gratuite**
Tickets and seat reservations for trains	110	**EC/IC trains**
Phone (nearly) free of charge; phone calls beginning with the numbers 1678 are counted as local calls. You only need to insert one token regardless of distance.	1678	**Numero verde nazionale**
Twenty-four-hour service for booking telephone calls to European countries; information in French and English	15	
Stock Exchange, Milan	193	**Borsa di Milano**
Information from ACI on everything of interest to tourists, e.g. road conditions, weather, petrol coupons, etc.	(06) 4214	**ACI (Automobile Club Italiana)**
Alitalia Information on flights and seat reservations	(06)	
. . . inland	5454	
. . . abroad	5455	
. . . general	5456	

Italian Telephone Alphabet

A	Ancona	J	I lunga	S	Savona
B	Bologna	K	Kursaal	T	Torino
C	Como	L	Livorno	U	Udine
D	Domodossola	M	Milano	V	Venezia
E	Empoli	N	Napoli	W	Washington
F	Firenze	O	Otranto	X	Ics
G	Genova	P	Padova	Y	York, yacht
H	Hotel	Q	Quarto	Z	Zara
I	Imola	R	Roma		

6

Leisure Time

6.1 Tourist information offices

Where's the tourist information centre, please?	**Dov'è l'ente turismo, per favore?**
When does it open/close?	**Qual è l'orario di apertura?**
Are there any sightseeing tours?	**Ci sono delle visite organizzate della città?**
Can you make a booking, please?	**Vorrei prenotare un posto?**
When's the sightseeing tour of the town/city?	**Quand'è il giro della città?**

What are the most interesting sights, please?
▶ the old town
▶ the library
▶ the botanical garden
▶ the monuments
▶ the cathedral/churches
▶ the market

Quali sono le cose più interessanti da vedere?
▶ **il centro storico**
▶ **la biblioteca**
▶ **l'orto botanico**
▶ **i monumenti**
▶ **la cattedrale/chiese**
▶ **il mercato**

▶ the museum   ▶ **il museo**
▶ the castle   ▶ **il castello**
▶ the university   ▶ **l'università**

Have you got a map of the town?	**Ha una pianta della città?**
– a list of events	**– calendario delle manifestazioni**
– a list of hotels	**– elenco degli alberghi**
– a bus timetable	**– orario autobus**
– in English, please	**– in inglese, per favore**
Have you got any information on . . .?	**Avete delle informazioni su . . .?**
Have you got any brochures in English about . . .?	**Avete degli opuscoli in inglese di . . .?**
Can you recommend a good restaurant, please?	**Mi può consigliare un buon ristorante?**
Thank you very much for your help	**Grazie tante/molte grazie/grazie per il Suo aiuto**
Three tickets, please	**Tre biglietti, per favore**
Two full price	**Due normali**
One half price	**Uno a prezzo ridotto**
Two adults, one child	**Due adulti e un bambino**
Where can I book seats for . . .?	**Dove posso prenotare dei biglietti per . . .?**
When do I have to pick them up?	**Quando devo venire a ritirarli?**
How much do I owe you?	**Quanto Le devo?**
Where's the town hall?	**Scusi, dov'è il municipio?**

▶ Straight on at the traffic lights   ▶ **continui dritto fino al semaforo**
▶ You can't miss it   ▶ **Non riesce a non vederlo**

■ Please note:

Most towns and holiday resorts have tourist information offices, tourist associations or travel agencies, where you can reserve a room, obtain information and booklets (street maps, entrance tickets, forthcoming events, programmes, etc.) and book excursions.

If you haven't thought of making enquiries or obtaining petrol coupons before leaving home from your local travel agent or the Italian State Tourist Office, you can still do this at the Italian frontier, e.g.: Italian/Austrian frontier Brennero–Lupo (Bolzano); Italian/Swiss frontier Ponte Chiasso–Brogeda (Como); Italian/French frontier Ponte S. Luigi–Grimaldi di Ventimiglia.

Ente Nazionale Italiano Turismo (ENIT):

The Italian State Tourist Office
Via Raimondi Garibaldi 7
00145 Roma
Tel: (06) 54571/5133733

The Italian State Tourist Office (ENIT)
1 Princes Street
London W1R 8AY
Tel: 071-408 1254
Fax: 071-493 6695

Addresses of local tourist associations can be found in Part III, 11.

6.2 Entertainment

Have you got an entertainments guide?

Avete un elenco delle manifestazioni?

What's on at the cinema/at the theatre?

Che cosa danno al cinema/al teatro?

Can you recommend a show?

Mi può consigliare qualcosa?

When does the performance begin?

Quando comincia la rappresentazioni?

Are there any tickets for . . .?
– the concert
– the exhibition
– the dance/the ball
– the circus
– the play

Avete biglietti per . . .?
– il concerto
– la mostra
– la danza
– il circo
– la rappresentazione

Can I book in advance?

Mi potete riservare il biglietto?

Are you doing anything tonight?	**Ha già un impegno questa sera?**
What about a film?	**Se andassimo al cinema?**
▶ That would be nice	▶ **Sarebbe bello**
▶ That's a good idea	▶ **Sarebbe una buon'idea**
▶ I'm not sure, I'd prefer a concert	▶ **Mah, non so, preferirei un concerto**
▶ I don't mind	▶ **Per me, va tutto bene**
Is there a good film on tonight?	**Danno un buon film stasera?**
Can you tell me when the performance finishes?	**Quando finisce la rappresentazione?**

You might hear or read the following in Italian:

Vendita Biglietti	Booking Office
Botteghino Prevendita	Advance Booking
Guardaroba	Cloakroom
Platea	Stalls
Prima Galleria	Dress Circle
Seconda Galleria	Upper Circle
Tutto esaurito	I'm sorry we're sold out

■ Please note:

You can find information on local events in the local diary of leisure activities, obtainable from the local tourist and information office. Local newspapers are also a good source, as well as the Saturday editions of *Mercurio* (*La Repubblica*) and *Corriere della Sera*.

You can also dial 116 to find out what's on.

To reserve tickets for the opera and theatre go to the box office or reserve them through your hotel or travel agent. There is no central booking service.

Museums in Italy are usually open in the mornings only. Many museums are closed on Mondays.

6.3 Invitations

Are you free tonight?	**Ha tempo questa sera?**
Are you doing anything tonight?	**Ha già un impegno questa sera?**
Could you come for dinner tomorrow?	**Può venire domani a cena?**
▶ I'd like to come	▶ **Con piacere!**
▶ I'm sorry, I can't make it	▶ **Mi dispiace, ma proprio non posso**
Can we meet tomorrow morning?	**Ci possiamo incontrare domattina?**
What about 10 o'clock?	**Per esempio alle dieci?**
Where shall we meet?	**Dove ci incontriamo?**
I'll pick you up at the hotel	**Vengo a prenderLa all'albergo**
Can I give you a lift?	**Posso darLe un passaggio?**
▶ Thank you, that's really not necessary	▶ **Grazie, ma non occorre**
Thank you very much for a delightful evening, I enjoyed it very much	**Grazie della bella serata, è stata una piacevolissima serata, mi è molto piaciuta**
Thank you very much for asking me out	**Grazie di avermi accompagnato**
▶ The pleasure was all mine	▶ **È stato un piacere**
Thank you very much for your hospitality	**Grazie dell'ospitalità**
The meal was delicious	**La cena** (dinner)/**il pranzo** (supper) **era ottima a(o)**
I'm afraid I must leave now	**Purtroppo devo andarmene ora**
Nice to have met you	**È stato un piacere averLa ospite**
It was very interesting	**È stato tutto molto interessante**

You might hear the following in Italian:

Diamo una festa venerdì. Ci	We're having a party on Friday.

viene anche Lei?	Would you like to come?
▶ **Molto volentieri**	▶ I'd love to
▶ **Come mi dispiace! Venerdì ho già un impegno**	▶ What a pity, I'm busy on Friday
Si senta come a casa sua	Make yourself at home
Desidera qualcosa da bere?	What are you drinking?
Si serva, prego	Please help yourself
Potrebbe passarmi il formaggio, per favore?	Could you pass me the cheese, please?
Desidera un altro po'di vino?	Would you like some more wine?
▶ **Volentieri**	▶ Yes, please
▶ **No, grazie**	▶ No thanks
Prenda ancora	Would you like some more?
Grazie, veramente basta così	I think I've had enough, thank you
Bella festa, no?	Great party, isn't it?
Grazie di essere venuto(a)	I'm so glad that you were able to come
Torni presto, mi raccomando	Come and see us again soon

■ Please note:

When you are invited to visit people it is customary in Italy to take chocolates or biscuits – 'paste' – with you from the 'pasticceria' (confectioner). You can also send flowers before or after the invitation.

If you have been invited for dinner you can wish one another 'buon appetito' (enjoy your meal), but this custom varies. You should leave this to your host.

If you want to send a thankyou letter for an invitation, you may find the model letters in the appendix useful.

 Model letters 16, 17 and 18

7

Problems

7.1 At the doctor's

Please call a doctor	**Chiami un medico, per favore**
Is there a doctor in the hotel?	**C'è un medico in albergo?**
What are the surgery hours?	**Quando riceve il dottore?**
Please call an ambulance	**Chiami un'autoambulanza**
I feel sick	**Mi sento male**
It hurts here	**Ho dolori qui**
I have a pain in . . .	**Ho dolori di . . .**
Can you give me something for . . .	**Può prescrivermi qualcosa contro . . .**
I suffer from . . .	**Suffro di . . .**
asthma	**asma**
attack/fit	**attacco**
back-ache	**dolori di schiena/mal di schiena**
blood pressure (too high/too low)	**pressione (troppo alta/bassa)**
bronchitis	**bronchite**
cancer	**il cancro**
circulatory trouble	**disturbi circolatori**
concussion	**commozione cerebrale**
constipation	**la stitichezza**
a cold	**il raffreddore**
cough	**la tosse**
diabetes	**diabete**
diarrhoea	**dissenteria/diarrea**
dizziness	**giramenti di testa/capogiro/ vertigine**
fever/temperature	**febbre/temperatura**
flu	**l'influenza**
fracture	**la frattura**

hayfever	**il raffreddore da fieno**
heart trouble	**disturbi cardiaci**
headache	**il mal di testa**
heartburn	**acidità di stomaco/bruciore di stomaco**
indigestion	**disturbi di digestione**
an infected wound	**l'infezione di una ferita**
infection	**l'infezione**
insomnia	**l'insonnia**
migraine	**l'emicrania**
nausea	**la nausea**
nephritis	**l'infiammazione renale**
phlebitis	**la flebite**
rheumatism	**i reumatismi**
sciatica	**la sciatica**
skin disease	**malattia della pelle**
a sore throat	**il mal di gola**
stomachache	**dolori di stomaco**
sunburn	**la scottatura solare**
toothache	**mal di denti**
upset stomach	**un'indigestione**
vomiting	**vomito**

At the doctor's you might hear the following:

Che disturbi si sente?	What's the trouble?
Dove Le fa male?	Where does it hurt?
Che cosa posso fare per Lei?	What can I do for you?
Si spogli, prego	Get undressed, please
Si distenda qui, per favore	Lie down here, please
Respiri profondamente	Breathe deeply, please
Apra la bocca	Open your mouth, please
Misuro la pressione	I'm going to take your blood pressure
Le faccio un'iniezione	I'm going to give you an injection
Deve farsi fare una radiografia	I'd like you to have an X-ray

Non è niente di grave	It's nothing serious
Le prescrivo qualcosa	I'll prescribe something for you
Prenda una pastiglia tre volte al giorno dopo i pasti	Take one pill three times a day after meals
È un antibiotico	This is an antibiotic
Le manderò il conto	I'll send you the bill
Deve restare a letto per tre giorni	You must stay in bed for three days
Ritorni fra tre giorni	Come back in three days
Reparto di pronto soccorso	Emergency ward

■ Please note:

If you need a doctor, ask if there is one available at the hotel. By phoning directory enquiries you will also be able to find out the names and addresses of doctors nearby. Lists of doctors can also be found in the 'Pagine Gialle' (Yellow Pages).

In an emergency dial 113. You can also go to the casualty department (Pronto soccorso) of the local hospital. In the major Italian newspapers you will find listed, under 'telefoni utili' and 'guardia medica permanente', details of round-the-clock medical services.

Travellers from Great Britain should bring with them an E111 form. This entitles them to receive treatment free of charge. Produce your E111 at the Unità Sanitaria Locale (USL), the local office of Italy's Health Service. The addresses and telephone numbers of the USL are listed under 'Unità Sanitarie Locali' in the local telephone directory (tutta città).

If a doctor asks for payment in advance be sure to ask for an itemized bill as this will help you get a refund when you return home.

7.2 At the chemist's

Where is the nearest chemist, please?	**C'è una farmacia qui vicino?**

Which chemist is open at night?	**Quale farmacia fa il turno di notte?**
I'd like some pills for . . .	**Vorrei delle pastiglie contro . . .**
Do I need a prescription?	**Ci vuole la ricetta?**
adhesive plaster	**cerotto**
aspirin	**aspirina**
after/before each meal	**dopo i pasti/prima dei pasti**
burn ointment	**pomata contro le bruciature**
charcoal (indigestion) tablets	**pasticche al carbone**
cotton wool	**cotone**
cough medicine	**medicina contro la tosse**
for external use	**ad uso esterno**
eye drops	**gocce per gli occhi**
first-aid kit	**cassetta di pronto soccorso**
headache tablets/analgesics	**pastiglie contro il mal di testa**
indigestion tablets	**pastiglie contro il mal di stomaco**
for internal use	**ad uso interno**
laxatives	**pasticche lassative**
pain-killers	**pastiglie antidolore**
pills/tablets	**pillole/pastiglie/pasticche/ compresse**
sleeping tablets	**sonniferi**
valerian (herbal antispasmodic)	**valeriana**

What you may read in pharmacies:

Questa farmacia effettua il turno di chiusura infrasettimanale Diurna: 8.30 – 21.00	Open daily from 8.30 am to 9 pm.
Notturna: 21.00 – 8.30	Night-service from 9 pm to 8.30 am (the names of pharmacies on night duty are then listed).
Chiusura settimanale sabato/ domenica 8.30 – 12.30/15.30 – 19.30	

■ Please note:

Pharmacies are usually indicated by the sign of a black, red and gold cross with the Aesculapian snake. There are other versions, too, and sometimes simply the sign 'Farmacia'.

In Italy there is no chain of chemists like Boots; they are all privately owned.

The range of goods in an Italian pharmacy is much more limited than in England. Also, medicines in Italy are more expensive.

The numbers of pharmacies are listed on the first pages of the telephone directory. Dial 116 if you need further help.

Remember, there is a difference between a 'farmacia' (chemist's) and a 'drogheria' (groceries, household goods).

You can buy cosmetics in a 'profumeria', but toiletries can be bought more cheaply at a supermarket.

7.3 Lost property

Where's the lost property office, please?	Scusi, dov'è l'ufficio oggetti smarriti?
I've lost my . . .	Ho perso . . .
. . . wallet	. . . il portafoglio
. . . handbag	. . . la borsetta
. . . identity card	. . . la carta d'identità
. . . passport	. . . il passaporto
. . . purse	. . . il portamonete
. . . cheque card/banker's card	. . . la carta assegni
. . . watch	. . . l'orologio

■ Please note:

If you have lost something, go to the local lost property office, or those of the railway station or local transport company. The police will also try to help you.

7.4 The police

Please call the police	**Per favore, chiami la polizia**
I've been robbed	**Sono stato derubato**
I'd like to report a theft/a crime	**Voglio denunciare un furto/un delitto**
My car has been broken into	**Hanno scassinato la mia macchina**
My briefcase is missing	**La mia borsa è scomparsa**
Thank you very much for your help	**Grazie dell'aiuto**
You've been very helpful	**Mi ha aiutato molto, grazie**
I'm very grateful	**Sono molto riconoscente**
You are very kind	**Lei è molto gentile**
Thank you very much	**Grazie tante**
▶ Don't mention it/Not at all	▶ **Di niente/non c'è di che**
Can anyone here speak English?	**C'è qualcuno qui che parli inglese?**
I need an interpreter	**Mi serve un interprete**
I need a lawyer	**Ho bisogno di un avvocato**
I'd like to speak to the British consul, please	**Vorrei parlare con il console britannico**
Where's the British embassy, please?	**Dov'è l'ambasciata della Gran Bretagna, per favore?**

Calls for help:

Help	**Aiuto**
Stop	**Alt**
Quick	**Presto**
Stop, thief	**Al ladro**
Fire	**Fuoco**
Watch Out/Careful	**Attenzione**

Poison	**Veleno**
Danger	**Pericolo**
Fire Brigade	**Pompieri**
Ambulance	**Autoambulanza**
Police	**Polizia/Carabinieri**

At a police station you may be asked the following:

Può darci una descrizione dell'oggetto scomparso?	Can you describe it for me, please?
Quando esattamente lo ha perduto?	When exactly did you lose it?
Posso vedere i documenti?	Can I see your papers, please?
Mi dia nome, cognome e indirizzo, d'identità per favore	May I have your name and address, please?

■ Please note:

Loss of documents or valuables, as well as theft, has to be reported to the police immediately or to the next carabiniere station.

To assist your claim against the insurance company you are advised to report the theft or loss of property to the police in writing and send a copy of the report to your insurance company.

Should you have any other problems, remember that you can always dial 116. You will be given additional help, or at least will be told which other authority to contact. This is a 24-hour service.

The telephone numbers 112 and 113 should only be used in emergencies – if you need an ambulance, a doctor, or if you have been involved in an accident.

When you dial 113 you will find that the information is often given via an interpreter.

Should you need to get in touch with a British consulate in Italy, there are consulates in: Cagliari, Florence, Genoa, Milan, Naples, Rome, Trieste and Venice.

British Embassy in Italy:

Ambasciata Britannica
Via XX Settembre 80A
00187 Roma
Tel: (06) 4755441/551

7.5 Accidents and breakdowns

I've had an accident	**Ho avuto un incidente**
My car has broken down	**Ho un guasto**
Could you take me to the nearest garage, please?	**Mi dà un passaggio fino alla prossima officina?**
Could you send someone to repair my car?	**Può mandare qualcuno che ripari la mia macchina?**
Can you tow the car into town?	**Può rimorchiare la mia macchina fino in città?**
Can you send a mechanic at once, please?	**Può mandare subito un meccanico, per favore?**
How long will it take?	**Quanto ci vorrà?**
How much do I owe you?	**Quanto devo?**
Here is proof of my insurance/ this is my insurance certificate	**Ecco i miei documenti dell'assicurazione/la mia polizza di assicurazione**

See also Part II, 3.5.

I think there's something wrong with the . . .	**Credo che . . . non funzioni**
accelerator	**l'acceleratore**
battery	**la batteria**
brake	**il freno**
bumper	**il paraurti**
clutch	**la frizione**
engine	**il motore**
exhaust	**il tubo di scappamento**

headlight	**il faro**
horn	**il clacson**
ignition	**accensione**
spark plugs	**candele**
starter	**l'avviatore**
steering wheel	**il volante**
windscreen wiper	**il tergicristallo**
wing mirror	**il parafango**
Have you got . . .?	**Scusi, ha un(a) . . .?**
– a rope	**– cavo da rimorchio**
– a spanner	**– una chiave per dadi**
– a screwdriver	**– un cacciavite**
– spare parts	**– pezzi di ricambio**
The engine is overheating	**Il motore è surriscaldato**
The keys are locked inside the car	**Ho lasciato le chiavi nella macchina**

■ Please note:

In the event of a breakdown or an accident, you can use the emergency telephone on the motorway or look up the number of the breakdown service in the local telephone directory under ACI (Automobil Club Italiano). Motoring organizations provide breakdown services (e.g. TCI).

If you have an accident you can phone the police or call an ambulance by dialling 112.

7.6 Problems when returning goods

Can you change this, please?	**Potrei cambiare questo(a) . . .?**
Can I return this?	**Posso restituirlo/renderlo?**
I bought this yesterday	**L'ho comprato ieri**
Here's the receipt	**Ecco la ricevuta**
This is dirty/torn/damaged	**E sporco/è lacero/è rovinato**

Can I have the money back?	**Potrei riavere la somma pagata?**
Can I see the manager, please?	**Potrei parlare al direttore?**

7.7 Problems with the tone of voice

If you hear the following expressions and sentences, you should know that you are probably being insulted or that you are not being treated very politely:

Questa cosa è molto seccante	This is a damn nuisance
La questione mi dà ai nervi	It really gets on my nerves
Ne ho abbastanza di . . .	I'm fed up (with . . .)
Ne ho fin sopra i capelli	I've just about had enough
Sciocchezze!	It's rubbish
Ma è ridicolo	Don't make me laugh
Sono prezzi da strozzini	It's a rip-off
Ebbè?	So what?
Non me ne importa/Me ne infischio	I couldn't care less
Beh, insomma!	Really!
Guai!	Don't you dare!
Stupidi stranieri	Stupid foreigners
Vattene!	Get lost
Taccia/Sta zitto	Shut up
Mi lasci in pace	Leave me alone
Ma che cosa crede di essere?/ Ma chi crede di essere?	What on earth do you think you're doing!

8

What You Say if You Want to . . .

8.1 . . . make a request

Scusi, può/potrebbe/Le dispiacerebbe?
Se non Le dispiace . . .
Potrebbe avere la gentilezza di . .?
Non so, se posso chiederLe questo favore?
Forse potrebbe . . .
Potrei chiederLe di . .?
Scusi il disturbo, ma . . .

. . . respond to a request

Ma certo
Certamente
Con piacere

Temo di no
Mi dispiace, ma non posso
Mi dispiace, ma è proprio impossibile

8.2 . . . say thank you

Grazie
La ringrazio tanto
Le sono veramente grato
Apprezzo molto il Suo aiuto
Le sono riconoscente di avermi aiutato

. . . respond to thanks

Di niente
È stato un piacere
Non c'è di che
Non è stato nessun disturbo
Sono contento di aver potuto essere di aiuto

8.3 . . . to ask for information

Posso/Potrei/È permesso?
Le dispiace se . .?
Le dispiacerebbe se . .?
Non so se posso . .?
Se non le fa niente, vorrei . . .

. . . grant or refuse permission

Certamente
Naturalmente
Affatto
Certo, faccia pure
Per me va benissimo
Temo di no
Mi dispiace
Preferirei non lo facesse
Temo che non sia possibile
Sarebbe veramente meglio che non lo facesse

8.4 . . . ask for something to be repeated

Scusi?
Non ho capito?
Mi scusi?
Scusi, non ho ben capito l'ultima parola?
Scusi, che chosa ha detto?
Può ripetere, per favore?
Potrebbe ripetere l'ultima frase, per favore?

. . . show that you are listening

Davvero
Davvero/Sul serio/Veramente?

. . . sum up

In breve, dunque . . .
In base . . .
Quello che stiamo dicendo è . . .

8.5 . . . ask for advice/suggestions

Che cosa dovrei fare?
Che cosa mi consiglia?
Che consiglio mi darebbe?
Che cosa farebbe Lei al mio posto?
Vorrei sentire il Suo consiglio riguardo . . .
Potrei chiederLe un consiglio riguardo . . .?

. . . offer advice/make a suggestion

Perchè non . . .?
Se fossi in Lei, non lo farei
Forse sarebbe un'idea . . .
Ha già pensato a/di . . .?
Penso che dovrebbe . . .
Penso che non dovrebbe . . .
Le raccomando
Posso suggerirLe di . . .?

. . . respond to some advice

Questa è un'ottima/eccellente idea
Si, va bene

Non, mi sembra una buona idea
Be', non la ritengo una buona cosa

8.6 . . . ask for someone's opinion

Che cosa ne pensa di . . .?
Potrebbe darmi qualche ragguaglio riguardo . .?
Conosce per caso . . .?
Le sarei grato di sentire la Sua opinione in materia

. . . give your opinion

Penso/credo
Secondo me/secondo la mia opinione
Per quanto ne so . . .
Ne sono perfettamente certo
Non mi pare ci siano dubbi di sorta . . .
Personalmente sono convinto che . . .
Trovo molto bene che . . .
Ci terrei a far presente che . . .

Dipende
Forse/probabilmente
Secondo me . . .
A me pare che tutto indichi che . . .

Non saprei dire . . .
Non lo posso dire di sicuro
Probabilmente, no
È molto poco probabile
Devo ammettere che non lo so
Non ne sono convinto
Temo che sia impossibile
Mi dispiace, ma non se ne parla nemmeno

8.7 . . . express delight

Magnifico!
Splendido!
Eccellente!
Che belle novità!
Sono felice di sentire ciò?
Che piacere di sentire ciò?

. . . show that you are angry

Mah, no!
No, questo poi no!
Che noia!
No, non è fatto come si deve
Non sono affatto contento di . . .
È una cosa molto noiosa

8.8 . . . make a complaint

Mi dispiace, ma . . .
Le dispiace di non . . .
Mi dispiace di dovermi
  lamentare . . .
Vorrei reclamare . . .
Non sono menomamente
  soddisfatto del (la) . . .
Forse ha ragione
Si, forse ha ragione su questo
  punto
È colpa mia
Mi dispiace molto. È tutto
  sbagliato

. . . apologize

Scusi!
Mi dispiace della cosa
Sono spiacente/mi rincresce
  di . . .
Mi scusi di . . .
Mi perdoni di . . .
Mi dispiace, è stata tutta colpa
  mia
Mi devo proprio scusare per . . .

. . . respond to an apology

Va bene, OK
Non importa
Tutto a posto
Non c'è di che scusarsi
Non si preoccupi
Spero che non succeda più

8.9 . . . invite someone

Che ne pensa?
Andiamo a cena insieme
  domani?
Perchè non . .?
Verrà con noi?
Sarei felice se venisse

. . . accept or decline an invitation

Va bene
Grazie mille
Molto gentile da parte Sua
Grazie, accetto volentieri

No, grazie
Vorrei molto, ma temo che . . .
È molto gentile da parte Sua,
  ma . . .

PART III

1

Abbreviations

a.	arrivo	arrival
abbr.	abbrevizzione	abbreviated
a.c.	anno corente	present year
a.C.	avanti Cristo	BC
ACI	Automobil Club Italiano	Automobile Association
a.D.	anno Domini	AD
all.	allegato/i	enclosure/s
app.	appendice	appendix
APT	Azienda di Promozione Turistica	tourist office
a.r.	andata e ritorno	return ticket
Avv.	avvocato	lawyer
B/L	polizza di carico marittimo	Bill of Lading
C	grado centigrado	degrees Celsius/ centigrade
ca.	circa	circa, about
CAP	Codice di avviamento postale	postcode
c/o	conto corrente	current account
C&F	costo e nolo	cost and freight
CIF	costo assicurazione e nolo	cost, insurance and freight
cit.	citato	quoted
c.m.	corrente mese	present month
Confin-dustria	Confederazione dell'Industrie Italiana	Federation of Italian Industry
CP	Casella Postale	Post Office Box
c.s.	come sopra	as above
C.so	Corso	avenue
c.to	Conto	account
D/A	documenti contro accettazione	documents against acceptance

d.C.	dopo Cristo	AD
div.	divisione	department
Dott./Dr.	dottore	Dr
ecc.	eccetera	et cetera, etc.
ENIT	Ente Nazionale Italiano per il Turismo	National Tourist Organisation
FAS	Franco sotto paranco	Free alongside ship
FS	Ferrovie dello Stato	railways
FOB	Franco bordo	Free on board
f.to	firmato	signed
ICE	Istituto per il Commercio Estero	Italian Institute for Foreign Trade
ISTAT	Istituto Centrale di Statistica	Central Institute of Statistics
IVA	Imposta sul Valore Aggiunto	VAT (Value-Added Tax)
L/C	Lettera di Credito	Letter of Credit
L.it.	Lire italiane	Italian Lire
mitt.	mittente	sender
n.	nome	name
NB	Nota Bene	please note
nc	nota di credito	credit note
nd	nota di debito	debit note
No.	Numero	number
pag/pagg	pagina/e	page/pages
p.es.	per esempio	for example, e.g.
PTT	Poste e Telecomunicazioni	post and telecommunications
p.v.	prossimo venturo	next month
p.za	Piazza	square
Rag.	ragioniere	accountant
RAI	Radio Audizioni Italiane	Italian Broadcasting Company
RSVP	Répondez s'il vous plaît	please reply

S./S.ta	San(to)/Santa	Saint, St
SAS	Società in Accomandita Semplice	limited partnership
SE & O	salvo errori ed omissioni	errors and omissions excepted
Sig.	Signor	Mr
Sig.a	Signora	Mrs
Sig.na	Signorina	Miss
SIP	Società Italiana per l'Esercizio delle Telecomunicazioni	Italian telephone company
Soc.	Società	Company
SNC	Società in Nome Collettivo	partnership
SpA	Società per Azioni	Italian public company
Srl.	Società a responsabilità limitata	Italian private company
TCI	Touring Club Italiano	Italian Touring Club
USL	Unità Sanitaria Locale	National Health Unit
v.le	Viale	avenue
VU.UU.	Vigili urbani	Traffic police

2

Signs

Accendere la Luce	Lights On
Accesso Libero per Confinanti	Access to Residents Only
Accesso Vietato	No Admission/No Admittance
Accesso Vietato ai Non Addetti	No Admission for Unauthorized Persons
Acqua Potabile	Drinking Water
Adulti	Adults
Ai Binari	To the Platforms
Al Piano Superiore	On the Top Floor

Alt	Stop
Aperto dalle . . . alle . . .	Open from . . . to . . .
Arrivi	Arrivals
Ascensore/Lift	Elevator/Lift
Attenti al Cane	Beware of the Dog
Attenzione	Attention, Caution
Attenzione, Fragile	Handle with Care
Attenzione, Scalino!	Mind the Step
Autoambulanza	Ambulance
Binario	Platform
Bussare	Please Knock (door)
Caldo	Hot
Camere Libere	Vacancies
Cassa	Cash Desk
Cassetta Lettere	Letterbox
Cassette Deposito Bagagli	Luggage Lockers
Cassiere/a	Cashier
Centralino	Operator
Chiuso	Closed
Circolazione rotatoria	Roundabout
Cuccetta	Couchette
Da Affittare/Affittasi	For Rent
Da Noleggiare/Tassi Libero	For Hire
Da Vendere/Vendesi	For Sale
Decolli	Departures (flights)
Deposito Bagagli	Left Luggage
Deviazione	Diversion
Divieto Di Accesso	No Through Road
Divieto di Fumare	No Smoking
Divieto di Inversione	No U-Turn
Divieto di Sorpasso	No Overtaking
Divieto di Svolta a Destra	No Right Turn
Divieto di Svolta a Sinistra	No Left Turn
Dogana	Customs
Donne/Signore	Women/Ladies' Room
Dritto	Straight on
Entrare Senza Bussare	Walk Straight In

Entrata	Entrance
Entrata/Uscita	Way In/Way Out
Entrata Libera	Admission Free
Entrata Solo Davanti	Enter at the Front
Esaurito	Sold out
Facchino/Portabagagli	Porter
Freddo	Cold
Freno di Emergenza	Emergency Brake
Fuoco	Fire
Fuori Servizio	Out of Order
Gabinetti/Tolette	Toilets
Gabinetti Pubblici/Latrine	Public Conveniences
Giorno di Riposo	Closed All Day
Guardaroba/WC	Cloakroom
Guida Turistica	Guide
In Alto	Upstairs
In Basso	Downstairs
Incrocio/Crocicchio	Crossroads
Ingresso	Entry
Ingresso Libero	Free Admittance
Intasamento di Traffico/ Ingorgo	Traffic Jam
Introdurre le Monete	Insert Coins
Istruzioni per l'Uso	Instructions for Use
Lavori in Corso	Roadworks
Levata	Collection
Libero	Vacant (toilets)
Limite di Velocità	Speed Limit
Mantenere la Sinistra/la Destra	Keep Left/Keep Right
Merce da Dichiarare	Goods to Declare
Metropolitana	Underground
Niente da Dichiarare	Nothing to Declare
Noleggio	To Let/For Hire
Non Aprire	Do Not Open
Non Disturbare	Do Not Disturb

Non Toccare	Do Not Touch
Occupato	Engaged/Occupied
Offerta Speciale	Special Offer
Oggetti Smarriti	Lost Property
Orario Apertura	Opening Hours
Ore Lavorative	Office Hours
Ospedale	Hospital
Parcheggio	Car Park
Parcheggio Custodito	Supervised Car Park
Parking/Garage a Più Piani	Multi-storey Car Park
Partenze	Departures
Passaggio Treni, Attenzione	Beware of the Train
Pedoni	Pedestrians
Pensione	Bed and Breakfast
Pericolo	Danger
Pericolo di Morte	Danger of Death
Pianterreno	Ground Floor
Pittura Fresca	Wet Paint
Polizia	Police
Prefisso Telefonico	Dialling Code
Premere/Spingere	Push
Primo Piano	First Floor
Proibito/Vietato	Prohibited
Pronto Soccorso	First Aid
Rallentare	Reduce Speed Now
Reception	Reception
Rifiuti	Litter
Riservato	Reserved
Ritorno/Restituzione Monete	Returned Coins
Sala da Pranzo	Dining Room
Sala di Attesta/di Aspetto	Waiting Room
Saldi	Clearance Sale
Saldo/Svendita	Sale
Scala Mobile	Escalator
Semafori	Traffic Lights
Senso Unico	One-Way Street
Servizio di Assistenza	Customer Service

Signore	Women/Ladies' Toilets
Signori/Uomini	Men's Toilets
Solo Uscita	Do Not Enter/No Entry
Sosta Vietata	No Parking
Sotterraneo	Basement
Spingere	Push
Spogliatoio	Dressing Room
Stampa	Press
Strada Privata	Private Road
Strada senza Sbocco	Dead End
Suonare	Ring (the bell)
Telefoni Pubblici	Public Telephones
Tener Libera l'Uscita	Keep Entrance Clear
Terreno Privato	Private Grounds
Tirare	Pull
Traffico di Transito	Through Traffic
Tutto Esaurito	No Vacancies/Sold Out
Ufficio Informazioni	Information Office
Ufficio Viaggi	Travel Agency
Uomini	Men's Toilets
Uscita	Exit
Uscita di Emergenza	Emergency Exit
Vagone Letto	Sleeper
Vagone Ristorante	Dining Car
Velocità Massima	Maximum Speed
Vendita Biglietti	Booking Office/Ticket Office
Vicolo Cieco	Dead End
Vietato	Forbidden
Vietato Calpestare l'Erba	Keep off the Grass
Vietato Fare Bagni	No Swimming
Vietato Gettare Rifiuti	No Littering
Vietato Girare a Sinistra	No Left Turn
Vietato l'Accesso	No Trespassing
Vietato Scaricare Rifiuti	No Dumping
Vietato Sporgersi	Do Not Lean Out
Volo in Orario	Scheduled Flight
Voltaggio	Voltage

3

Numbers

0	zero	18	diciotto
1	uno	19	diciannove
2	due	20	venti
3	tre	21	ventuno
4	quattro	22	ventidue
5	cinque	30	trenta
6	sei	40	quaranta
7	sette	50	cinquanta
8	otto	60	sessanta
9	nove	70	settanta
10	dieci	80	ottanta
11	undici	90	novanta
12	dodici	100	cento
13	tredici	1,000	mille
14	quattordici	10,000	diecimila
15	quindici	100,000	centomila
16	sedici	1,000,000	un milione
17	diciassette	1,000,000,000	un miliardo

Please note:

137	centotrentassette
9465/9.465	novemilaquattrocentosessantacinque

Decimal fractions: a comma is used rather than a point: 2.5123 becomes 2,5123 in Italian.

Fractions:

a half	una metà, un mezzo
a third	un terzo
a quarter	un quarto
three-quarters	tre quarti
two-tenths	due decimi

Ordinal Numbers:

first	1°	primo/a
second	2°	secondo/a

third	3°	terzo/a
fourth	4°	quarto/a
fifth	5°	quinto/a
sixth	6°	sesto/a
seventh	7°	settimo/a
eighth	8°	ottavo/a
ninth	9°	nono/a
tenth	10°	decimo/a
eleventh	11°	undicesimo/a
twelfth	12°	dodicesimo/a
thirteenth	13°	tredicesimo/a
twentieth	20°	ventesimo/a
twenty-first	21°	ventunesimo/a
twenty-second	22°	ventiduesimo/a
thirtieth	30°	trentesimo/a
thirty-first	31°	trentunesimo/a

4

Weights and Measures

Misure di lunghezza: Lengths:

1 chilometro	km	0.6214 miles
		1.0936 yards
1 metro	m	3.2808 feet
		39.3701 inches
1 centimetro	cm	0.3937 inches
1 millimetro	mm	0.0394 inches

Misure di superficie: Areas:

1 chilometro quadrato	km²	0.3861 square miles
1 ettaro	ha	0.0039 square miles
1 metro quadrato	m²	{ 1.1960 square yards / 10.7639 square feet
1 centimetro quadrato	cm²	0.1550 square inches

Misure di capacità: ## Volumes:

1 metro cubo	m³	1.3079 cubic yards
		35.3148 cubic feet
		219.9736 gallons (imperial)
1 litro	l	0.2200 gallons (imperial)
		1.7596 pint

Misure di peso: ## Weights:

1 tonnellata (1000 kg)	t	0.9843 ton
1 chilo	kg	2.2046 pound
1 mezzo chilo (0,5 kg)		1.102 pound
100 grammi (1 etto)		3.53 ounces
1 grammo	g	0.0353 ounces

Celsius and Fahrenheit:

Temperatures are given in degrees Celsius (centigrade) in Italy.

Celsius	−10	−5	0	10	21
Fahrenheit	−14	23	32	50	70

To convert Fahrenheit into Celsius subtract 32, then multiply by five, and divide by nine. To convert Celsius to Fahrenheit, multiply by nine and divide by five, then add 32.

5

The Calendar

Days of the week:

Monday	lunedì
Tuesday	martedì
Wednesday	mercoledì
Thursday	giovedì
Friday	venerdì

Saturday	**sabato**
Sunday	**domenica**

Months:

January	**gennaio**
February	**febbraio**
March	**marzo**
April	**aprile**
May	**maggio**
June	**giugno**
July	**luglio**
August	**agosto**
September	**settembre**
October	**ottobre**
November	**novembre**
December	**dicembre**

Seasons:

spring	**la primavera** *f*
summer	**l'estate** *f*
autumn	**l'autunno** *m*
winter	**l'inverno** *m*

Public holidays in Italy:

1 January	New Year's Day	**Capodanno**
6 January	Epiphany	**Epifania**
25 April	Liberation Day	**Anniversario della Liberazione**
1 May	May Day	**Festa del Lavoro**
2 June or the following Sunday	National Day	**Festa della Repubblica**
15 August	Assumption Day	**Assunzione, Ferragosto**
1 November	All Saints' Day	**Organissanti**
8 December	Immaculate Conception	**Immacolata Concezione**
25 December	Christmas	**Natale**
26 December	St Stephen's Day	**S. Stefano**

Movable bank holidays in Italy:

Easter Sunday	**Pasqua**
Easter Monday	**Lunedì dell'Angelo**
Whit Sunday	**Pentecoste**

An Italian calendar will also give you all the bank holidays.

6

Job Titles

acquisitore/acquisitrice	buyer
addetto al magazzino	warehouseman/woman
addetto alla statistica	statistician
agente immobiliare	estate agent, property agent
agente viaggi	travel agent
allenatore	sports coach
analitico per sistemi da computer	systems analyst
archeologo/a	archaeologist
architetto	architect
archivario/a	archivist
artista	artist
assistente di laboratorio	laboratory technician
assistente ricerche	research assistant
assistente sociale	social worker
attore/attrice	actor/actress
avvocato	lawyer, solicitor, barrister
bambinaia	nurse, nanny
barbiere	barber
biochimico/a	biochemist
biologo/a	biologist
birrario	brewer
botanico	botanist

cameriere	waiter/waitress
capo formazione professionale	training manager
capo reparto acquisti	purchasing manager
capo reparto fabbricazione	production engineer
capoufficio	office manager
carabiniere	police officer
commercialista	(business) economist
commerciante	trader, dealer, business person
compratore/compratrice	purchaser
consulente marketing	marketing consultant
consulente su campo professionale	careers officer
contabile	bookkeeper
controllatore qualità	quality controller
costruttore armamenti	scaffolder
costruttore attrezzi	toolmaker
decoratore/decoratrice	window dresser
dentista	dentist
designer, disegnatore	designer (graphic, fashion)
dirigente, dirrettore	director, general manager(ess)
direttore alberghiero	hotel/catering manager
direttore di società immobiliare	building society manger(ess)
dottore	doctor
economista	economist
editore/editrice	editor
fabbro	blacksmith
facchino	porter
farmacista	pharmacist
fiorista	florist
fisico/a	physicist
fotografo	photographer
geologo/a	geologist
geometra	surveyor
giardiniere	gardener
giornalista	journalist
idraulico	plumber

imbianchino	decorator
impaccatore/impaccatrice	packer
impiegato/a	clerk
impegiato/a bancario	bank clerk
impiegato/a dirigente export	export executive
impiegato/a ferroviario/a	railwayman/woman
impegiato/a public relations	public relations officer
imfermiera/e	nurse/male nurse
ingegnere	engineer, civil engineer
ingegnere aeronautico	aeronautical engineer
ingegnere chimico	chemical engineer
ingegnere elettrico	electrical engineer
ingegnere meccanico	mechanical engineer
ingegnere minerario	mining engineer
ingegnere servizio assitenza	maintenance engineer
insegnante	teacher
interprete	interpreter
lastricatore	plasterer
libraio/a	librarian
macellaio	slaughterman
maestro di scuola guida	driving instructor
manager	manager(ess)
matematico/a	mathematician
meccanico (autoveicoli)	(car) mechanic
mediatore di asscurazioni	insurance broker
mediatore di borsa	stockbroker
mercante	trader, dealer
metallurgio	metallurgio
medico	doctor
meteorologo/a	meteorologist
montatore	assembler, fitter
molatore, molatrice	grinder
mugnaio	miller
muratore	bricklayer
operaio d'acciaieria	steelworker
orologiaio	watch and clock repairer
oste	publican
ottico	optician

parrucchiere	hairdresser
pianificatore urbanistico	town planner
pilota aeronautico	airline pilot
poliziotto	police officer
portiere alberghiero	(hotel) receptionist
portinaio	housekeeper
portobagagli	porter
programmatore per computer	computer programmer
pubblicista	advertising media executive
pulitore/pulitrice di vetri	window cleaner
ragioniere	accountant
revisore dei conti	chartered accountant
rappresentante vendite	sales representative
saldatore	welder
sarto/a	tailor, dressmaker
scienziato chimico	chemist (scientist)
tapezziere	upholsterer, decorator
tassista	taxi driver
technico/a dentario	dental technician
technico/a per telecomunicazioni	telecommunications technician
technico/a specializzato	technician, engineer
technico/a tessile	textile worker
traduttore/traduttrice	translator
trapanatore	driller
ufficiale aste pubbliche	auctioneer
veterinario	veterinary surgeon
vetraio	glazier
vetrinista	window dresser
vigile	police officer, traffic warden
zoologo/a	zoologist

7

Information on the Single European Market

Europe: Population and GNP of EC States (1989)

Country		Population (millions)	GNP (billion ECU)
UK	**Gran Bretagna**	55.8	565
Belgium	**Belgio**	9.9	120
Denmark	**Danimarca**	5.1	90
France	**Francia**	55.6	740
Germany	**Germania**	78.1*	1070 (estimated West and East)
Greece	**Grecia**	10.0	40
Ireland	**Irlanda**	3.5	25
Italy	**Italia**	57.3	650
Luxembourg	**Lussemburgo**	0.4	5
The Netherlands	**Paesi Bassi/ Olanda**	14.7	185
Portugal	**Portogallo**	10.4	30
Spain	**Spagna**	38.8	250
Total EC		339.5	3770
Comparison with the USA:		245.5	3870

*Since October 1990
1 ECU = US $1.00 (approx.).
Source: EC, Brussels

Trade between the UK and the European Community (1989)

	Imports	Exports
	(in million pounds)	
Total World	120,788	93,249
Germany, West	20,005	11,110
Germany, East	169	106
France	10,785	9,462
The Netherlands	9,586	6,515
Belgium and Luxembourg	5,701	4,873
Ireland	4,279	4,715
Italy	6,702	4,631
Spain	2,772	3,138
Denmark	2,229	1,209
Portugal	1,041	916
Greece	395	571
Total EC	63,664	47,246
Comparison with North America:	15,349	14,346

Source: DTI

Trade between Italy and the European Community (1988)

	Imports	Exports
	(in million Lire)	
Total World	180,013,548	166,380,067
Germany, West	39,202,693	30,058,306
France	26,721,675	27,598,034
UK	9,165,419	13,370,683
Spain	4,346,978	6,751,502
The Netherlands	10,305,639	5,124,085
Belgium and Luxembourg	8,800,838	5,616,748
Greece	1,562,486	2,686,825
Portugal	581,523	2,000,765

Denmark	1,767,543	1,297,514
Ireland	1,067,980	432,794
Germany, East	275,399	338,297
Total EC	103,522,774	94,937,255
Comparison with the USA	10,090,589	14,791,453

Source: ISTAT, 1989

EC Countries/Languages/Currencies/ECU Parities

Country	Language	Currency	Parity 1 ECU* corresponds to:
Belgio/Belgium	fiammingo/ Flemish francese/French	franco belga/ Belgian franc	42.9990 FB
Danimarca/ Denmark	danese/Danish	corona danese/ Danish Krone	7.9623 DKr
Germania/ Germany	tedesco/ German	marco tedesco/ Deutsche Mark	2.0481 DM
Francia/France	francese/French	franco francese/ French Franc	6.9653 FF
Gran Bretagna/ Great Britain	inglese/English	libbra sterling/ English Pound	0.7064 L
Grecia/Greece	greco/Greek	dracma/ Drachma	183.6220 Drch
Irlanda/Ireland	English/Gaelic	libbra irlandese/ Irish Pound	0.6905 IrP
Italia/Italy Lussemburgo/ Luxembourg	italiano/Italian francese/ French	lira/Italian Lira franco lussemburghese/ Luxembourg Franc	1506.3400 Lit
Paesi Bassi Olanda/ The Netherlands	olandese/Dutch	fiorino/Dutch Guilder	2.3116 hfl

Portogallo/ Portugal	portoghese/ Portuguese	scudi portoghesi/ Portuguese Escudo	176.3210 esc
Spagna/Spain	spagnolo/ Spanish	pesete spagnole/ Spanish Peseta	131.3480 pst

*Source: *The European*, 3.1.91

If you have any questions on the Single European Market you can contact various institutions, e.g. the Chambers of Commerce and Industry, etc.:

Association of British Chambers of Commerce
9 Tufton Street
London SW1P 3QB
Tel: 071-222 1555

British Chamber of Commerce (in Italy)
Via Agnello 8
20121 Milano
Tel: (02) 876981/877798

British Government Trade Office
Massimo d'Azelio 60
10126 Torino
Tel: (011) 687832
Telex: 221464 BRITRAD I

Italian Chamber of Industry and Commerce (in the UK)
296 Regent Street
London W1R 6AE
Tel: 071-637 3153/3062
Fax: 071-436 6037

Euro-Chambers
B-1000 Brussels
Tel: 010 322 230 0038

Associazioni delle Camere di Commercio
Italiano all Estero
(Association of Italian Chambers of
Commerce Abroad)
Piazza Sallustio 21
00187 Roma
Tel: (06) 4743488/4750854
Telex: 622327 Unicam I

Camera di Commercio Industria
Artigianato e Agricultura di Milano
(Foreign Trade Office at the Chamber of
Commerce, Industry, Crafts and
Agriculture, Milan)
Via Asperto 5
20123 Milano
Tel: (02) 85155248
Telex: 312 481 Comcam

Istituto Nazionale per il Commercio Estero
(ICE)
(Italian Foreign Trade Institute)
Via Liszt 21
00100 Roma
Tel: (06) 59921
Telex: 610160/612282 ICERM I

as well as:

Department of Trade and Industry
1 Victoria Street
London SW1H 0ET
Tel: 071-210 3000

DTI Hotline
Tel: 071-2000 1992

Further addresses:

SME Task Force
200 rue de la Loi
B-1049 Brussels
Tel: 010 322 236 1676
Telex: 61.655 BURAP B
Fax: 010 322 236 1241

The SME Task Force was set up by the European Commission to help small- and medium-sized businesses.

CBI
(The Confederation of British Industry)
Centre Point
103 New Oxford Street
London WC1A 1DU
Tel: 071-379 7400
Telex: 21322

The Confederation of British Industries represents many branches of industry. It can supply a great deal of material, especially on aspects of the Single European Market.

Commission of the European Communities
(Brussels Office)
200 rue de la Loi
B-1049 Brussels
Tel: 010 322 235 1111
Telex: 21877

European Investment Bank
(Head Office)
100 boulevard Konrad Adenauer
2950 Luxembourg
Tel: 010 352 43791
Telex: 3530

Department of Official Publications of the
  European Community
2 rue Mercier
2985 Luxembourg
Tel: 010 352 499281
Telex: 1324 pubog lu

Addresses of some Euro-Info-Centres in Great Britain

Birmingham Chamber of Industry and
  Commerce
75 Harbone Road
PO Box 360
Birmingham B15 3DH
Tel: 021-454 6171

Scottish Development Agency
Atrium House
50 Waterloo Street
Glasgow G2 6HO
Tel: 041-221 0999

Department of Employment
Small Firms Services
Ebury Bridge House
2–18 Ebury Bridge Road
London SW1W 8QD
Tel: 071-730 8451

Ireland:

European Business Information Centre
Irish Export Board/Coras Trachtala
Merrion Hall
PO Box 203
Strand Road
Sandymount
Dublin 4
Tel: 010 353 1 61695011

179

The above list is necessarily incomplete since Euro-Info-Centres are still being established. Please write to the European Community for an update:

Office in the United Kingdom
Jean Monnet House
8 Storey's Gate
London SW1P 3AT
Tel: 071-222 8122
Telex: 23 208 EURUK GB

or

Jean-Pierre Haber
Commission of the European Communities
GD XIII
200 rue de la Loi
B-1049 Brussels
Tel: 010 322 235 0538

There are a number of EC Advice Centres in Italy called 'Eurosportello' in: Bologna, Florence, Genoa, Perugia, Milan, Bari, Ravenna, Catania, Cagliari, Palermo, Rome.

Eurosportello di Milano
Via delle Orsole 4
Milano
Tel: (02) 85151

The Commission of the European Community has some offices in Italy:

EC Ufficio in Italia
Via Poli 29
00187 Roma
Tel: (06) 6789722
Telex: 610 184 EUROMA I

Corso Magenta 59
20123 Milano
Tel: (02) 801505
Telex: 316200 EURMIL I

Book tips on the Single European Market:

In Italian:
Guida al Mercato Unico
(*Guide to the Single Market*)
Andrea Forti
ISEDI, Turin, 1988

La sfida del 1992: Una grande scommessa per l'Europa
(*The Challenge of 1992: A great gamble for Europe*)
Sperling e Kupfer, Milan

Il mercato unico europeo: Norme e funzionamento
(*The Single European Market: directives and rules of the game*)
Alfonso Mattera Ricigliano
UTET, Turin

In English:
Promotion of Research and Technology by the EC:
A manual for applicants
Commission of the European Communities

Publications of statistics from various fields, e.g. foreign trade and industry, obtainable from:

> **Office of Statistics of the European**
>   **Communities**
> **Bâtiment Jean Monnet**
> **rue Alcide de Gasperi**
> **L-2920 Luxembourg**

The Times Guide to 1992: Britain in a Europe without Frontiers
Richard Owen and Michael Dynes
Times Books Limited, London, 1989

1992 – The Facts and Challenges
Catherine Taylor and Alison Press
Industrial Society Press, London, 1989

Completing the Internal Market of the European Community:
1992 Handbook
Mark Brealey and Conor Quigley
Graham and Trotman, London, 1989

Setting up a Company in the European Community:
A country by country guide
Brebner and Co., International Solicitors
Kogan Page, London, 1989

1992: Strategies for the Single Market
James W. Dudley
Kogan Page, London, 1989

The EC-Twelve Economic Situation
BfAi No. 27.001.90
Telex: 8 882 735 bfa d

Free EC publications:

You can obtain EC publications free of charge from the press and information offices of the EC Commission:

In Great Britain:

Jean Monnet House
8 Storey's Gate
London SW1P 3AT
Tel: 071-222 8122

Windsor House
9/15 Bedford Street
Belfast BT2 7EG
Tel: (0232) 240 708

4 Cathedral Road
Cardiff CF1 9SG
Tel: (0222) 371 631

7 Alva Street
Edinburgh EH2 4PH
Tel: 031-226 4105

In Ireland:

39 Molesworth Street
Dublin 2
Tel: 010-353 1 712 244

EC databanks:

Access to EC databanks can be made through:

> **ECHO Customer Service**
> **European Commission Host Organisation**
> **BP 2373**
> **177 Route d'Esch**
> **L-1023 Luxembourg**
> **Tel: 010 352 48804 1**
> **Telex: 2181 euro lu**
> **Fax: 010 352 48804 0**

Through ECHO access to one of the most interesting databanks is possible: **TED (Tenders Electronics Daily)** (Data Bank Supplement of the Official Gazette of the EC) (Survey of Public Contracts, Invitations to Tender and Supplement Contracts)

Italian databank:

> **CERVED**
> **Società Nazionale di Informatica delle**
> **Camere di Commercio Italiane**
> **(National Institute for Information of the**
> **Italian Chambers of Commerce)**
>
> **Via Meravigli 9b**
> **20123 Milano**
> **Tel: (02) 85151**
>
> **Via Appia Nuovo 696**
> **00179 Roma**
> **Tel: (06) 79341**

Demand from foreign companies for Italian products is registered daily.

If you see offers on the monitor which interest you, you can find all the details of the companies offering the goods by dialling numero verde 1678–25008 of the Chamber of Commerce and Industry in Milan. This service is free of charge. Regardless of where in Italy you make the call you will only have to pay for one unit: Tel: 1678 25008.

8

Reference Libraries and Bookshops

The City Business Library
106 Fenchurch Street
London EC3M 5JB
Tel: 071-638 8215

Department of Industry Library
Ashdowne House Library
123 Victoria Street
London SW1E 6RB
Tel: 071-212 0164

Department of Trade Library
1 Victoria Street
London SW1H 0ET
Tel: 071-215 3124

Reference Library
London Chamber of Commerce and
    Industry
69 Cannon Street
London EC4N 5AB
Tel: 071-248 4444

London Business School Library
Sussex Place
Regent's Park
London NW1 4SA
Tel: 071-262 5050

Statistics and Market Intelligence Library
1 Victoria Street
London SW1H 0ET
Tel: 071-215 7877

Europe and International Policy Group
Confederation of British Industry
Centre Point
103 New Oxford Street
London WC1A 1DU
Tel: 071-379 7400

Centro Studi e Documentazione sulle
  Comunità Europea
(Centre for Studies and Documentation on
  the European Community)
Corso Magenta 61
20123 Milano

Libreria Pirola Maggioli
(Pirola Bookshop)
Via Meravigli
(opposite the Chamber of Commerce
  and Industry)
20123 Milano

Libreria Hoepli
(Hoepli Bookshop)
Via Hoepli 5
20121 Milano
Tel: (02) 865446
Fax: (02) 8052886

An interesting list of ICC Publications is available. See p. 28 for the address.

■ Please note:

Opening hours of the Chambers of Industry and Commerce are generally restricted to mornings only.

You can, of course, obtain information from the reference libraries of the Chambers of Industry and Commerce in Italy.

9

Newspapers and Magazines

The following Italian newspapers and magazines will probably be of interest to businessmen and women:

Il Sole–24 Ore
Italia Oggi
Mondo Economico
Espansione
Europa Domani
Capital
Gente Money
Milano Finanza
Il Mondo
Business
Città
Corriere dell'Economia
Dimensione
Economia & Management

Europaforum
L'Impresa
Management
Messaggero Economico
Tempo Economico
Italiano per Gran Bretagna e il Commonwealth
Eise News
International Business Contacts
The British Italian Trade Review della Camera di Commercio Italiana per la Gran Bretagna e il Commonwealth

10

Useful UK addresses for Part I

→1

Market Research Society
175 Oxford Street
London W1R 1TA

European Marketing and Statistics
Euromonitor Publications
87–88 Turnmill Street
London EC1 5QU

→2   **Advertising Association**
Abford House
15 Wilton Road
London SW1V 1NJ

Institute of Practitioners in Advertising
44 Belgrave Square
London SW1X 8QS

→3   **British Telecom**
Bureaufax International Centre
BTI Communication Centre
9 St Botolph Street
London EC3A 7DT

The centre provides an extensive Italian/English and English/Italian translation service: interpreters are available when required.

→4   **British Exporters Association**
16 Dartmouth Street
London SW1H 9BL

SITPRO
(Simplification of International Trade
    Procedures)
Almack House
26–28 King Street
London SW1Y 6QW

Department of Trade and Industry
Export Initiative
1 Victoria Street
London SW1H 0ET

→5   **Institute of Freight Forwarders Ltd**
Redfern House
Browells Lane
Feltham
Middlesex TW13 7ET

Freight Transport Association
Hermes House
St John's Road
Tunbridge Wells
Kent TN4 9UZ

→6   Lloyd's of London
51 Lime Street
London EC3M 7DQ

→7   British Institute of International and
Comparative Law
Charles Clore House
17 Russell Square
London WC1B 5DR

The Law Society
113 Chancery Lane
London WC2A 1PL

→8   Italian Chamber of Industry and Commerce
in the UK
296 Regent Street
London W1R 6AE

Italian Trade Centre
37 Sackville Street
London W1X 2DQ

Italian Centre
90 St Vincent Street
Glasgow G2 5UB

11

Addresses of Chambers of Commerce and Tourist Information Centres

Bologna 40125
P. za Mercanzia 4
Tel: (051) 213111
Telex: 510240 PALAF
Fax: (051) 213451

Firenze 50122
P. za dei Giudici 3
Tel: (055) 27951
Telex: 570406 CCIAAFI
Fax: (055) 2795259

Genova 16124
Via Garibaldi 4
Tel: (010) 20941
Telex: 286325 COMGINI
Fax: 2094200

Milano 20123
Via Meravigli 9/B 11
Tel: (02) 85181
Telex: 312482 COMCAMI
Fax: 85154245

Napoli 80133
P. za Bovio
Tel: (081) 207222 206144
Telex: 710644 CAMCONA
Fax: (081) 207374

Roma 00186
Via de'Burrò 147
Tel: (06) 570071
Telex: 616376 CAROMAI
Fax: (06) 57007617

189

Torino 10123
Via S. Francesco da Paola 24
Tel: (011) 57161
Telex: 221247 CCTO
Fax: (011) 5716450

Venezia 30124
Via XXII Marzo 2032
Tel: (041) 5289580 786111
Telex: 410662 CAMVEI

■ Please note:

The office hours of the Chambers of Commerce and Industry are very often limited to mornings only.

Main Tourist Information Centres in Italy:

Ente Provinciale per il Turismo	EPT
Azienda di Promozione turistica	APT
Ufficio Provinciale per il Turismo	UPT

APT Bologna
Via Marconi 45
40122 Bologna
Tel: (051) 237413

EPT Firenze
Via Manzoni 16
50121 Firenze
Tel: (055) 2478141

EPT Genova
Via Roma 11
16121 Genova
Tel: (010) 581407

APT Milano
Via Marconi 1
20123 Milano
Tel: (02) 870016

EPT Napoli
Via Partenope 10 A
80121 Napoli
Tel: (081) 418988

EPT Roma
Via Parigi 11
00185 Roma
Tel: (06) 461851

APT Torino
Via Roma 222
10121 Torino
Tel: (011) 535181

APT Venezia
Rialto 4089
30122 Venezia
Tel: (041) 5226110

12

Reference Books

Annuario Kompass
(*Kompass Year Book*)
The Italian version of Kompass contains detailed information
about the activities, products and services of 35,000 Italian firms.
The Italian Kompass is published in 30 countries. The products are
listed according to the various branches. The three volumes can be
ordered from:

Kompass Italia
Via S. Rita da Cascia 33
20143 Milano
Tel: (02) 8910775
Fax: (02) 8910454

Annuario SEAT
(*SEAT Year Book*)
This comprises ten volumes and gives an overall picture of the Italian economy, professional activities and commercial undertakings, listed according to products and services.

SEAT Direct
Telephone directory containing the names of about a million firms and private subscribers.

Europages – L'Annuario degli affari in Europa
(*Year Book of European Business*)
This gives information on the following nine countries: Belgium, Germany, Spain, France, Great Britain, Italy, Switzerland, Luxembourg and The Netherlands. It reports on 140,000 international firms, and is an excellent aid to making initial contact within the Single Market.

Elenco degli Utenti del Servizio Telefax
(*Directory of Telefax Numbers*)

Pagine Gialle Elettroniche
(*Electronic Yellow Pages*)
A teledata service containing adverts of more than 1,000,000 Italian firms and technical and commercial information on about 100,000 of them.

If you want further information on the above-mentioned reference books, please write to:

> **SEAT Divisione STET**
> **Marketing Prodotti Editoriali**
> **(Marketing for publications)**
> **Via A. Saffi 18**
> **10138 Torino**

Guida Monaci – Annuario Generale Italiano
(*Italian General Directory*)

Duns Europa
(*35,000 leading companies in Europe*)
(Dun & Bradstreet International, High Wycombe)

ABC
Europ Production (Europex), the universal register of European trade (32 countries), gives information on more than 200,000 industrial, commercial and service firms and associations.

Statistica del Commercio
(*Statistical Year Book for Commerce*)
The Italian Office for Statistics (ISTAT)

> **Piazza Repubblica 22**
> **20123 Milano**
> **Tel: (02) 6595133**

Catalogo dei Periodici Italiani
(*Catalogue of Italian Magazines*)

> **Editrici Biografica**
> **Vle V. Veneto 24**
> **20124 Milano**

CERVED (Società Nazionale di Informatica delle Camere di Commercio Italiane)
(*National Institute for Information of the Italian Chambers of Commerce*)

> **Via Meravigli 9b**
> **20123 Milano**
> **Tel: (02) 85151**

> **Via Appia Nuovo, 696**
> **00179 Roma**
> **Tel: (06) 79341**

Demand from foreign companies for Italian products is registered daily.

If you see offers on the monitor which interest you, you will be given all the details of the companies offering the goods by dialling the green number 1678–25008 of the Chamber of Commerce and Industry in Milan. This service is (nearly) free of charge. You will only have to pay for one unit no matter from where in Italy you dial.

APPENDIX

1

Model Letters

 Model letter 1

Rif.:		reference
Torino, 21 dicembre 1991 <21.12.91>		name of city, date
(1) Spett. Ditta	(2) Dr. Mario Rossi	inside address
Marcello S.p.A.	Marcello S.p.A.	(two various forms)
Via Dolorosa 9		(1), (2)
20123 Milano		
Oggetto:		subject line
	(1) no salutation	salutation
	(2) Egregio Dottore	(two various forms, corresponding to the address) (1), (2)
		body of the letter
(1) Distinti saluti	(2) Cordiali saluti	complimentary
	(3) Distintamente	close (three various forms)
		signature
(Giorgio Bonnetto)		name
Direttore		job title

Model Letter 2

Oggetto: Fiera di elettrotecnica 1992

Quali commercianti specializzati per arredamenti elettrotecnici abbiamo l'intenzione di partecipare alla Fiera suddetta.

Vi saremmo grati per ulteriori dettagliate informazioni relative alle condizioni di partecipazione nonché per l'invio del modulo d'iscrizione.

RingraziandoVi in anticipo per una sollecita risposta, Vi salutiamo distintamente.

Model Letter 3

Dal Suo annuncio nel . . . abbiamo appreso che offre . . .

Lavoriamo nel campo importazione . . . e siamo interessati a contattare fornitori di tale merce.

La preghiamo di inviarci il Suo catalogo di data più recente assieme al listino prezzi.

Ringraziando in anticipo e con distinti saluti.

Model Letter 4

Con riferimento alla Vs richiesta del . . ., Vi possiamo fare la seguente offerta:

(merchandise, quantity, price)

termine di pagamento: pagamento al momento del recapito della merce

sconto del 2% per pagamento in contanti

termine di consegna: non appena ricevuto l'ordine

Siamo certi che la ns. merce risponderà alle Vs. aspettative e restiamo in attesa della Vs. pregiata ordinazione.

Distinti saluti

 # Model Letter 5

Oggetto: ns. ordinazione No. . . .

Vi ringraziamo della Vs. offerta dell'11 agosto 1992

Vi preghiamo di fornirci la seguente merce alle condizioni sottoelencate:

(merchandise, quantity)

Prezzo: Lit . . . cada uno/a
              franco fabbrica,
              imballaggio compreso
Pagamento: gg. 10 dopo racapito fattura
Consegna: entro il 15 aprile presso i ns. agenti di Brindisi

Con preghiera di volerci gentilmente confermare la presente ordinazione, Vi porgiamo distinti saluti.

Enrico Faghera
Direttore acquisti

 Model Letter 6

Oggetto: No. . . . del 03. 01. 1992

Siamo assai spiacenti dover informarLa che l'ordinazione No. . . . non è stata eseguita in modo soddisfacente.

Esaminando la merce, ci siamo resi conto che non corrispondeva allo standard da noi ordinato.

Accludiamo alla presente un campione affinché Lei possa verificare la ragione del reclamo.

La preghiamo di occuparsi al più presto del fatto e comunicarci come intendete procedere.

Distinti saluti

Allegato

 Model Letter 7

Siamo molto spiacenti di sentire che la ns. consegna non Vi ha soddisfatti.

Abbiamo attentamente esaminato i campioni inviatici e non abbiamo potuto verificare nessun difetto del materiale, ragione per cui non siamo in grado di accettare il reclamo.

Distintamente

Model Letter 8

Accusiamo ricevuta della Vs. del . . . relative alla consegna No. . . .

Ci rincresce assai di sentire che non siete rimasti soddisfatti della merce ed abbiamo provveduto alla sostituizione. Al tempo stesso Vi preghiamo di rinviarci a ns. spese la merce difettosa.

PregandoVi nuovamente di scusare il contrattempo, Vi porgiamo distinti saluti.

Model Letter 9

Accludiamo un assegno per l'ammontare di . . . emesso dalla Banco . . . quale saldo della Vs. fattura.

Distinti saluti

Allegato

Model Letter 10

In data odierna abbiamo incaricato la ns. banca di rimetterVi l'ammontare di L /£ . . . presso la . . . (Banca).

Distintamente

Model Letter 11

Come da allegato Vi ricordiamo l'ammontare in sofferenza.

Vi saremmo grati per un sollecito saldo a mezzo assegno.

Distinti saluti

Allegato

Model Letter 12

Con la precedente in data del . . . Vi abbiamo ricordato l'importo ancora in sospeso di £ . . .

Non avendo ancora ricevuto niente, Vi preghiamo provvedere al saldo entro 10 giorni.

Distintamente

 # Model Letter 13

Raccomandata

Oggetto: pareggiamento conto

Con riferimento alle nostre du lettere del . . . con le quali Vi ricordavamo il versamento di £ . . .

Fino ad oggi non avete effettuato nessun pagamento in merito. Se tale versamento non avverrà entro il . . . saremo obbligati ad iniziare atti giudiziari a mezzo del ns. legale.

Distinti saluti

 # Model Letter 14

Privato e confidenziale

La ditta nominata in allegato vorrebbe entrare in relazione d'affari con noi.

Non conoscendo la sunnominata ditta, Vi preghiamo di darci informazioni dettagliate in merito.

Sarebbe possibile fidarsi di un credito per l'ammontare di . . . ?

Qualsiasi informazione verrà trattata con la massima discrezione e riservatezza.

Vi ringraziamo fin d'ora e Vi salutiamo distintamente

Allegato

Model Letter 15

Curriculum Vitae

Cognome

Nomi di Battesimo

Indirizzo

No. di Telefono

Data e Luogo di Nascita

Nazionalità

Stato Civile

Scuole

Qualifiche

Esperienza

Attuale Datore di Lavoro

Referenze

 # Model Letter 16

Caro Signor Blackfield,

Siamo lieti di invitarLa assieme a Sua moglie per un cocktail, l'11 agosto alle ore 17.30.

Con preghiera di risposta.

Cordiali saluti

Model Letter 17

Caro Signor Faghera,

La ringraziamo vivamente per il gentile invito al cocktail dell'11 agosto ed accettiamo con piacere.

Cordialmente

 # Model Letter 18

Caro Signor Faghera,

La ringraziamo vivamente dell'invito per sabato, 11 agosto. Purtroppo per lo stesso giorno avevamo un impegno e quindi ci rincresce non poter accettare.

Con i più cordiali saluti

 # Model Letter 19

Caro Signor Marcello,

Ci tengo a ringraziarLa del Suo gentile aiuto durante il mio soggiorno a Milano.

La Sua collaborazione mi è stata preziosa e spero poter contraccambiare la Sua ospitalità in occasione della Sua visita a Sheffield in maggio.

Ringraziando nuovamente, Le invio cari saluti

Ronald Piggott

2

Presentation of a Balance Sheet

Assets

Unpaid capital, called up
Expenses incurred in connection with the start-up or expansion of the business

A Fixed Assets
I *Intangible assets*
1 Licences, trade marks and patents, etc., as well as licences to such rights and assets
2 Goodwill
3 Advances paid on intangible assets

II *Tangible assets*
1 Land, rights similar to land, and buildings, including buildings on property owned by others
2 Technical equipment and machinery
3 Other equipment, office furniture and equipment
4 Advances paid on fixed assets, and assets under construction

III *Financial assets*
1 Shares in group companies
2 Loans to group companies
3 Participating interests of 25% or more
4 Loans to entities with which the enterprise is linked by virtue of participating interests of 25% or more
5 Other investments – long term
6 Other loans

B Current assets
I *Inventories*
1 Raw materials and supplies
2 Work in progress; uncompleted projects
3 Finished goods and goods for resale
4 Advance payments on stocks

II *Receivables and other current assets*
1 Trade receivables
2 Amounts due from group companies
3 Receivables from entities with which the enterprise is linked by virtue of participating interests of 25% or more
4 Other current assets

III *Securities*
1 Shares in group companies
2 Treasury stock
3 Other securities

IV *Cheques, Cash, Deposits with Federal Bank and with Bank of Federal Postal System, Deposits with Commercial Banks*

C Pre-paid Expenses
Excess of liabilities over assets to the extent not covered by shareholders' equity

Schema Tipo di Stato Patrimoniale

Attivo

Capitale non versato, con indicazione della parte di cui è stato chiesto il versamento
Spese di costituzione (o di ampliamento)

A Attività Fisse
I *Attività immateriali*
   1 Brevetti, marchi di fabbrica e simili, o concessioni su tali diritti
   2 Avviamento
   3 Anticipi sull'acquisizione di attività immateriali

II *Immobilizzazioni tecniche e civili*
   1 Terreni (proprietà o altri diritti reali di godimento) e fabbricati, compresi quelli costruiti su terreni altrui
   2 Impianti e macchinari
   3 Altre immobilizzazioni tecniche, mobili e macchine per ufficio
   4 Anticipi a fornitori e costruzioni in corso

III *Immobilizzazioni finanziarie*
   1 Partecipazione in imprese consociate
   2 Finanziamenti a imprese consociate
   3 Partecipazioni superiori al 25%
   4 Finanziamenti a società con partecipazione superiore al 25%
   5 Altri investimenti di lungo periodo
   6 Altri finanziamenti

B Attività correnti
I *Magazzino*
   1 Materie prime e materiali di consumo
   2 Semilavorati; opere in corso di laborazione
   3 Merci e prodotti finiti
   4 Acconti a fornitori

II *Crediti e altre attività correnti*
   1 Crediti commerciali
   2 Crediti verso imprese consociate
   3 Crediti verso società con partecipazione superiore al 25%
   4 Altre attività correnti

III *Titoli*
   1 Partecipazioni in società consociate
   2 Azioni proprie
   3 Altri titoli

IV *Assegni, Cassa, Depositi presso la banca federale, Depositi postali, Depositi bancari*

C Rate e risconti attivi
   Perdite eccedenti il patrimonio netto

Liabilities and Shareholders' Equity

A Shareholders' equity
I *Share capital*
II *Capital reserve*
III *Earnings reserve*
    1 Legal reserve
    2 Reserve for treasury stock
    3 Statutory reserves
    4 Other earnings reserves

IV *Retained earnings/Accumulated deficit brought forward from previous year*

V *Net income/Loss for the year*
Special reserves, to be taxed in subsequent years

B Accruals
    1 Accruals for pensions and benefits
    2 Accrued taxes
    3 Other accruals

C Liabilities
    1 Debenture loans (convertible)
    2 Amounts due to banks
    3 Advance payments received
    4 Trade payables
    5 Notes payable
    6 Amounts due to group companies
    7 Amounts owed to entities with which the enterprise is linked by virtue of participating interests of 25% or more
    8 Other liabilities
      taxes
      in respect of social security

D Deferred income

Contingencies and commitments
Discounted notes, guarantees, guarantees given on notes and loans, other warranties, pledges on company assets to secure another party's liabilities, other contingencies and commitments

Passivo

A Patrimonio netto
I *Capitale sociale*
II *Riserve di capitale*
III *Riserve di utili*
   1 Riserva legale
   2 Riserva azioni proprie
   3 Riserva statutaria
   4 Altre riserve di utili

IV *Utili/perdite di esercizi precedenti*
V *Utile/perdita di esercizio*
Riserve speciali in sospensione d'imposta

B Fondi passivi
   1 Accantonamento per pensioni e impegni sociali
   2 Fondo imposte
   3 Altri fondi passivi

C Debiti
   1 Obbligazioni, con indicazione della parte costituita da obbligazioni
     convertibili
   2 Debiti verso Banche
   3 Anticipi da terzi
   4 Debiti commerciali
   5 Effetti passivi
   6 Debiti vs. società consociate
   7 Debiti vs. società con partecipazione superiore al 25%
   8 Altri debiti
     di cui per imposte
     di cui per contributi previdenziali

D Ratei e risconti passivi

Conti d'ordine
Effetti allo sconto, garanzie fideiussori, fideiussioni su cambiali e altri
finanziamenti, altre garanzie, attività impegnate a garanzia di debiti a
terzi, altri impegni e rischi.

3

Presentation of a Statement of Earnings

1 Sales
2 Increase or decrease in finished goods and work in progress
3 Other capitalized labour, overheads and materials
4 Other operating income
5 Materials
  (a) raw materials, supplies and purchased goods
  (b) purchased services (e.g. utilities, subcontracting costs, etc.)
6 Personnel costs
  (a) wages and salaries
  (b) social security and pension costs, benefits
7 Depreciation, amortization and special provisions
  (a) on intangible and tangible assets, and on capitalized business start-up or expansion costs
  (b) on current assets to the extent that usual provisions made by corporations are exceeded
8 Other operating expenses
9 Income from participating interests of 25% or more, income from group companies
10 Income from group companies' other securities and long term financial investments
11 Other interest and similar income from group companies
12 Write-down of financial assets and of securities included in currrent assets
13 Interest and similar expenses incurred by subsidiary companies
14 Results of ordinary operations
15 Extraordinary income
16 Extraordinary expenses
17 Extraordinary net
18 Taxes on income
19 Other taxes
20 Net income loss for the year

Income and expenses arising from profit and loss pooling arrangements and similar contracts are to be presented as separate line items.

Schema Tipo del Conto Profitti e Perdite

1 Vendite
2 Incrementi o decrementi di magazzino
3 Lavori in economia
4 Altri ricavi della gestione caratteristica
5 Acquisti
   (a) materie prime, materie accessorie, merci,
   (b) prestazioni di servizi
6 Oneri retributivi
   (a) salari e stipendi,
   (b) oneri sociali con indicazione della parte costituita da oneri
      pensionistici
7 Ammortamenti
   (a) delle attività immobilizzare immateriali e materiali e delle spese di
      costituzione e di ampliamento
   (b) delle attività correnti qualora eccedano il limite generalmente
      consentito
8 Altri oneri aziendali
9 Proventi dalla partecipazione in società consociate, con indicazione di
   quelli da società con partecipazione superiore al 25%
10 Proventi da altri titoli e da finanziamenti di lungo periodo, con
   indicazione di quelli da imprese del gruppo
11 Altri interessi e proventi simili, con indicazione di quelli da altre imprese
   del gruppo
12 Svalutazione di attività finanziarie e titoli inclusi tra le attività correnti
13 Interessi passivi e oneri simili, con indicazione di quelli verso altre
   imprese del gruppo
14 Risultato operativo
15 Proventi straordinari
16 Oneri straordinari
17 Utile/perdita al lordo delle imposte
18 Imposte sul reddito
19 Altre imposte
20 Utile netto (o perdita)

Gli utili e le perdite derivanti dalla partecipazione in associazioni in
partecipazioni, da accordi di cointeressenza agli utili o da accordi simili
devono essere evidenziati separamente.

4

English–Italian Index of Technical Vocabulary with a Phonetic Transcription

f feminine
m masculine
pl plural

to accept an offer	**accettare un'offerta** *f*	attʃet'tare un of'fɛrta
accepted in the trade	**d'uso** *m* **commerciale**	d'uzo kommer'tʃale
in accordance with your order	**in base** *f* **alla Vs. ordinazione** *f*	in 'baze alla 'vɔstre ordɪnat'tsjone
account	**conto** *m*	'konto
accountant, bookkeeper	**contabile** *m*, **ragioniere** *m*	kon'tabile, radʒo'njɛre
accounting, bookkeeping	**contabilità** *f*	kontabili'ta
accruals	**spese** *f pl* **da pagare**	'spese da pa'gare
acknowledgement of order	**conferma** *f* **dell'ordine** *m*	kon'fɛrma del'ordine
to acquire a licence	**acquisire una licenza** *f*	akkwi'zire una lɪ'tʃentsa
acquisition	**acquisto** *m*, **acquisizione** *f*	ak'kwisto, akkwizit'tsjone
additional period of time	**periodo** *m* **addizionale**	pe'rɪodo addittsjo'nale
address	**indirizzo** *m*	ɪndɪ'rɪttso
to adjust prices	**equiparare i prezzi** *m pl*, **equiparazione** *f*	ekwɪpa'rare ɪ 'prɛttsɪ, ekwɪpara'tsjone
adjustment	**regolare il reclamo** *m*	rego'lare ɪl re'klamo
administration expenses	**spese di amministrazione** *f pl*	'spese dɪ ammɪn-ɪstrat'tsjone
in advance	**in anticipo** *m*	ɪn an'tɪtʃɪpo
advance order	**ordine** *m* **anticipato**	'ordine antɪtʃɪ'pato

210

English	Italian	Phonetic
advance payment	pagamento m anticipato	paga'mento antit∫ı'pato
advertisement	inserzione f, annuncio m	ınser'tsjone, an'nunt∫o
advertising, commercial	pubblicità f	pubblıt∫ı'ta
advertising gimmick	omaggio m di pubblicità f	o'maddʒıo dı pubblıt∫ı'ta
affidavit	affidavit m	
after-sales service	assistenza f post vendita f	assıs'tentsa post 'vendıta
after-tax profit	utile m tasse f pl detratte	'utıle 'tasse de'tratte
agenda	ordine m del giorno m	'ordıne del 'dʒorno
agent, representative	agente m, rappresentante m	a'dʒɛnte, rapprezen'tante
agreement	accordo m	ak'kordo
air cargo, airfreight	carico m aereo	'karıko a'erıo
air transport	trasporto aereo m	tras'porto a'ɛreo
air waybill	lettera f di trasporto m aereo	'lɛttera dı tras'porto a'ɛreo
all-in costs	spese f pl totali	'spese to'tali
all-in price	prezzo m complessivo	'prɛttso komples'sıvo
to allow a claim	riconoscere un reclamo m	rıko'no∫∫ere un re'klamo
to amend a contract	modificare un contratto m	modıfı'kare un kon'tratto
amortization rate	tasso m d'ammortamento m	'tasso d'ammorta'-mento
amount overdue	importo m in sofferenza f	ım'porto ın soffe'rɛntsa
annual financial statement	bilancio m annuale/ documenti m pl contabili annuali	bı'lant∫o annu'ale/ doku'mentı kon'tabılı annu'alı
annual general meeting of the shareholders	assemblea f generale annuale	assem'blɛa dʒene'rale annu'ale

annual report	relazione *f* annuale del bilancio *m*	relɑt'tsjone ɑnnu'ɑle del bɪ'lɑntʃɔ
application	domanda *f* d'impiego *m*	do'mɑndɑ d'ɪm'pjegɔ
to apply for	applicarsi	ɑpplɪ'kɑrsɪ
to apply for a patent	depositare *f* domanda di brevetto *m*	depozɪ'tɑre do'mɑndɑ dɪ bre'vettɔ
to appreciate	apprezzare	ɑppret'tsɑre
apprentice	apprendista *m/f*	ɑppren'dɪstɑ
arrears	arretrati *m pl*	ɑrre'trɑtɪ
as per contract	conforme a contratto *m*	kon'forme ɑ kon'trɑttɔ
as per invoice	conforme a fattura *f*	kon'forme ɑ fɑt'turɑ
as per your order/in accordance with your order	secondo la Vs. ordinazione *f* (in base alla Vs. ordinazione)	se'kondɔ lɑ vɔstro ordɪnɑt'tsjone (ɪn' bɑze ɑllɑ vɔstro ordɪnɑt'tsjone)
assembly	montaggio *m*	mon'tɑddʒɔ
assembly instructions	istruzioni *f pl* per il montaggio *m*	ɪstrut'tsjonɪ per ɪl mon'tɑddʒɔ
assembly line	catena *f* di montaggio *m*	kɑ'tenɑ dɪ mon'tɑddʒɔ
assets	attivo *m*	ɑt'tivɔ
assignment of a debt	cessione *f* di credito *m*	tʃes'sjone dɪ 'kredɪtɔ
at cost	a prezzo *m* di costo *m*	ɑ 'prettsɔ dɪ kɔstɔ
at half price	a metà *f* prezzo *m*	ɑ me'tɑ 'prettsɔ
at your/our expense	a Vostre (Vs.)/nostre (ns) spese *f*	ɑ vɔstre/nostre 'spese
attached	allegato *m*	ɑlle'gɑtɔ
attachment (seizure of goods)	pignoramento *m*	pɪnjorɑ'mento
to attend (a conference)	partecipare ad una conferenza *f*	pɑrtetʃɪ'pɑre ɑd 'unɑ konfe'rɛntsɑ
auditing	revisione *f*	revɪ'zjone
bad debt	credito *m* inesigibile	'kredɪtɔ ɪnezɪ'dzɪbɪle
bag, sack	sacco *m*	'sɑkkɔ

balance	saldo *m*, bilancio *m*	'saldo, bı'lantʃσ
to balance an account	pareggiare un conto *m*	pared'dʒare un 'kontσ
balance sheet	bilancio *m*	bı'lantʃσ
bankruptcy, liquidation	fallimento *m*, liquidazione *f*	fallı'mentσ, lıkwıdat'tsjone
to bargain	mercanteggiare	merkanted'dʒare
barrel	botte *f*, barile *m*	'botte, ba'rıle
to become contractual	obbligarsi per contratto *m*	σbblı'garsı per kon'trattσ
beneficiary, payee	beneficiario/a *m/f*	benefı'tʃarıσ/a
to bill, to invoice	emettere una fattura *f*, fatturare	e'mettere 'una fat'tura, fattu'rare
bill of exchange (B/E)	cambiale *f*	kam'bjale
Bill of Lading (B/L)	polizza *f* di carico *m* marittima, Bill of Lading *m*	'pɔlıttsa dı 'karıkσ ma'rıttıma
bill overdue	cambiale *f* in sofferenza *f*	kam'bjale ın soffe'rɛntsa
blank, space	spazio *m*	'spattsjσ
blend	miscela *f*	mıʃ'ʃela
to book (tourism)	prenotare	prenσ'tare
to book, to enter a booking	registrare	redʒıs'trare
to book exhibition space	noleggiare un'area *f* dell'esposizione *f*	noled'dʒare un'area del'espozıt'tsjone
to book in conformity	registrare in conformità *f*	redʒıs'trare ın konformı'ta
book value	valore *m* contabile	va'lore kon'tabıle
bookings	ordini *m pl* pervenuti, acquisizioni *f pl* di ordini *m pl*	'ordını pervenutı, akkwızıt'tsjonı dı'ordını
bookkeeper, accountant	contabile *m*	kon'tabıle
bookkeeping, accounting	contabilità *f*	kontabılı'ta
booth	stand *m* della fiera *f*	stænd 'della 'fjɛra
borrowed capital	capitale *m* prestito	kapı'tale 'prɛstıto
boss, foreman	capo *m*	'kapσ

to bounce (cheque)	**essere respinto al beneficiario** *m*	'ɛssere res'pɪntɔ al benefɪ'tʃarjɔ
branch	**filiale** *m*	fɪl'ljale
brand	**marchio** *m*	'markjɔ
to bring an action against somebody	**iniziare un'azione** *f* **legale**	ɪnɪt'tsjare un at'tsjone le'gale
to bring forward a motion	**presentare una mozione** *f*	prezen'tare una mot'tsjone
brochure, leaflet	**opuscolo** *m*	ɔ'puskolɔ
broker, dealer, trader	**commerciante** *m* **su commissione** *f*	kommer'tʃante su kommɪs'sjone
brought forward (b/f)	**riporto**	rɪ'pɔrtɔ
bulk goods	**merci** *f pl* **alla rinfusa** *f*	'mɛrtʃɪ 'alla rɪn'fuza
bulk haulage	**trasporto** *m* **alla rinfusa** *f*	tras'pɔrtɔ 'alla rɪn'fuza
business, company, firm	**compagnia** *f*, **ditta** *f*, **società** *f*	kompaɲ'ɲia, 'dɪtta, sotʃe'ta
business letter	**lettera** *f* **commerciali**	'lettera kommert'ʃale
business partnerships	**partecipazioni** *f pl* **commerciali**	partetʃɪpat'tsjonɪ kommert'ʃalɪ
business reply card	**cartolina** *f* **con risposta** *f* **pagata**	kartɔ'lɪna kon rɪ'posta pa'gata
business reputation	**reputazione** *f* **sul campo** *m* **affari** *m pl*	reputat'tsjone sul'kampɔ af'farɪ
business, to do . . .	**fare affari** *m pl*	'fare af'farɪ
to buy, to purchase	**acquistare, comprare**	akkwɪs'tare, kom'prare
buyer	**acquirente** *m*, **compratore** *m*	akkwɪ'rɛnte, kompra'tore
buying conditions	**condizioni** *f pl* **di acquisto** *m*	kondɪt'tsjonɪ dɪ ak'kwɪstɔ
c/o (care of)	**presso, c/o**	'prɛsɔ
cable connection	**allacciamento** *m* **via cavo** *m*	allattʃa'mento 'vɪa 'kavɔ
to calculate	**calcolare**	kalko'lare
calculation	**calcolo** *m*	'kalkolɔ
calculator	**calcolatrice** *f*	kalkola'trɪtʃe

call-money	denaro m rimborsabile a richiesta f	de'naro rɪmbor'sabɪle a rɪ'kjɛsta
can, metal container, case	scatola f	'skatola
to cancel	stornare	stor'nare
to cancel a contract	stornare/disdire un contratto m	stor'nare/dɪz'dɪre un kon'tratto
capital gains tax	imposta f sulla plus valenze f pl	ɪm'pɔsta 'sulla plus va'lɛntse
capital goods	beni m pl strumentali	'bɛnɪ strumen'talɪ
capital structure	struttura f finanziaria	strut'tura finan'tsjarja
cardboard box, carton	cartone m	kar'tone
cargo, freight, carriage	carico m	'karɪko
carriage, removal	trasporto m merci f pl., carreggio m, rimozione f	tras'pɔrto 'mɛrtʃɪ, kar'rɛdʒo, rɪmot'tsjone
carrier, forwarder	spedizioniere m	spedɪttsjo'njɛre
to carry a motion	adottare una mozione f	adot'tare 'una mot'tsj'one
to carry forward	riportare	rɪpor'tare
carry-over	riporto	rɪ'pɔrto
case	scatola f	'skatola
cash	contanti m pl	kon'tantɪ
cash against documents (CAD)/ documents against payment (D/P)	pagamento m contro documenti m pl	paga'mento 'kontro doku'mentɪ
cash discount	sconto m per contanti m pl/sconto m di cassa f	'skonto per kon'tantɪ 'skonto dɪ 'kassa
cash flow	cash flow	
cash on delivery (COD)	pagamento m alla consegna f	paga'mento 'alla kon'seɲɲa
cash with order (CWO)	pagamento m all'ordinazione f	paga'mento 'all'-ordɪnat'tsjone
catalogue (latest)	catalogo m (di data f recentissima)	ka'talogo dɪ data reʃen'tɪsɪma

215

central processing unit (CPU)	unità centrale di elaborazione *f* CPU	unɪ'ta tʃen'trale dɪ elabɔrat'tsjone
to certify	certificare, attestare	tʃertɪfɪ'kare, attes'tare
to certify a contract	vidimare/legalizzare un contratto *m*	vidi'mare, legalɪd'dʒare un kon'trattɔ
chairperson	presidente *m/f*	presɪ'dɛnte
charge, fee	tassa *f*	'tassa
to charge	fatturare, addebitare	fattu'rare, addebɪ'tare
chartered accountant	revisore *m* dei conti *m pl*, ragioniere *m* professionista *m*	revɪ'zore deɪ 'kontɪ, radʒɔ'njere profjessjɔ'nɪsta
circular	circolare *f*	tʃɪrko'lare
circumstances beyond our control	circostanze *f pl* imprevedibili	tʃɪrkos'tantse ɪmpreve'dɪbɪlɪ
claim	domanda *f*, diritto *m*	do'manda, dɪ'rɪttɔ
to clarify a position	chiarire una posizione *f*	kja'rire una pozɪt'tsjone
classifications	classificazioni *f pl*	klassɪfɪkat'tsjonɪ
clerk	impiegato/a *m/f* commerciale	ɪmpje'gato/a kommer'tʃale
to close a meeting	chiudere una seduta *f*	'kjudere 'una se'duta
to close an account	chiudere un conto *m*	'kjudere un 'konto kodʒes'tjone
collection agency	ufficio *m* di incasso *m*	kollabɔrat'tsjone uf'fitʃɔ dɪ ɪn'kassɔ
commercial (radio, television)	pubblicità *f* (radio/televisione)	pubblɪtʃɪ'ta
commercial invoice	fattura *f* commerciale	fat'tura kommer'tʃale
commercial quality	qualità *f* d'uso *m* commerciale	kwalɪ'ta d'uzɔ kommer'tʃale
commercial settlement of a dispute	composizione *f* d'una lite *f*	kompozɪt'tsjone d'una 'lite
commission	provvigione *f*	provvɪ'dʒone
commission agent	commissionario *m*, intermediario *m*	kommɪssjɔ'narjɔ, interme'djarjɔ

commodity, goods, merchandise	merce *f*, merci *f pl*, mercanzia *f*	'mɛrtʃe, 'mɛrtʃɪ, merkan'tsɪa
common market	mercato comune *m*	mer'kato ko'mune
communication line	linea di comunicazione *f*	'lɪnea dɪ komunɪkat'tsjone
Community Transport Procedure (CTP)	procedimento m comune di spedizione *f*	protʃedɪ'mento ko'mune dɪ spedɪt'tsjone
company, firm, business	dittà *f*, società *f*, compagnia *f*	'dɪtta, sotʃe'ta, kompaɲ'ɲɪa
to compel	obbligare, forzare	obblɪ'gare, for'tsare
to compensate	risarcire, indennizzare	rɪsar'tʃɪre, ɪndennɪd'dzare
compensation	risarcimento *m* dei danni *m pl*, indennizzo *m*	rɪsartʃɪ'mento 'dannɪ, ɪnden'nɪddzo
to compete	competere, concorrere	kom'pɛtere, kon'korrere
competition	concorrenza *f*, competitività *f*	konkor'rɛntsa, kompetɪtɪvɪ'ta
competitive price	prezzo *m* competitivo	'prettso kompetɪ'tɪvo
competitor	concorrente *m*	konkor'rɛnte
to complain about	lamentarsi di	lamen'tarsɪ dɪ
complaint	reclamo *m*	re'klamo
composition	composizione *f*, concordato *m*	kompozɪt'tsjone, konkor'dato
compound interest	interesse *m* composto	ɪnte'resse kom'posto
compulsory sale	vendita *f* forzata	'vendɪta for'tsata
concern, group, consortium	consorzio *m*, gruppo *m*	kon'sortsjo, 'gruppo
concerning	riguardo a	rɪ'gwardo a
conditions, terms	condizioni *f pl*	kondɪt'tsjonɪ
conditions of participation	condizioni *f pl* di partecipazione *f*	kondɪt'tsjonɪ dɪ partetʃɪpat'tsjone
conference	conferenza *f*	konfe'rɛntsa
consignee	destinatario/a *f/m*, consegnatario/a *f/m*	destɪna'tarjoa, konseɲɲa'tarjo/a

English	Italian	Phonetic
consignment note, waybill	lettera *f* di vettura *f*	'lɛttera dɪ vet'tura
consignment, shipment	spedizione *f*, consegna *f*	spedɪt'tsjone, kon'seɲɲa
consignor, shipper	mittente *m*	mɪt'tɛnte
consortium	consorzio *m*	kon'sɔrtsjɔ
to constitute a quorum	raggiungere il quorum *m*	rad'dʒundʒere ɪl 'kwɔrum
consular invoice	fattura *f* consolare	fat'tura konso'lare
consumer goods	beni *m pl* di consumo *m*	'bɛnɪ dɪ kon'sumɔ
consumer price	prezzo *m* al consumo *m*	'prɛttsɔ al kon'sumɔ
container	container *m*, contenitore *m*	kontenɪ'tore
to contract, enter into a contract	stipulare un contratto *m*	stɪpu'lare un kon'trattɔ
contract clause	clausola *f* contrattuale	'klauzola kontrattu'ale
contract of employment	contratto *m* d'impiego *m*	kon'trattɔ d'ɪm'pjɛgɔ
contract of sale	contratto *m* di vendita *f*	kon'trattɔ dɪ 'vendɪta
the contract expires . . .	il contratto *m* scade . . .	ɪl kon'trattɔ 'skade
the contract is null and void	il contratto *m* è nullo e senza effetto *m*	ɪl kon'trattɔ e 'nullɔ e 'sɛntsa ef'fɛttɔ
contracting parties	parti *f pl* contraenti	'partɪ kontra'ɛntɪ
contractors, suppliers	ditta *f* fornitrice *f*	'dɪtta fornɪ'trɪtʃe
to control, check	controllare	kontrol'lare
convenience, at your earliest . . .	con cortese sollecitudine *f*	kon kor'teʒe solletʃɪ'tudɪne
co-operation	collaborazione *f*	kollaborat'tsjone
corporation tax	imposta *f* sulla società *f*	ɪm'pɔsta 'sulla sotʃe'ta
cost price	prezzo *m* di costo *m*	'prɛttsɔ dɪ 'kɔstɔ
cost covering	che copre i costi *m pl*	ke 'kopre ɪ 'kɔstɪ
cost-effective	costo *m* efficace	'kɔstɔ effɪ'katʃe

cost-free, free of charge	franco di spese *f pl*, gratis, gratuito	'franko dı 'spese, 'gratıs, gra'tuıto
costs	costi *m pl*	'kɔstı
country of destination	paese *m* di destinazione *f*	pa'eze dı destınat'tsjone
courtesy	cortesia *f*	korte'zıa
to cover a risk	coprire un rischio *m*	ko'prıre un 'rıskjo
cover (insurance)	copertura *f*	koper'tura
crate	cassa *f* da imballaggio *m*, crate *m*	'kassa da ımbal'laddʒo
credit, short-/medium-/long-term	credito *m* a breve/medio/lungo termine *m*	'kredıto a 'brɛve/'medjo 'lungo 'termine
to credit	accreditare	akkredı'tare
credit inquiry	richiesta *f* di informazioni *f pl* commerciali	rı'kjesta dı ınformat'tsjonı kommer'tʃalı
credit insurance	assicurazione *f* di crediti *m pl*	assıkurat'tsjone dı 'kredıtı
credit note	nota *f* d'accredito *m*	'nota d'ak'kredıto
credit rating	credito *m*	'kredıto
creditor	creditore *m*	kredı'tore
current account	conto *m* corrente	'konto kor'rɛnte
current assets	attivo *m*, realizzabile attività *f pl*, correnti	at'tıvo, realıd'dzabıle attıvı'ta, kor'rɛntı
curriculum vitae	curriculum vitae *m*	kur'rıkulum 'vıtɛ
customer	cliente *m*	klı'ɛnte
daisy wheel	margherita *f* di stampa *f*	marger'ıta dı 'stampa
damage	danno *m*	'danno
database	base *f* di dati *m pl*, database *m*	'baze dı 'datı
data transfer	trasferimento *m* dati *m pl*	trasferı'mento datı
date of invoice	data *f* della fattura *f*	'data 'della fat'tura
date of shipment	data *f* di spedizione *f*	'data dı spedıt'tsjone
deadline	termine *m* ultimo	'termine 'ultımo

deadlines	limite *m* determinato per prestazioni *f pl*	'limite determi'nato per prestat'tsjoni
debit note	nota *f* d'addebito *m*	'nɔta d'ad'debito
debt	credito *m*, debito *m*	'kredito, 'debito
debtor	debitore *m*	debi'tore
to decide on a motion	prendere una decisione *f* riguardo a una mozione *f*	'prendere 'una detʃi'zjone, rigwardo a 'una mot'tsjone
defect	difetto *m*, guasto *m*	di'fetto, 'gwasto
defective goods	merce *f* difettosa	'mɛrtʃe difet'tosa
delay	ritardo *m*	ri'tardo
to deliver	recapitare, consegnare	rekapi'tare, konseɲ'ɲare
to deliver within the specified time	consegnare entro il termine previsto *m*	konseɲ'ɲare 'entro il 'tɛrmine pre'visto
delivery	consegna *f*, fornitura *f*	kon'seɲɲa, forni'tura
delivery note	bolla *f* di consegna *f*	'bɔlla di kon'seɲɲa
demand	domanda *f*	do'manda,
to demand compensation	chiedere un indennizzo *m*	'kjedere un inden'niddzo
to demand payment	invitare al pagamento *m*, ingiungere il pagamento *m*	invi'tare al paga'mento, in'dʒundʒere il paga'mento
demonstration	presentazione *f*	prezentat'tsjone
density	densità *f*	densi'ta
deposit/savings account	conto *m* di risparmio *m*/di deposito *m*	'konto di ris'parmjo, di de'pɔzito
depreciations	ammortamenti *m pl*	ammorta'menti
detailed information about	informazioni *f pl* dettagliate su	informat'tsjoni detta'ʎʎate su
development (of a product)	attività *f* di sviluppo *m*	attivi'ta di zvi'luppo
development (of business), growth	sviluppo *m* commerciale	zvi'luppo kommer'tʃale

direct labour	manodopera f diretta	manoˈdɔpera dɪˈrɛtta
direct material	materiale m diretto	mateˈrjale dɪˈrɛttɔ
direct memory access	accesso m diretto alla memoria f	atˈtʃessɔ dɪˈrɛttɔ ˈalla meˈmɔrja
discount	sconto m, ribasso m	ˈskonto, rɪˈbassɔ
discount rate	tasso m della sconto m	ˈtassɔ ˈdella ˈskontɔ
disk (computers)	disco m	ˈdɪskɔ
disk operating system (DOS)	sistema m operativo (DOS)	sɪˈstɛma operaˈtɪvɔ
disk storage	memoria f, a massa f	meˈmɔrja, a ˈmassa
to dismantle a stand	smontare lo stand m	zmonˈtare lo stœnd
dismissal	licenziamento m	lɪtʃentsjaˈmentɔ
to dispatch, to send off, to ship, to forward	inviare, spedire	ɪnvɪˈare, speˈdɪre
dispatch department	reparto m spedizione f	reˈpartɔ spedɪtˈtsjone
dispatch note	avviso m di spedizione f	avˈvɪsɔ dɪ spedɪtˈtsjɔne
display, screen	video m, schermo m	ˈskermɔ
display material	materiale m da esposizione f	mateˈrjale da espozɪtˈtsjone
dispute	lite f, causa f	ˈlite, ˈkauza
distribution network	rete f di distribuzione f	ˈrete dɪ dɪstrɪbutˈtsjone
dividend	dividendi m pl	dɪvɪˈdɛndɪ
documents against acceptance (D/A)	documenti m pl contro accettazione f	dokuˈmentɪ ˈkontro attʃettatˈtsjone
domestic market	mercato m nazionale	merˈkatɔ nattsjoˈnale
doubtful debt	credito m di dubbia esazione f	ˈkredɪtɔ dɪ ˈdubbja ezatˈtsjone
down-payment, payment on account	acconto m	akˈkontɔ
draft	tratta f	ˈtratta
to draw a cheque	emettere un assegno m	eˈmettere un asˈseɲɲa
to draw money from an account	prelevare denaro m da un conto m	preleˈvare deˈnarɔ da un ˈkontɔ

drive (disk)	drive *m*, unità *f* (disco *m*, nastro *m*)	unɪ'ta ('dɪsko, 'nastrɔ)
due date	scadenza *f*, data *f* di rimborso *m*	ska'dɛntsa, 'data dɪ rɪm'borsɔ
dunning letter, reminder letter	lettera *f* di sollecitazione *f*	'lɛttera dɪ sollɛtʃɪtat'tsjone
duplicate consignment note	duplicato *m* della lettera *f* di vettura *f*	duplɪ'katɔ 'della 'lɛttera dɪ vet'tura
E & OE (errors and omissions excepted)	SE & O (salvo errori ed omissioni)	'salvɔ er'rorɪ ed omɪs'sjonɪ
economic position	situazione *f* economica	sɪtuat'tsjone eko'nɔmɪka
education, training	istruzione *f*, formazione *f* professionale	ɪstrut'tsjone, format'tsjone professjɔ'nale
to effect delivery	eseguire una consegna *f*	eze'gwɪre una kon'seɲɲa
to effect payment	pagare	pa'gare
electronic data processing (EDP)	elaborazione *f* elettronica dei dati *m pl*	elaborat'tsjone elet'trɔnɪka deɪ 'datɪ
electronic mail/E-mail	posta *f* elettronica	'pɔsta elet'trɔnɪka
to employ, to engage, to take on	assumere	as'sumere
employee	impiegato/a *m/f*, dipendente *m/f*	ɪmpje'gatɔ/a, dɪpen'dɛnte
employer	datore *m* di lavoro *m*	da'tore dɪ la'vorɔ
enclosure, attached	allegato *m*	alle'gatɔ
to engage, to employ, to take on	assumere	as'sumere
engineering	progettazioni *f pl* tecniche	prodʒettat'tsjonɪ 'technike
to enter/book an order	prenotare un'ordinazione *f*	preno'tare un ordɪnat'tsjone
to enter into a contract	stipulare un contratto *m*	stɪpu'lare un kon'trattɔ
to entrust a firm with the agency	affidare la rappresentanza *f*	affɪ'dare la rapprezen'tantsa
entry	registrazione *f*	redʒɪstrat'tsjone

equity capital	**patrimonio** *m* **netto**	patrɪˈmɔnjɔ ˈnettɔ
to erase (computer data)	**cancellare**	kantʃelˈlare
error, oversight	**svista** *f*, **errore** *m*	ˈzvista, erˈrore
to establish, to found	**fondare**	fonˈdare
estimate	**preventivo** *m* **di spesa** *f*	prevenˈtivɔ dɪ ˈspesa
estimated annual turnover	**movimento** *m* **anno** *m* **stimato**	moviˈmentɔ ˈannɔ stɪˈmatɔ
to exchange the goods	**cambiare la merce** *f*	kamˈbjare la ˈmertʃe
excise tax	**imposta** *f* **sul consumo** *m*	ɪmˈpɔsta sul konˈsumɔ
to execute an order	**eseguire un ordine** *m*	ezeˈgwire un ˈordɪne
executive, manager(ess)	**dirigente** *m*	dɪrɪˈdʒente
exhibit	**oggetto** *m* **d'esposizione** *f*	odˈdʒettɔ dˈespozɪtˈtsjone
to exhibit, to show	**esporre**	esˈporre
exhibition	**fiera** *f*, **mostra** *f*, **esposizione** *f*	ˈfjɛra, ˈmostra, espozɪtˈtsjone
exhibition centre	**centro** *m* **della fiera** *f*	ˈtʃentro della ˈfjɛra
exhibition regulations	**regolamento** *m* **della fiera** *f*	regolaˈmentɔ della ˈfjɛra
exhibitor	**espositore/espositrice** *m/f*	espozɪˈtore, espozɪˈtrɪʃe
expected growth	**sviluppo** *m* **previsto**	zvɪˈluppo preˈvistɔ
expenses, expenditure	**spese** *f pl*	ˈspese
expert	**esperto/a** *m/f*	esˈpɛrtɔ/a
to exploit a patent	**utilizzare un brevetto** *m*	utɪlɪdˈdzare un breˈvettɔ
to export	**esportare**	esporˈtare
export packing	**imballaggio** *m* **per esportazione** *f*	ɪmbalˈladdʒɔ per esportatˈtsjone
exporter	**esportatore/ esportatrice** *m/f*	esportaˈtore/ esportaˈtrɪʃe
to extend a contract	**prolungare un contratto** *m*	prolunˈgare un konˈtrattɔ
extension	**proroga** *f*	ˈprɔroga
extras	**spesa** *f* **extra**	ˈspese ˈɛkstra

factoring	**factoring** *m*	
factory gate price	**prezzo** *m* **alla produzione** *f*	'prɛttsɔ 'alla produt'tsjone
fair	**fiera** *f*	'fjɛra
fair average quality (faq)	**qualità** *f* **buona media**	kwalı'ta 'bwɔna 'mɛdja
fair management	**direzione** *f* **della fiera** *f*	dıret'tsjone 'della 'fjɛra
fair pass	**tessera** *f* **d'espositore** *m*	'tɛssera d'espozıtore
fair price	**prezzo** *m* **ragionevole**	'prɛttsɔ radʒɔ'nevole
to fall due	**scadere**	ska'dere
fault	**errore** *m*, **sbaglio** *m*	er'rore, zbaʎʎɔ
faulty material	**materiale** *m* **difettoso**	mater'jale dıfet'tosɔ
favourable price	**prezzo** *m* **favorevole**	'prɛttsɔ favo'revole
fee	**tassa** *f*	'tassa
file	**file** *f*, **archivio** *m*	ar'kıvjɔ
to file for bankruptcy	**presentare istanza** *f* **di**	prezen'tare ı'stantsa dı
file protection	**protezione** *f* **degli archivi** *m pl*	protet'tsjone deʎʎı ar'kıwı
financial standing	**stato** *m* **patrimoniale**	'stato patrımɔ'njale
finished goods	**prodotti** *m pl* **finiti**	pro'dotti fınıtı
firm, business, company	**ditta** *f*, **società** *f*, **compagnia** *f*	'dıtta, sotʃe'ta, kompaɲ'ɲıa
first-class quality	**di prima qualità** *f*	dı 'prıma kwalı'ta
fixed assets	**attivo** *m* **fisso**	at'tıvo 'fısso
fixed costs	**spese** *f pl* **fisse**	'spese 'fısse
fixed price	**prezzo** *m* **fisso**	'prɛttso 'fıssɔ
flat rate	**tasso** *m* **forfettario**	'tassɔ forfe'tarjɔ
flexible working hours, flexi-time	**orario** *m* **di lavoro** *m* **flessibile**	o'rarjɔ dı la'vorɔ fles'sıbıle
floating point (computers)	**virgola** *f* **mobile**	'virgola 'mobıle
floor plan	**pianta** *f*	'pjanta
floor space	**area** *f* **dell'esposizione** *f*	'area dell'espozıt'tsjone

flowchart	**diagramma** *m* **di flusso** *m* **dei dati** *m pl*	dɪɑ'grɑmmɑ dɪ 'flussɔ'deɪ 'dɑtɪ
follow-up letter	**lettera** *f* **pubblicitaria susseguente**	'lɛtterɑ pubblɪtʃɪ'tɑrjɑ susse'gwente
for the attention of . . .	**all'attenzione di . . .**	all'atten'tsjone dɪ
foreign currency	**valuta** *f* **estera**	vɑ'lutɑ 'ɛsterɑ
foreign exchange department	**reparto** *m* **di cambio** *m* **(sull'estero)**	re'pɑrtɔ dɪ 'kɑmbjɔ
foreign language secretary	**segretaria** *f* **di lingue** *f pl*	segre'tɑrjɑ dɪ 'lɪngwɑ
to forward, to send off, to ship, to dispatch	**spedire, inviare**	spe'dɪre, ɪnvɪ'ɑre
forwarder, carrier	**spedizioniere** *m*	spedɪttsjɔ'njɛre
forwarding/freight charges	**spese** *f pl* **di trasporto** *m*, **nolo** *m*	'spese dɪ trɑs'pɔrtɔ, 'nɔlɔ
forwarding agent's certificate of receipt (FAC)	**certificato** *m* **di accettazione** *f* **dello spedizionere** *m*	tʃertɪfɪ'kɑtɔ dɪ attʃettɑt'tsjone 'dellɔ spedɪt'tsjonere
to found, to establish	**fondare**	fon'dɑre
franchise	**concessione** *f*, **franchise**	kontʃes'sjone
franchised dealer	**concessionario** *m*	kontʃessjɔ'nɑrjɔ
free of charge, cost-free	**franco di spese** *f pl*, **gratis, gratuito**	frɑnkɔ dɪ 'spese, 'grɑtɪs, grɑ'tuɪtɔ
free sample	**campione** *m* **pubblicitario**	kɑm'pjone pubblɪtʃɪ'tɑrjɔ
freight, cargo, carriage	**trasporto** *m*	trɑs'pɔrtɔ
freight/forwarding charges	**spese** *f pl* **di nolo** *m*	'spese dɪ 'nɔlɔ 'nɔlɔ
freight collect	**nolo** *m* **assegnato**	asseɲ'ɲɑtɔ
freight included	**nolo** *m* **incluso**	'nɔlɔ ɪn'kluzɔ
freight rate	**rata** *f* **di nolo** *m*	rɑtɑ dɪ 'nɔlɔ
fringe benefit	**indennità** *f* **accessoria addizionale** *f*	ɪndennɪ'tɑ attʃes'sɔrjɑ/ addɪttsjɔ'nɑle
fulfilment of contract	**adempimento** *m* **del contratto** *m*	ɑdempɪ'mentɔ del kon'trɑttɔ

full-time workers	chi lavora a tempo *m* pieno	kı la'vora a 'tɛmpo 'pjɛno
to furnish a customer with goods, to supply	fornire un cliente *m* con merci *m pl*, consegnare	for'nıre un klı'ɛnte kon 'mɛrtʃı konseɲ'ɲare
general agency	rappresentanza *f* generale	rapprezen'tantsa dʒene'rale
general meeting of the shareholders	assemblea *f* generale	assem'blɛa dʒenerale
giro account	giroconto *m*	dʒıro'konto
to give notice	dare il preavviso *m* a	'dare ıl preav'vızo a
to go bankrupt	fare fallimento *m*, fallire	'fare fallı'mento, fal'lıre
goods, commodity, merchandise	merci *f pl*, merce *f*, mercanzia *f*	'mɛrtʃı, 'mɛrtʃe, merkan'tsıa
grade	qualità *f*, classe *f*, categoria *f*, grado *m*	kwalı'ta, 'klasse, katego'rıa, 'grado
to grant an allowance	concedere/fare uno sconto *m*	kon'tʃedere 'fare un 'skonto
to grant an extension	accordare una proroga *m*	akkor'dare una 'prɔrɔga
to grant sole selling rights	dare diritto *m* esclusivo di vendita *f*	'dare dı'rıtto esklu'zıvo dı 'vendıta
gross profit	profitto *m* lordo	pro'fıtto 'lordo
gross weight	peso *m* lordo	'peso lordo
group, concern (business)	gruppo *m*	'gruppo
guarantee, warrant	garanzia *f*, mandato *m*	garan'tsıa, man'dato
hall/room plan	pianta *f* della sala *f*	'pjanta 'della 'sala
handbill	volantino *m*	volan'tıno
hard disk	disco *m* rigido/fisso	'dısko 'rıdʒıdo/ 'fısso
haulage, bulk . . .	trasporto *m* alla rinfusa *f*	tras'pɔrto alla rın'fuza
to have in stock	avere in magazzino *m*	a'vere ın magad'dzıno

head office	sede *f* principale/ centrale	'sɛde prɪntʃɪ'pɑle/ tʃen'trɑle
hidden defect	difetto *m* nascosto	dɪ'fɛtto nɑs'kostɔ
highly competitive market	mercato *m* altamente competitivo	mer'kɑtɔ ɑltɑ'mente kompetɪ'tɪvɔ
hire purchase	acquisto *m* a rate *f pl*	ɑk'kwɪstɔ ɑ 'rɑte
holding/parent company	holding/società *f* madre *f*	sotʃe'tɑ 'mɑdre
honest	onesto/a	o'nɛstɔ/ɑ
hostess (fair)	hostess della fiera *f*	'houstɪs 'dellɑ 'fjɛrɑ
immediate	immediamente	ɪmmedjɑtɑ'mente
to import	importare	ɪmpor'tɑre
import licence	licenza *f* d'importazione *f*	lɪ'tʃentsɑ d'ɪmportɑt'- tsjone
importer	importatore *m*	ɪmportɑ'tore
in advance	in anticipo	ɪn ɑn'tɪtʃɪpɔ
in transit	in transito *m*	ɪn 'trɑnsɪtɔ
included	incluso, compreso	ɪn'kluzɔ, kom'presɔ
income tax	imposta *f* sul reddito *m*	ɪm'pɔstɑ sul 'reddɪtɔ
indebtedness	indebitamento *m*	ɪndebɪtɑ'mentɔ
in-depth knowledge of the trade	profonda conoscenza *f* del settore *m*	pro'fondɑ konoʃ'ʃentsɑ del set'tore
industrial fair	fiera *f* industriale	'fjɛrɑ ɪndus'trjɑle
industrial plant	impresa *f* industriale	ɪm'presɑ ɪndus'trjɑle
industrial production	produzione *f* industriale	produt'tsjone ɪndus'trjɑle
industrial standard	standard *m* industriale	'stɑndɑrd ɪndus'trjɑle
to inform	informare	ɪnfor'mɑre
inheritance tax	imposta *f* di successione *f*	ɪm'pɔstɑ dɪ suttʃes'sjone

initial order	**prima ordinazione** f	'prima ordinat'tsjone
input	**entrata** f, **ingresso** m, **input**	en'trata, in'grɛssɔ, 'input
inquiry	**richiesta** f, **domanda** f	ri'kjɛsta, do'manda
insolvency	**insolvenza** f	insol'vɛntsa
instalment	**rata** f	'rata
to instruct, to train	**istruire, formare professionalmente**	istru'ire, for'mare professjonal'mente
instruction leaflet	**foglio** m **di istruzioni** f pl, **volantino**	'fɔʎʎɔ di istrut'tsjoni, volan'tino
insurance	**assicurazione** f	assikurat'tsjone
insurance against loss on the exchange rate	**assicurazione** f **contro le perdite** f **sul cambio** m	assikurat'tsjone kontro le 'pɛrdite sul 'kambjɔ
insurance certificate	**certificato** m **d'assicurazione** f	tʃertifi'katɔ d'assiku'rat'-tsjone
insurance company	**compagnia** f **di assicurazione** f pl	kompaɲ'ɲia di assikurat'tsjone
insurance policy	**polizza** f **di assicurazione** f	'polittsa di assikurat'tsjone
to intend	**avere l'intenzione** f	a'vere l'intent'tsjone
interest against default	**interesse** m **di mora** f	inte'rɛsse di 'mɔra
interested, to be . . . in	**essere interessati in**	'ɛssere interes'sati in
interests	**interesse** m	inte'rɛsse
interface	**interfaccia** f	inter'fattʃa
interview (person)	**colloquio** m **per un impiego** m	kol'lɔkwjɔ per un im'pjɛgɔ
inventories	**stocks** m pl, **provviste** f pl, **scorte** f pl	prov'viste, 'skɔrte
inventory	**inventario** m	inven'tarjɔ
to investigate	**investigare**	investi'gare
investment	**investimento** m	investi'mentɔ
invoice, bill	**fattura** f	fat'tura

English	Italian	Phonetic
to invoice, to bill	**emettere una fattura** f, **fatturare**	eˈmettere ˈuna fatˈtura, fattuˈrare
invoice amount	**somma** f/**importo** m **della fattura** f	ˈsomma, ımˈpɔrtɔ ˈdella fatˈtura
invoice number	**numero** m **della fattura** f	ˈnumero ˈdella fatˈtura
invoicing	**fatturazione** f	fatturatˈtsjone
issue of a magazine	**edizione** f **per una rivista** f	edıtˈtsjone per una rıˈvısta
to issue, to make out (cheque)	**emettere/fare (un assegno** m**)**	eˈmettere, ˈfare (un asˈseɲɲɔ)
item	**voce** f, **articolo** m	ˈvɔtʃe, arˈtıkolɔ
job, position	**posto** m **di lavoro** m, **posizione** f	ˈpɔstɔ dı laˈvorɔ, pozıtˈtsjone
to join a firm	**entrare in una ditta** f	enˈtrare ın ˈuna ˈdıtta
joint venture	**joint venture, associazione** f **in partecipazione** f	assotʃatˈtsjone ın partetʃıpatˈtsjone
to keep the minutes	**redigere il verbale** m	reˈdıdʒere ıl verbale
keyboard	**tastiera** f	tasˈtjera
label	**etichetta** f	etıˈketta
latest catalogue	**catalogo** m **di data** f **recentissima**	kaˈtalogɔ dı ˈdata retʃenˈtıssıma
lawsuit, litigation	**processo** m, **causa** f	proˈtʃɛssɔ, ˈkauza
lawyer	**legale** m, **avvocato** m	leˈgale, avvɔˈkatɔ
leaflet, instructions	**volantino** m, **foglio** m **di istruzioni** f pl	volanˈtınɔ, fɔʎʎɔ dı ıstrutˈtsjonı
to lease to/from someone	**dare/prendere in affitto** m	ˈdare/ˈprendere ın afˈfıttɔ
ledger	**mastro** m /**libro mastro** m	ˈmastrɔ/lıbro ˈmastrɔ
legal reserves	**riserve** f pl **legali**	rıˈsɛrvı leˈgalı

229

legally protected	**legalmente protetto**	legal'mente prɔ'tɛttɔ
letter of credit (irrevocable and confirmed)	**lettera f di credito m (irrevocabile e confermata)**	'lettera dı 'kredıtɔ (ırrevɔ'kabıle e konfer'matɔ)
letter of intent	**lettera f d'intenti m pl**	'lettera d'ın'tɛntı
liabilities	**passivo m**	pas'sıvɔ
liability	**responsabilità f**	respɔnsabılı'ta
liable for tax	**soggetto a tasse f pl**	sod'dʒɛttɔ a 'tasse
liquid funds	**attivo m liquido**	at'tıvɔ 'lıkwıdɔ
liquidation, bankruptcy	**liquidazione f, fallimento m**	lıkwıdat'tsjone, fallı'mentɔ
liquidity	**liquidità f**	lıkwıdı'ta
list of exhibitors	**elenco m degli espositori m pl**	ɛ'lɛnkɔ 'deʎʎı espozı'tore
list of products	**elenco m della merce f**	e'lɛnkɔ 'della 'mertʃe
list price	**prezzo m di listino m**	'prettsɔ dı lıs'tınɔ
litigation, lawsuit	**causa f, processo m**	'kauza, prɔ'tʃɛssɔ
to load, to unload	**caricare, scaricare**	karı'kare, skarı'kare
loan	**prestito m**	'prestıtɔ
long hauls	**traffico m merci f pl a lunga distanza f**	'traffıkɔ 'mertʃı a 'lunga dıs'tantsa
loss	**perdita f**	'perdıta
lot	**partita f di merci f pl**	par'tıta dı 'mertʃı
lump sum	**somma forfettaria f**	'somma forfe'tarja
machine shop	**officina f meccanica**	ɔffı'tʃına mek'kanıka
magnetic head	**testa f magnetica**	'testa maɲ'ɲetıka
magnetic tape	**nastro m magnetico**	'nastrɔ maɲ'ɲetıkɔ

mail circular, mail-shot	**spedizione** *f* **postale cumulativa**	spedıt'tsjone pos'tale kumula'tıva
maintenance contract	**contratto** *m* **di manutenzione** *f*	kon'trattɔ dı manuten'tsjone
to make out/to issue a cheque	**fare un assegno** *m*	'fare un as'seɲɲɔ
to manage	**dirigere, amministrare**	dı'rıdʒere, ammınıs'trare
management	**management, direttivo** *m*	dıret'tıvɔ
manager(ess)	**gerente** *m*, **dirigente** *m*, **direttore/ direttrice** *m/f*	dʒe'rɛnte, dırı'dʒente, dıret'tore/ dıret'trıʃe
managing director	**amministratore** *m* **delegato**	ammınıstra'tore dele'gatɔ
manual	**manuale** *m*	manu'ale
to manufacture, to produce, to make	**produrre**	pro'durre
to manufacture under licence	**fabbricare su licenza** *f*	fabbrı'kare su lı'tʃentsa
marginal costs	**costi** *m pl* **marginali**	'kostı mardʒı'nalı
market	**mercato** *m*	mer'katɔ
market analysis	**analisi** *f* **di mercato** *m*	a'nalızı dı mer'katɔ
market research	**ricerca** *f* **di mercato** *m*	rı'tʃerka dı mer'katɔ
market situation	**situazione** *f* **del mercato** *m*	sıtuat'tsjone del mer'katɔ
market survey	**indagine** *f* **del mercato** *m*	ın'dadʒine del mer'katɔ
marketing	**marketing, distribuzione** *f*, **vendita** *f*	dıstrıbut'tsjone, 'vendıta
mask, picture	**maschera** *f*	'maskera
mass production	**produzione** *f* **in serie** *f*	produt'tsjone ın 'sɛrje
master	**mastro** *m*	'mastrɔ
master file	**archivio** *m* **principale**	ar'kıvjɔ prıntʃı'pale
maturity date of contract	**scadenza** *f* **del contratto** *m*	ska'dentsa del kon'trattɔ
meetings	**sedute** *f pl*, **riunioni** *f pl*, **assemblee** *f pl*	se'dute, rıu'njonı, assem'blɛɛ

memory (computers)	memoria f	me'mɔrja
memory protection	protezione f della memoria f	protet'tsjone 'della me'mɔrja
merchandise, commodity, goods	merci f pl, merce f, mercanzia f	'mertʃı, 'mertʃe, merkan'tsıa
merchant trader	commerciante m	kommer'tʃante
to merge	fondere, fondersi	'fondere, fon'dersı
merger	fusione f	fu'zjone
metal container	bidone m	bı'done
minutes, to keep the . . .	redigere/stendere il verbale m di . . .	re'dıdʒere/ 'stendere ıl ver'bale dı
model, pattern, specimen	modello m, campione m	mo'dɛllʊ, kam'pjone
monopoly	posizione f di monopolio m	pozıt'tsjone dı monʊ'pɔljʊ
mortgage	ipoteca f	ıpo'tɛka
to negotiate the conditions of a contract	negoziare le condizione f pl di un contratto m	negot'tsjare le kondıt'tsjonı dı un kon'trattʊ
net cash	contante m netto	kon'tante 'nettʊ
net weight	peso m netto	'peso 'nettʊ
non-conformity with sample	non conformità f al campione m	non konformı'ta al kam'pjone
notes payable	cambiali f pl passive	kam'bjali pas'sıvı
notification	notificazione f	notıfıkat'tsjone
notification address	indirizzo m d'avviso m	ındı'rıttsʊ d'av'vızʊ
number, a limited . . . of	numero m limitato di	'numerʊ lımı'tatʊ dı
to object to something	opporsi a	op'porsı a
to offer (make a firm offer)	offrire a prezzo m e condizioni f pl fissi	of'frıre a 'prɛttso e kondıt'tsjonı 'fıssı
to offer subject to confirmation	offrire salvo approvazione f	of'frıre 'salvʊ approvat'tsjone
offer, proposal	offerta f	of'fɛrta
office automation	automazione f	automat'tsjone
official receiver	curatore m fallimentare	kura'tore fallımen'tare

on-the-job training	formazione f professionale	formɑt'tsjone professjo'nɑle
one-off production	produzione f singola	produt'tsjone 'sɪngolɑ
to open a fair	inaugurare una fiera f	ɪnɑugu'rɑre 'unɑ 'fjɛrɑ
to open a meeting	aprire una seduta f	ɑ'prɪre unɑ se'dutɑ
to open an account	aprire un conto m	ɑ'prɪre un 'konto
opening, vacancy	posto m vacante	'posto vɑ'kɑnte
operating expenses and revenue	spese f pl e proventi m di gestione f	'spese e pro'vɛntɪ dɪ dʒes'tjone
operating instructions	istruzioni f per il funzionamento m	ɪstrut'tsjonɪ per ɪl funtsjonɑ'mento
operating system	sistema m operativo	sɪ'stɛmɑ operɑ'tɪvo
operations program	programma m operativo	pro'grɑmmɑ operɑ'tɪvo
order	ordine m, ordinazione f	'ordɪne, ordɪnɑt'tsjone
order book	libro m delle commissioni f pl	'lɪbro 'delle komɪs'sjonɪ
order form	modulo m d'ordinazione f, cedola f, commissione f	modulo d'ordɪnɑt'tsjone, 'tʃedolɑ, kommɪs'sjone
order number	ordine m no.	'ordɪne
orders on hand	ordinazioni f pl a disposizione f	ordɪnɑt'tsjonɪ ɑ dɪsposɪt'tsjone
to organize a fair	organizzare una fiera f	orgɑnɪd'dʒɑre 'unɑ 'fjɛrɑ
organizer (of a fair)	organizzatore m della fiera f	orgɑnɪddzɑ'tore 'dellɑ 'fjɛrɑ
to outline	dare un sommario m	'dɑre un som'mɑrjo
output	output m, rendimento m, produzione f	rendɪ'mento, produt'tsjone
outstanding accounts	crediti pendenti m pl	'kredɪtɪ pen'dɛntɪ
outstanding quality	qualità f eccellente/ primissima	kwɑlɪ'tɑ ettʃel'lente/ prɪ'mɪssɪmɑ
overdraft credit	credito m in conto m corrente	'kredɪto ɪn 'konto kor'rɛnte

233

to overdraw on an account	trarre allo scoperto *m*	'trarre 'allo sko'pɛrtʊ
overdue	in sofferenza *f*, scaduto *m*	ɪn soffe'rɛntsa, ska'dutʊ
overheads	costi *m pl* indiretti	'kostɪ ɪndɪ'rɛttɪ
overhead charges	imputazione *f* dei costi *m pl* comuni	ɪmputat'tsjone deɪ 'kostɪ ko'munɪ
package	collo *m*	'kɔllʊ
packing	imballaggio *m*	ɪmbal'laddʒʊ
packing at cost	imballaggio *m* al prezzo di costo *m*	ɪmbal'laddʒʊ al prɛttsʊ di 'kostʊ
packing list	distinta *f* pesi *m pl*	dɪs'tɪnta 'pesɪ
pallet	pallet	
paper feed	alimentazione *m* carta *f*	alɪmentat'tsjone 'karta
parent/holding company	società *f*, madre *f*, holding *f*	sotʃe'ta, 'madre
part payment	pagamento *m* parziale	paga'mentʊ par'tsjale
to participate in a fair	partecipare ad una fiera *f*	partetʃɪ'pare ad 'una 'fjɛra
part-time workers	chi lavora part-time/a tempo *m* parziale	kɪ la'vora . . ., a 'tɛmpo par'tsjale
password	parola *f* d'ordine *m*, password	pa'rɔla d''ordɪne
patented	brevettato	brevet'tatʊ
pattern	stampo *m*	'stampʊ
to pay	pagare	pa'gare
pay into an account	versare	ver'sare
payee	beneficiario/a *m/f*	benefɪ'tʃarjʊ/a
payment against bank guarantee	pagamento *m* contro garanzia *f* bancaria *f*	paga'mentʊ 'kontro garan'tsɪa ban'karja
payment by acceptance	pagamento *m* contro accettazione *f*	paga'mentʊ 'kontrʊ attʃetat'tsjone
payment by cheque	pagamento *m* mediante assegno *m*	paga'mentʊ me'djante as'seɲɲʊ

payment by irrevocable confirmed documentary letter of credit	pagamento *m* a mezzo credito *m* documentario *m* confermato e irrevocabile	paga'mento a 'meddzo 'kredıtʊ dokumen'tarjʊ konfer'matʊ e ırrevʊ'kabıle
payment by sight draft	pagamento *m* a mezzo tratta a vista *f*	paga'mentʊ a 'meddzo 'tratta a 'vısta
payment of the balance	pagamento restante *m*	paga'mento res'tante
payment on account	acconto *m*	ak'kontʊ
payment on recipt of goods (ROG)	pagamento *m* al recapito *m* della merce *f*	paga'mentʊ al re'kapıtʊ 'della 'mertʃe
payment, settlement	pagamento *m*	paga'mento
payroll	conteggio del salario *m*, elenco del personale *m*	kon'teddʒʊ del sa'larjʊ, e'lɛnkʊ del perso'nale
penalties	pena *f* convenzionale	'pena konventsjo'nale
pension fund	fondo *m* pensioni *f pl*	'fondʊ pen'sjonı
percentage	percentuale *f*	pertʃen'tuale
period of contract	durata *f* di un contratto *m*	du'rata dı un kon'tratto
period of limitation	prescrizione *f* contrattuale	preskrıt'tsjone kontrattu'ale
personal data sheet	curriculum vitae breve *m*	'brɛve
personal secretary	segretario/a (del capo) *m/f*	segre'tarjʊ/a (del 'kapʊ)
personnel, workforce, staff	personale *m*, forza *f* di lavoro *m*	perso'nale, 'fɔrtsa dı lav'orʊ
personnel manager	capo *m* del personale *m*	'kapʊ del perso'nale
personnel matters	affari *m pl* concernenti il personale *m*	af'farı kontʃer'nentı ıl perso'nale
piggyback (combined road and rail) service	traffico *m* combinato strada-rotaia *f*	'traffikʊ kombı'natʊ 'strada-ro'taja
to place an order, to commission	dare un'ordinazione *f*, commissionare	'dare un'ordınat'tsjone, kommıssjo'nare

place of destination	**luogo** *m* **di destinazione** *f*	'lwɔgɔ dɪ destɪnat'tsjone
place of dispatch	**luogo** *m* **di spedizione** *f*	'lwɔgɔ dɪ spedɪt'tsjone
plant manager	**direttore di stabilimento** *m*	dɪret'tore dɪ stabɪlɪ'mentɔ
plotter	**plotter**	
policy holder	**titolare** *f/m* **di una polizza** *f,* **assicuratore** *m*	tɪto'lare d'una 'pɔlɪttsa, assɪkura'tore
poor quality	**scadente qualità** *f*	ska'dɛnte kwalɪ'ta
position, job	**posizione** *f,* **posto di lavoro** *m*	pozɪt'tsjone, 'posto dɪ la'vorɔ
postage	**affrancatura** *f*	affranka'tura
poster	**cartellone** *m,* **affisso** *m,* **poster** *m*	kartel'lone, af'fɪssɔ
power supply	**alimentatore** *m*	alɪmenta'tore
premium	**premio** *m*	'prɛmjɔ
pre-tax profit	**utile tassabile** *m*	'utile tas'sabile
price deduction	**riduzione** *f* **di prezzo** *m*	rɪdut'tsjone dɪ 'prɛttsɔ
price increase	**aumento** *m* **dei prezzi** *m pl*	au'mentɔ dei 'prɛttsɪ
price list	**listino** *m* **dei prezzi** *m pl*	lɪs'tɪnɔ dei 'prɛttsɪ
price maintenance	**mantenimento** *m* **del prezzo** *m* **di vendita** *f*	mantenɪ'mentɔ del 'prɛttsɔ dɪ 'vendɪta
prices	**prezzi** *m pl*	'prɛttsɪ
printed letterhead	**intestazione** *f* **(di lettera)**	ɪntestat'tsjone (dɪ 'lɛttera)
probation period	**periodo** *m* **di prova** *f*	pe'rɪodɔ dɪ 'prɔva
to produce	**produrre**	pro'durre
product description	**descrizione** *f* **dei prodotti** *m pl*	deskrɪt'tsjone dei pro'dottɪ
product liability	**responsabilità** *f* **per il prodotto** *m*	responsabɪlɪ'ta per ɪl pro'dottɔ
production	**produzione** *f*	produt'tsjone
production costs	**costi** *m pl* **di produzione** *f*	'kostɪ dɪ produt'tsjone
production period	**periodo** *m* **di produzione** *f*	pe'rɪodɔ dɪ produt'tsjone

production	programma *m*	pro'gramma
programme	**produttivo**	produt'tivo
production schedule	**programma *m* di**	pro'gramma dı
	fabbricazione *f*	fabrıkat'tsjone
professional	**esperienza *f***	espe'rjentsa
experience	**professionale**	professjo'nale
profit and loss account	**conto *m* profitti *m pl* e**	'konto pro'fıttı e
	perdite *f pl*	'pɛrdıte
profit margin	**margine *m* degli**	'mardzıne deʎʎı
	utili *m pl*	'utıle
profit mark-up	**aumento *m* degli**	au'mentʊ
	utili *m pl*	'deʎʎı 'utılı
profit sharing	**compartecipazione *f***	kompartetʃıpat'-
	agli utili *m pl*	tsjone 'aʎʎı
		'utılı
profit tax	**imposta *f* sui**	ım'pɔsta suı
	profitti *m pl*	pro'fıttı
profitability	**redditività *f***	reddıtıvı'ta
pro-forma invoice	**fattura *f* proforma**	fat'tura pro'forma
programming	**linguaggio *m* di**	lın'gwaddʒʊ dı
language	**programmazione *f***	programmat'-
		tsjone
to prolong, to extend	**prolungare**	prolun'gare
prolongation	**proroga *f***	'prɔroga
promotion (of a	**promozione *f***	pro'mot'tsjone
person)		
promotional letter	**lettera *f* pubblicitaria**	'lɛttera
		pubblıtʃı'tarja
property	**proprietà *f***	prɔprje'ta
property tax	**imposta *f***	ım'pɔsta
	patrimoniale	patrımo'njale
prospectus, catalogue	**prospetto *m***	pros'pɛttʊ
proxy	**procuratore *m***	prokura'tore
public relations	**pubbliche relazioni**	'pubblıke
	_f pl_, public relations	relat'tsjonı
publicity agency	**agenzia *f* pubblicitaria**	adʒen'tsıa
		pubblıtʃı'tarja
publicity campaign	**campagna *f***	kam'paɲɲa
	pubblicitaria	pubblıtʃı'tarja
publicity expenditure	**spese *f pl* pubblicitarie**	'spese
		pubblıtʃı'tarje
purchase	**acquisto *m*, compera *f*,**	ak'kwıstʊ,
	compra *f*	'kompera,
		'kompra

to purchase	acquistare, comprare	ɑkkwıs'tɑre, kom'prɑre
purchase price	prezzo di acquisto *m*	'prɛttsɔ dı ɑk'kwıstɔ
purchasing power	potere d'acquisto *m*	pɔ'tere d'ɑk'kwıstɔ
qualification	qualificazione *f*, qualifica *f*	kwɑlıfıkɑt'tsjone, kwɑ'lıfıkɑ
quality	qualità *f*	kwɑlı'tɑ
quality control	controllo *m* della qualità *f*	kon'trɔllɔ 'dellɑ kwɑlı'tɑ
quantity	quantità *f*	kwɑntı'tɑ
quantity discount	sconto *m* sulla quantità *f*	'skontɔ 'sullɑ 'kwɑntı'tɑ
questionnaire	questionario *m*	kwestjɔ'nɑrjɔ
quotation	quotazione *f* prezzo corrente *m*	kwotɑt'tsjone 'prɛttsɔ kor'rɛnte
to quote prices	quotare prezzi *m pl*	kwo'tɑre 'prɛttsı
rail transport	trasporti *m pl* ferroviari	trɑs'pɔrtı ferro'vjɑrı
railway consignment note	lettera *f* di vettura *f* ferroviaria	'letterɑ dı vet'turɑ ferrɔ'vjɑrjɑ
random-access memory (RAM)	memoria *f* ad accesso *m* casuale (RAM)	me'mɔrjɑ ɑd ɑt'tʃessɔ kɑzu'ɑle
range, a wide . . . of	scelta *f*, una grande . . . di	'ʃeltɑ, 'unɑ 'grɑnde dı
rate of interest	tasso *m* d'interesse *m*	'tɑssɔ d'ınte'rɛsse
raw materials	materie *f pl* prime	mɑ'tɛrje 'prıme
read-only memory (ROM)	memoria *f* a sola lettura *f* (ROM)	me'mɔrjɑ ɑ 'solɑ 'letturɑ
receipt	ricevuta *f*	ritʃe'vutɑ
receipts	entrate *f pl*, proventi *m pl*	en'trɑte, pro'vɛntı
receivables	titoli *m pl* esigibili	'tıtolı ezı'dʒıbılı
receiving order	sentenza *f* iniziale di fallimento *m*	sen'tɛntsɑ ınıt'tsjɑle dı fɑllı'mentɔ
recourse	regresso *m*	re'grɛssɔ
to refer to	rivolgersi a	rıvɔldʒersı ɑ

reference (business letter)	**riferimenti** *m pl*	rɪferɪˈmentɪ
references	**referenze** *f pl*	refeˈrɛntse
to refund	**rifondere, rimborsare**	rɪˈfondere, rɪmborˈsɑre
refund of costs	**rimborso** *m* **di spese** *f pl*	rɪmˈbɔrsɒ dɪ ˈspese
to refuse a claim	**rifiutare un reclamo** *m*	rɪfjuˈtɑre un reˈklɑmɒ
regarding	**concernente, circa, quanto a**	kontʃerˈnente, tʃɪrkɑ, ˈkwantɒ ɑ
registered office	**sede** *f* **legale**	ˈsede leˈgɑle
registered trade mark	**marchio** *m* **registrato**	ˈmarkjɒ redʒɪˈstrɑtɒ
to regret	**essere spiacenti, rincrescere**	ˈessere spjaˈtʃentɪ, rɪnˈkreʃʃere
to reject a motion	**rifiutare una mozione** *f*	rɪfjuˈtɑre una motˈtsjone
reliability	**fidatezza** *f*	fɪdaˈtettsɑ
reloading, transshipment	**trasbordo** *m*	trazˈbordɒ
reluctantly	**malvolentieri**	malvolenˈtjɛrɪ
to remind somebody of something	**ricordare a**	rɪkorˈdare ɑ
reminder, dunning letter	**lettera di sollecitazione** *f*	ˈlɛttera dɪ solletʃɪtatˈtsjone
to remit, to transfer	**rimettere, trasferire**	rɪˈmettere, trasfeˈrɪre
remittance	**rimessa** *f*	rɪˈmessa
to rent	**dare in affitto, prendere in affitto, noleggiare**	ˈdare ɪn afˈfɪto, ˈprendere in afˈfɪtɒ, noledˈdʒare
repeat order	**ordine** *m* **susseguente**	ˈordɪne susseˈgwente
replacement	**fornitura** *f* **di ricambio** *m*	fornɪˈtura dɪ rɪˈkambjɒ
representative, agent	**rappresentante** *m*, **agente** *m*	rapprezenˈtante, aˈdʒente
to request	**richiedere**	rɪˈkjedere
requirements	**richieste** *f pl*, **fabbisogno** *m*	rɪˈkjeste, fabbɪˈzoɲɲɒ

research	attività f di ricerca f scientifica	attɪvɪ'ta dɪ rɪ'tʃerka ʃen'tɪfɪka
reservation of title	riserva f di proprietà f	rɪ'serva dɪ proprje'ta
result, trading . . .	risultato m	rɪsul'tato
retail price	prezzo m al minuto	'prettso al mɪ'nuto
retailer	commerciante m al minuto	kommer'tʃante al mɪ'nuto
return, yield	redditività f, rendita f	reddɪtɪvɪ'ta, 'rendɪta
returnable container	recipienti m pl a rendere	retʃɪ'pjente a 'rendere
revenues	ricavati m pl, ricavi m pl	rɪka'vatɪ, rɪ'kavɪ
to revoke an offer	revocare un'offerta f	revo'kare un'of'ferta
rise	aumento m di stipendio m	au'mento dɪ stɪ'pendjo
road transport	trasporto m su strada f	tras'porto su 'strada
roll-on/roll-off service	servizio m roll-on/roll-off	ser'vɪttsjo
royalties	diritti m pl di licenza f, royalties	dɪ'rɪttɪ dɪ lɪ'tʃentsa
to run a business	gestire un'impresa f	dʒes'tɪre un'ɪmpresa
sack, bag	sacco m	'sakko
salary	stipendio m, salario m	stɪ'pendjo, sa'larjo
sale	vendita f	'vendɪta
sale on a trial basis	acquisto m a prova	ak'kwɪsto a 'prova
sale or return	vendita f con patto m di riscatto m	'vendɪta kon 'patto dɪ rɪs'katto
sales	vendite f pl	'vendɪte
sales letter, promotional letter	lettera f pubblicitaria	'lettera pubblɪtʃɪ'tarja
sales on commission	vendita f su base f di commissione f	'vendɪta su 'baze dɪ kommɪs'sjone
sales potential	potenziale m di vendita f	poten'tsjale dɪ 'vendɪta

sales promotion	promozione f delle vendite f pl	promot'tsjone 'delle 'vendıte
sales territory	zona di vendita f	'dzɔna dı 'vendıta
sample	campione m, provino m	kam'pjone, prɔ'vıno
sample collection	campionario m	kampjɔ'narjɔ
sample of no commercial value	campione m senza valore m	kam'pjone 'sɛntsa va'lore
savings/deposit account	conto m di risparmio m/di deposito m	'kontɔ dı rıs'parmjɔ/dı de'pɔzıtɔ
scanner	scanner m	
school leaving certificate	licenza f scolastica	lı'tʃɛntsa sko'lastıka
screen, monitor	schermo m, monitor m	'skermɔ
seaworthy packing	imballaggio m per trasporto m marittimo	ımbal'laddʒɔ per tras'pɔrtɔ ma'rıttımɔ
second-rate quality	di seconda qualità f	dı se'konda kwalı'ta
secretary (to XY)	segretario/a m/f di . . .	segre'tarjɔ/a dı
security	sicurezza f	sıku'rettsa
selection of samples	campionario m	kampjɔ'narjɔ
to sell	vendere	'vɛndere
to sell as sole agent	vendere come rappresentante m esclusivo	'vɛndere 'kome rapprezen'tante esklu'zıvɔ
to sell goods on commission	vendere merce f in commissione f	'vɛndere 'mertʃe ın komıs'sjone
to sell off	svendere	'zvendere
seller	venditore m	vendı'tore
selling conditions	condizioni f pl di vendita f	kondıt'tsjonı dı 'vendıta
selling expenses	spese f pl di vendita f	'spese dı vendıta
selling price	prezzo m di vendita f	'prettsɔ dı 'vendıta
semi-finished goods	prodotti m pl semilavorati	pro'dottı semılavo'ratı
to send off, to ship, to forward, to dispatch	inviare, spedire	ınvı'are, spe'dıre
to serve an apprenticeship	fare un tirocinio m	'fare un tırɔ'tʃınjɔ
service	servizio m	ser'vıttsjɔ

service manual	istruzioni *f pl* di manutenzione *f*	ıstrut'tsjonı di manuten'tsjone
to set up a business	mettersi in proprio	met'tersı ın 'prɔprjɔ
to set up a stand	montare lo stand *m*	mon'tɑre lo stænd
to settle a claim	regolare un sinistro *m*	regɔ'lɑre un sı'nıstrɔ
to settle an account	saldare un conto *m*	sal'dɑre un 'kɔntɔ
settlement	liquidazione *f*	lıkwıdɑt'tsjone
share	azione *f*	at'tsjone
shift work	lavoro *m* a turno *m*	la'vorɔ a 'turnɔ
to ship	inviare, spedire	ınvı'are, spe'dıre
shipment/ consignment	spedizione *f*	spedıt'tsjone
shipping documents	documenti *m pl* di spedizione *f*	doku'mentı dı spedıt'tsjone
shipping marks	marcatura *f* di spedizione *f*	mɑrka'turɑ dı spedıt'tsjone
short hauls	traffico *m* merci *f pl* a breve distanza *f*	'traffıko 'mertʃı a 'breve dıs'tantsa
shortage	quantità *f* mancante	kwantı'ta man'kante
to show, to exhibit	esporre	es'porre
showroom	sala *f* d'esposizione *f*	'sala d'espozıt'tsjone
signature	firma *f*	'fırma
single European market	mercato *m* unico europeo	mer'kato 'unıko euro'pɛɔ
size	misura *f*	mı'zura
skid (rollers)	slittamento *m*	zlıtta'mentɔ
skilled worker	operaio/a *m/f*, specializzato/a *m/f*	ope'rajɔ/a, spetʃalıd'dzatɔ/a
software	software *m*	
sole proprietorship	impresa *f* individuale, unico proprietario *m*	ım'presa ındıvıdu'ale, 'unıkɔ proprje'tarjɔ
solicitor	avvocato *m*	avvo'katɔ
solvency	solvenza *f*	sol'ventsa

to sort	assortire, smistare	ɑssor'tɪre, zmɪs'tɑre
sound	sicuro	sɪ'kurɒ
space, blank	spazio *m*	'spɑttsjɒ
special design	produzione *f* fuori serie *f*	prɒdut'tsjone fwɔrɪ 'sɛrje
special discount	sconto *m* speciale	'skontɒ spe'tʃɑle
special packing	imballaggio *m* speciale	ɪmbɑl'laddʒɒ spe'tʃɑle
special price	prezzo *m* speciale	'prɛttsɒ spe'tʃɑle
specialized fair	fiera *f* specializzata	'fjɛrɑ spetʃɑlɪd'dzɑta
specification	elenco *m*, dettagliato specificazione *f*	e'lɛnkɒ, dettaʎ'ʎato spetʃɪfɪkɑt'tsjone
to specify the delivery route	specificare la via *f* di spedizione *f*	spetʃɪfɪ'kɑre la 'via dɪ spedɪt'tsjone
specimen, model, sample	modello *m*, campione *m*	mo'dɛllɒ, kɑm'pjone
spreadsheet	modulo multiplo *m*, spreadsheet *m*	'mɔdulɒ 'multɪplɒ
staff, workforce, personnel	forza *f* di lavoro *m*, personale *m*	'fɔrtsɑ dɪ la'vorɒ, perso'nɑle
stand, stall, booth	stand *m* della fiera *f*	stænd 'della 'fjɛrɑ
stand rental	noleggio *m* stand *m*	no'leddʒɒ stænd
standard quality	qualità *f* corrente	kwɑlɪ'ta kor'rɛnte
standing order	ordine *m* permanente	'ordɪne permɑ'nɛnte
statement of account	estratto *m* conto *m*	es'trɑtto 'kontɒ
statement of earnings	rendiconto *m*	rendɪ'kontɒ
statistics	statistica *f*	stɑ'tɪstɪkɑ
stipulated	convenuto/a	konve'nutɒ/ɑ
stock	scorte *f pl*	'skɔrte
to stock, to store	immagazzinare	ɪmmɑgɑddzɪ'nɑre
stock clerk	magazziniere *m*	mɑgɑddzɪ'njɛre
stock control	controllo *m* delle scorte *f pl*	kon'trɔllɒ 'delle 'skɔrte

stock rotation	**rotazione** f **delle scorte** f pl	rotat'tsjone 'delle 'skɔrte
storage	**magazzinaggio** m	magaddzɪ'naddʒɔ
to store, to stock	**immagazzinare**	ɪmmagaddzɪ'nare
strictly confidential	**strettamente confidenziale**	stretta'mente konfɪden'tsjale
subcontractor	**subappaltatore** m	subappalta'tore
subject line (letter)	**riguardo** m, **oggetto** m	rɪ'gwardɔ, ɔd'dʒettɔ
subject to payment of royalties	**sottomesso a diritti** m pl **di licenza** f	sotto'messɔ a dɪ'rɪttɪ di lɪ'tʃentsa
to submit an offer	**presentare un'offerta** f	prezen'tare un'of'ferta
subscription price	**prezzo** m **di sottoscrizione** f	prettsɔ dɪ sottɔskrɪt'tsjone
subsidiary	**società** f **affiliata/ sussidiaria**	sotʃe'ta affɪ'ljata/ sussɪ'djarja
subsidy	**sovvenzione** f	sovven'tsjone
substitute	**consegna** f sostituita	kon'seɲɲa sostɪ'tuta
superannuation fund, pension fund	**fondo** m **pensioni** f pl	'fɔndɔ pen'sjoni
superior	**superiore** m/f	supe'rjore
supplier	**fornitore/ fornitrice** m/f	fornɪ'tore/ fornɪ'tritʃe
suppliers, contractors	**ditta** f **fornitrice** f	'ditta fornɪ'tritʃe
to supply, to furnish a customer with goods	**consegnare, fornire un cliente** m **con merci** f pl	konseɲ'ɲare, for'nire un klɪ'ente kon 'mertʃɪ
supply contract	**contratto** m **di consegna** f	kon'trattɔ dɪ kon'seɲɲa
surcharge	**maggiorazione** f **del prezzo** m	maddʒorat'tsjone del 'prettsɔ
surtax	**tassa** f, **supplementare soprattassa** f	'tassa, supplemen'tare sopra'tassa
to take out insurance	**stipulare un'assicurazione** f	stɪpu'lare un assɪkurat'tsjone

to take stock	fare l'inventario m	'fare l'ınven'tarjɔ
to take the goods back	riprendere la merce f	rı'prendere la 'mɛrtʃe
take-over	take-over, assorbimento m	assorbı'mentɔ
tape drive unit	unità f a nastro m, stazione f	unı'ta a 'nastrɔ, stat'tsjone
tare	tara f	'tara
tariff zone	zona f tariffaria	'dzɔna tarıf'farja
tax	imposta f, tassa f	ım'pɔsta, 'tassa
tax allowance	detrazione f fiscale	detrat'tsjone fıs'kale
tax consultant	consulente m fiscale	konsu'lɛnte fıs'kale
tax exemption	esenzione f fiscale	ezent'tsjone fıs'kale
tax-favoured	con agevolazione f fiscale	kon adʒevolat'tsjone fıs'kale
tax-free	esente da tasse f pl/da imposte f pl	e'zɛnte da 'tasse/ da ım'pɔste
teleprocessing	elaborazione f dati m pl a distanza f	elaborat'tsjone 'datı a dıs'tantsa
temporary staff	manodopera f avventizia	'manɔd'ɔpera avven'tıttsja
tender	offerta f d'appalto m	ɔf'fɛrta d'ap'paltɔ
terms	condizioni f pl	kondıt'tsjonı
terms of contract	condizioni f pl di contratto m	kondıt'tsjonı dı kon'trattɔ
terms of payment	condizioni f pl di pagamento m	kondıt'tsjonı dı paga'mentɔ
testimonial	attestato m del datore di lavoro m	attes'tatɔ del da'tore dı la'vɔrɔ
third-party insurance	assicurazione f di responsabilità f civile	assıkurat'tsjone dı respɔnsabılı'ta tʃı'vıle
tool	attrezzo m, utensile m	at'trettsɔ, uten'sıle

total (sum) amounting to £ . . .	**somma totale** *f* **per un ammontare** *m* **di £ . . .**	'sɔmma to'tale per un ammon'tare dı £ . . .
trade	**commercio** *m*	kom'mɛrtʃɔ
to trade	**commerciare**	kommer'tʃare
trade custom	**uso** *m* **commerciale**	'uzɔ kommer'tʃale
trade discount	**sconto** *m* **commerciale**	'skontɔ kommer'tʃale
trade fair	**fiera** *f* **commerciale**	'fjera kommer'tʃale
to trade in	**dare in pagamento** *m*	'dare ın paga'mentɔ
trade margin, make-up	**margine** *m* **commerciale**	'mardʒıne kommer'tjale
trade mark	**marchio** *m*	'markjɔ
trade relations	**relazioni** *f pl* **commerciali**	relat'tsjonı kommer'tʃalı
trade union	**sindacato** *m*	sında'katɔ
trader, dealer	**commerciante** *m*	kommer'tʃante
trading result	**risultato** *m* **di gestione** *f*	rısul'tatɔ dı dʒes'tjone
to train, to instruct	**formare professionalmente, istruire**	for'mare professjɔnal'mente, ıstru'ıre
training, education	**formazione** *f,* **professionale istruzione** *f*	format'tsjone, professjo'nale ıstrut'tsjone
training courses for salespersons	**formazione** *f* **per addetti** *m pl* **alla vendita** *f*	format'tsjone per ad'dettı 'alla 'vendıta
to transfer, to remit	**trasferire, rimettere**	trasfe'rıre, rı'mettere
transit, in . . .	**transito** *m,* **in . . .**	'transıto, ın . . .
transmission channels	**canali** *m pl* **di trasmissione** *f*	ka'nalı dı trazmıs'sjone
transport	**trasporto** *m*	tras'pɔrtɔ
transport insurance	**assicurazione** *f* **trasporto** *m*	assıkurat'tsjone tras'pɔrtɔ
transshipment, reloading	**trasbordo** *m*	traz'bordɔ
to treat	**trattare**	trat'tare
trend	**trend** *m*	

trial sample	**campione di saggio** *m*/**di prova** *f*	kɑm'pjone dɪ 'saddʒɔ/dɪ 'prɔva
trustee	**curatore fallimentare** *m*	kurɑ'tore fallɪmen'tare
turnover	**giro** *m* **d'affari** *m pl*, **fatturato** *m*	'dʒɪrɔ d'af'farɪ, fattu'ratɔ
turnover tax	**imposta** *f* **sulla cifra** *f* **d'affari** *m pl*	ɪm'pɔsta 'sulla 'tʃɪfra d'af'farɪ
typist	**dattilografa/o** *f*/*m*	dattɪ'lɔgrafa/ɔ
unanimous(ly)	**unanime**	u'nanime
under patent law	**secondo diritto** *m* **di brevetto** *m*	se'kɔndɔ dɪ'rɪttɔ dɪ bre'vettɔ
under reserve	**con riserva** *f*	kon rɪ'sɛrva
to undercut	**offrire a minor prezzi** *m pl*	ɔf'frɪre a mɪnor 'prɛttsɪ
undermentioned	**sotto indicato**	'sɔttɔ ɪndɪ'katɔ
to underwrite a risk	**assicurare contro il rischio** *m*	assɪku'rare 'kontrɔ ɪl 'riskjɔ
underwriter	**assicuratore** *m*	assɪkura'tore
unemployment	**disoccupazione** *f*	dɪzɔkkupat'tsjone
unit cost	**costo** *m* **unitario**	'kɔstɔ unɪ'tarjɔ
unit price	**prezzo** *m* **unitario**	'prɛttsɔ unɪ'tarjɔ
to unload	**scaricare**	skarɪ'kare
update	**aggiornamento** *m*	addʒorna'mentɔ
user identification	**identificativo** *m* **utente** *m*	ɪdentɪfɪka'tivɔ u'tɛnte
utility (program)	**utilità** *f*	utɪlɪ'ta
VAT (Value-Added Tax)	**imposta** *f* **sul valore** *m* **aggiunto (IVA)**	ɪm'pɔsta sul va'lore ad'dʒuntɔ pɔstɔ va'kante
valid	**valido**	'valɪdɔ
valuation	**valutazione** *f*	valutat'tsjone
variable costs	**costi** *m pl* **variabili**	kɔstɪ va'rjabɪlɪ
venture capital	**capitale** *m* **di rischio** *m*	kapɪ'tale dɪ 'riskjɔ

via . . .	via . . .	'vɪɑ . . .
to visit a fair	visitare una fiera f	vɪzɪ'tɑre 'unɑ 'fjɛrɑ
visitor at a fair	visitatore della fiera f	vɪzɪtɑ'tɔre 'dellɑ 'fjɛrɑ
vocational training	formazione f professionale	format'tsjone professjɔ'nɑle
to vote for/against	votare per/contro	vo'tɑre per/'kontrɔ
voucher	buono m, documento giustificativo m	'bwɔnɔ, doku'mentɔ dʒustɪfɪkɑ'tɪvɔ'
wage(s)	paga f	'pɑgɑ
warehouse	magazzino m	mɑgɑd'dzɪnɔ
warehouse company	società f magazzini generali m pl	sotʃe'tɑ mɑgɑd'dzɪnɪ dʒene'rɑlɪ
warrant, guarantee	garanzia f	gɑrɑn'tsɪɑ
water transport	trasporto m fluviale/ marittimo	tras'pɔrtɔ flu'vjɑle/ mɑ'rɪttɪmɔ
waybill, consignment note	lettera f di vettura f	'letterɑ dɪ vet'turɑ
wealth tax	imposta f sul patrimonio m	ɪm'pɔstɑ sul pɑtrɪ'monjɔ
well-founded complaint	reclamo m fondato/ giustificato	re'klɑmɔ fon'dɑtɔ, dʒustɪfɪ'kɑtɔ
wholesale price	prezzo all'ingrosso	prettsɔ al' ɪn'grɔssɔ
wholesaler	grossista m, commerciante m	gros'sɪstɑ, kommer'tʃɑnte
without charge	senza addebitamento m	'sɛntsɑ addebɪtɑ'mentɔ
without obligation	senza impegno m	'sɛntsɑ ɪm'peɲɲɔ
word processing	elaborazione f testi m pl	elɑbɔrɑt'tsjone tɛstɪ
work in progress	prodotti m pl in corso m di lavorazione f	pro'dottɪ ɪn 'kɔrsɔ dɪ lavorat'tsjone
to work overtime	fare le ore f pl straordinarie	'fare le 'ore straordɪ'narje
worker participation (in decision-making)	cogestione f	kodʒes'tjone

workforce, staff, personnel	forza *f* di lavoro *m*, personale *m*	'fɔrtsa dı la'vɔrɔ, persɔ'nale
working hours	orario *m* lavorativo	ɔ'rarjɔ lavɔra'tıvɔ
working storage (computers)	memoria *f* lavoro *m*	me'mɔrja dı la'vɔrɔ
works council member	membro *m* consiglio *m* di gestione *f*	'mɛmbrɔ kɔn'sıʎʎɔ dı dʒes'tjone
workshop	officina *f* meccanica *f*	ɔffı'tʃına mek'kanıka
wrapping	imballaggio *m*	ımbal'laddʒɔ
to write off	ammortare	ammɔr'tare
write-head (computers)	testina *f* di stampa *f*	tes'tına dı 'stampa
write-lock (computers), file protection	protezione *m* da scrittura *f*/del file *m*	protet'tsjone da skrıt'tura/del 'fıle
year under review	anno *m* in esame *m*	'annɔ ın e'zame
yield, return	redditività *f*, rendita *f*	reddıtıvı'ta, 'rendıta
zero-rated	senza IVA	'sɛntsa IVA

5

Italian–English Index of Technical Vocabulary

f feminine
m masculine
pl plural

a metà *f* prezzo *m*	at half price
a prezzo *m* di costo *m*	at cost
a Vostre (Vs.)/nostre (ns.) spese *f pl*	at your/our expense

accesso *m* diretto alla memoria *f*	direct memory access
accettare un'offerta *f*	to accept an offer
acconto *m*	down payment, payment on account
accordare una proroga *m*	to grant an extension
accordo *m*	agreement
accreditare	to credit
acquirente *m*, compratore *m*	buyer
acquisire una licenza *f*	to acquire a licence
acquisizione *f*, acquisto *m*	acquisition
acquisizioni *f pl* di ordini *m pl*, ordine *m pl* pervenuti	bookings
acquistare, comprare	to buy, to purchase
acquisto *m*, acquisizione *f*	acquisition
acquisto *m*, compera *f*, compra *f*	purchase
acquisto *m* a prova *f*	sale on a trial basis
acquisto *m* a rate *f*	hire-purchase
addebitare, fatturare	to charge
adempimento *m* del contratto *m*	fulfilment of contract
adottare una mozione *f*	to carry a motion
affari *m pl* concernenti il personale *m*	personnel matters
affidare la rappresentanza *f*	to entrust a firm with the agency
affidavit *m*	affidavit
affisso *m*, cartellone *m*, poster *m*	poster
affrancatura	poster
agente *m*, rappresentante *m*	agent, representative
agenzia *f* pubblicitaria	publicity agency
aggiornamento *m*	update
alimentatore *m*	power supply
alimentazione *m* carta *f*	paper feed
allacciamento *m* via cavo *m*	cable connection
all'attenzione *f* di . . .	for the attention of . . .
allegato *m*	enclosure, attached
amministrare, dirigere	to manage
amministratore *m*, delegato *m*	managing director

ammortamenti *m pl*	depreciations
ammortare	to write off
analisi *f* **di mercato** *m*	market analysis
anno *m* **in esame** *m*	year under review
annuncio *m*, **inserzione** *f*	advertisement
applicarsi	to apply for
apprendista *m/f*	apprentice
apprezzare	to appreciate
aprire un conto *m*	to open an account
aprire una seduta *f*	to open the meeting
archivio *m*	file (computers)
archivio *m* **principale**	master file
area *f* **dell'esposizione** *f*	floor space
arretrati *m pl*	arrears
articolo *m*, **voce** *f*	item
assemblea generale annuale *f*	shareholders' annual general meeting
assemblee *f pl*, **riunioni** *f pl*, **sedute** *f pl*	meetings
assicurare contro il rischio *m*	to underwrite a risk
assicuratore *m*	underwriter
assicuratore *m*, **titolare** *m*, **di una polizza** *f*	policy holder
assicurazione *f*	insurance
assicurazione *f* **contro le perdite** *f* **sul cambio** *m*	insurance against loss on the exchange rate
assicurazione *f* **di crediti** *m pl*	credit insurance
assicurazione *f* **di responsabilità** *f* **civile**	liability insurance (personal)
assicurazione *f* **trasporto** *m*	transport insurance
assistenza *f* **post vendita** *f*	after-sales service
associazione *f* **in partecipazione** *f*, **joint venture**	joint venture
assortire, smistare	to sort
assumere	to employ, to engage, to take on
attestare, certificare	to certify
attestato *m* **del datore** *m* **di lavoro** *m*	testimonial

attività *f pl* **correnti, attivo** *m* **realizzabile**	current assets
attività *f* **di ricerca** *f* **scientifica**	research
attività *f* **di sviluppo** *m*	development (of a product)
attivo *m*	assets
attivo *m* **fisso**	fixed assets
attivo *m* **liquido**	liquid funds
attivo *m* **realizzabile, attività** *f* **correnti**	current assets
attrezzo *m*, **utensile** *m*	tool
aumento *m* **degli utili** *m pl*	profit margin, mark-up
aumento *m* **dei prezzi** *m pl*	price increase
aumento *m* **di stipendio** *m*	rise
automazione *f*	office automation/ computerization
avere in magazzino *m*	to have in stock
avere l'intenzione *f* **di**	to intend to
avviso *m* **di spedizione** *f*	dispatch note
avvocato *m*, **legale** *m*	lawyer, solicitor
azione *f*	share
barile *m*, **botte** *f*	barrel
base *f* **di dati** *m pl*, **database**	database
beneficiario/a *m/f*	beneficiary, payee
beni *m pl* **di consumo** *m*	consumer goods
beni *m* **strumentali** *m pl*	capital
bidone *m*	metal container
bilancio *m*	balance sheet
bilancio *m*, **saldo** *m*	balance
bilancio *m* **annuale, documenti** *m pl* **contabili annuali**	annual financial statement
bolla *f* **di consegna** *f*	delivery note
botte *f*, **barile** *m*	barrel
brevettato	patented
buono *m*, **documento** *m* **giustificativo**	voucher
calcolare	to calculate
calcolatrice *f*	calculator
calcolo *m*	calculation

cambiale *f*	bill of exchange (B/E)
cambiali *f pl* passive	notes payable
cambiale *f* in sofferenza *f*	overdue bill
cambiare la merce *f*	to exchange the goods
campagna *f* pubblicitaria	publicity campaign
campionario *m*	selection of samples
campione *m*, modello *m*, provino *m*	model, pattern, specimen, sample
campione *m* di saggio *m*/di prova *f*	trial sample
campione *m* pubblicitario	free sample
campione *m* senza valore *m*	sample of no commercial value
canali *m pl* di trasmissione *f*	transmission channels
cancellare	to erase (computer data)
capitale *m* di rischio *m*	venture capital
capitale *m* prestito	borrowed capital
capo *m*	boss, foreman
capo *m* del personale *m*	personnel manager
caricare, scaricare	to load, to unload
carico *m*	cargo, freight, carriage
carico *m* aereo	air cargo, airfreight
carreggio *m*, trasporto *m* merci *f pl*	carriage
cartellone *m*, affisso *m*, poster *m*	poster
cartolina *f* con risposta pagata *f*	business reply card
cartone *m*	cardboard box, carton
cash flow	cash flow
cassa *f* da imballaggio *m*, crate	crate
catalogo *m*	catalogue
catalogo *m* di data *f* recentissima	latest catalogue
categoria *f*, grado *m*, classe *f*, qualità *f*	grade
catena *f* di montaggio *m*	assembly line
causa *f*, lite *f*	dispute
causa *f*, processo *m*	lawsuit, litigation
centro *m* della fiera *f*	exhibition centre
certificare, attestare	to certify
certificato *m* d'assicurazione *f*	insurance certificate

certificato *m* di accettazione *f* dello spedizioniere *m*	forwarding agent's certificate of receipt (FAC)
cessione *f* di credito *m*	assignment of a debt
che copre i costi *m pl*	cost-covering
chi lavora a tempo pieno *m*	full-time workers
chi lavora part-time/a tempo parziale *m*	part-time workers
chiarire una posizione *f*	to clarify a position
chiedere un indennizzo *m*	to demand compensation
chiudere un conto *m*	to close an account
chiudere una seduta *f*	to close a meeting
circolare *f*	circular
circostanze imprevedibili *f pl*	circumstances beyond our control
classe *f*, categoria *f*, grado *m*, qualità *f*	grade
classificazioni *f pl*	classifications
clausola contrattuale *f*	contractual clause
cliente *m*	customer
cogestione *f*	worker participation (in decision-making)
collaborazione *f*	co-operation
collo *m*	package
colloquio *m* per un impiego *m*	job interview
commerciante *m*	dealer, trader
commerciante *m* al minuto	retailer
commerciante *m* all'ingrosso, grossita *m*	wholesaler
commerciante *m* su commissione *f*	dealer
commerciare	to trade
commercio *m*	trade
commissionario *m*, intermediario *m*	commission agent
compagnia *f*, ditta *f*, società *f*	business, company, firm
compagnia *f* di assicurazioni *f pl*	insurance company
compartecipazione *f* agli utili *m pl*	profit sharing
compera *f*, acquisto *m*, compra *f*	purchase

competere, concorrere	to compete
competitività f	competition
composizione f, **concordato** m	composition
composizione f **d'una lite** f	commercial settlement of a dispute
compra f, **compera** f, **acquisto** m	purchase
comprare, acquistare	to buy, to purchase
compratore m, **acquirente** m	buyer
compreso, incluso	included
con agevolazione f **fiscale**	tax favoured
con cortese sollecitudine f . . .	convenience, at your earliest . . .
con riserva f	under reserve
concedere/fare uno sconto m	to allow a discount
concernente, circa, quanto a	regarding
concessionario m	franchised dealer
concessione f, **franchise**	franchise
concordato m, **composizione** f	composition
concorrente m	competitor
concorrenza f	competition
concorrere, competere	to compete
condizioni f pl	conditions, terms
condizioni f pl **di acquisto** m	buying conditions
condizioni f pl **di contratto** m	terms of contract
condizioni f pl **di pagamento** m	terms of payment
condizioni f pl **di partecipazione** f	conditions of participation
condizioni f pl **di vendita** f	selling conditions
conferenza f	conference
conferma f **dell'ordine** m	acknowledgement of order
conforme a contratto m	as per contract
conforme a fattura f	as per invoice
consegna f, **fornitura** f	delivery
consegna f, **spedizione** f	consignment, shipment
consegna f **sostituita**	substitute
consegnare	to deliver, to supply
consegnare, fornire un cliente m **con merci** f pl	to supply, to furnish a customer with goods
consegnare entro il termine m **previsto**	to deliver within the specified time

255

consegnatario/a *m/f*	consignee
destinario/a *m/f*	recipient
consorzio *m*, gruppo *m*	concern, group, consortium
consulente *m* fiscale	tax consultant
contabile *m*, ragioniere *m*	accountant, bookkeeper
contabilità *f*	accounting, bookkeeping
contante *m* netto	cash
conteggio *m* del salario *m*, elenco *m* del personale *m*	payroll
contenitore *m*, container	container
conto *m*	account
conto *m* corrente	current account
conto *m* di risparmio *m*/di deposito *m*	savings/deposit account
conto *m* profitti *m pl* e perdite *f pl*	profit and loss account
contratto *m* di consegna *f*	supply contract
contratto *m* di manutenzione *f*	maintenance contract
contratto *m* di venita *f*	contract of sale
contratto *m* d'impiego *m*	contract of employment
il contratto *m* è nullo e senza effetto *m*	the contract is null and void
il contratto *m* scade ...	the contract expires ...
controllare	to control, to check
controllo *m* della qualità *f*	quality control
controllo *m* delle scorte *f pl*	stock control
convenuto	stipulated
copertura *f*	cover
coprire un rischio *m*	to cover a risk
cortesia *f*	courtesy
costi *m pl*	costs
costi *m pl* di produzione *f*	production costs
costi *m pl* indiretti	overheads, indirect costs
costi *m pl* marginali	peripheral costs
costi *m pl* variabili	variable costs
costo *m* efficace	cost effective
costo *m* unitario	unit cost
crediti *m pl* pendenti	outstanding accounts
credito *m*	credit rating
credito *m*, debito *m*	debt

credito *m* a breve/medio/lungo termine *m*	short-/medium-/long-term credit
credito *m* di dubbia esazione *f*	doubtful debt
credito *m* in conto *m* corrente	overdraft
credito *m* inesigibile	bad debt
creditore *m*	creditor
curatore fallimentare *m*	official receiver, trustee
curriculum vitae *m*	curriculum vitae
curriculum vitae breve *m*	personal data sheet
danno *m*	damage
dare diritto *m* esclusivo di vendita *f*	to grant sole selling rights
dare il preavviso *m* a	to give notice, resign
dare in affitto, noleggiare	to lease, to rent out
dare in pagamento *m*	to trade in
dare un sommario *m*	to outline
dare un'ordinazione *f*, commissionare	to place an order
data *f* della fattura *f*	date of invoice
data *f* di rimborso *m*, scadenza *f*	due date
data *f* di spedizione *f*	date of shipment
datore *m* di lavoro *m*	employer
dattilografa/o *f/m*	typist
debito *m*, credito *m*	debt
debitore *m*	debtor
denaro *m* rimborsabile a richiesta *f*	call-money
densità *f*	density
depositare domanda *f* di brevetto *m*	to apply for a patent
descrizione *f* dei prodotti *m pl*	product description
destinatario/a *f/m*, consegnatario/a *f/m*	consignee
detrazione *f* fiscale	tax allowance
di prima qualità *f*	first-class quality
di seconda qualità *f*	second-rate quality
diagramma *m* di flusso *m* dei dati *m pl*	flowchart
difetto *m*, guasto *m*	defect
difetto *m* nascosto	hidden defect

257

dipendente *f/m*, impiegato/a *m/f*	employee
direttivo *m*, **management**	management
direttore/direttrice *m/f*, gerente *m*, dirigente *m*	manager/ess
direttore *m* di stabilimento *m*	plant manager
direzione *f* della fiera *f*	fair management
dirigente *m*	executive, manager/ess
dirigere, amministrare	to manage
diritti *m pl* di licenza *f*, **royalties**	royalties
diritto *m*, domanda *f*	claim
disco *m*	disk (computers)
disco *m* rigido/fisso	hard disk
disoccupazione *f*	unemployment
distinta *f* pesi *m pl*	packing list
distribuzione *f*, vendita *f*, **marketing**	marketing
ditta *f*, società *f*, compagnia *f*	company, firm, business
ditta fornitrice *f*	suppliers, contractors
dividendi *m pl*	dividend
documenti *m pl* contro accettazione *f*	documents against acceptance (D/A)
documenti *m pl* di spedizione *f*	shipping documents
documento *m* giustificativo, buono	voucher
domanda *f*	demand
domanda *f*, diritto *m*	claim
domanda *f* d'impiego *m*	application
drive, unità *f* a (disco *m*, nastro *m*)	(disk drive)
duplicato *m* della lettera *f* di vettura *f*	duplicate consignment note
durata *f* di un contratto *m*	period of contract
edizione *f* per una rivista *f*	issue of a magazine
elaborazione *f* dati *m pl* a distanza *f*	teleprocessing
elaborazione *f* elettronica dei dati *m pl*	electronic data processing (EDP)
elaborazione *f* testi *m pl*	word processing
elenco *m* degli espositori *m pl*	list of exhibitors

elenco *m* del personale *m*, conteggio *m* del salario *m*	payroll
elenco *m* della merce *f*	list of products
elenco *m*, dettagliato specificazione *f*	specification
emettere un assegno *m*	to draw a cheque
emettere una fattura *f*, fatturare	to invoice, to bill
emettere/fare (un assegno *m*)	to issue, to make out (cheque)
entrare in una ditta *f*	to join a firm
entrata *f*, ingresso *m*, input	input
entrate *f pl*, proventi m pl	receipts
equiparare i prezzi *m pl*	to adjust prices
equiparazione *f*, regolare il reclamo *m*	adjustment
errore *m*, sbaglio *m*	fault, error
eseguire un ordine *m*	to execute an order
eseguire una consegna *f*	to effect delivery
esente da tasse *f pl*/da imposte *f pl*	tax-free
esenzione *f* fiscale	tax exemption
esperienza *f* professionale	professional experience
esperto/a *m/f*	expert
esporre	to exhibit, to show
esportare	to export
esportatore/esportatrice *m/f*	exporter
espositore/espositrice *m/f*	exhibitor
esposizione *f*, fiera *f*, mostra *f*	exhibition
essere interessati in	interested, to be . . . in
essere respinto al beneficiario *m*	to bounce (cheque)
essere spiacenti, rincrescere	to regret
estratto conto *m*	statement of account
etichetta *f*	label
fabbisogno *m*, richieste *f pl*	requirements
fabbricare su licenza *f*	to manufacture under licence
factoring	factoring
fallimento *m*, liquidazione *f*	bankruptcy, liquidation
fallire, fare fallimento *m*	to go bankrupt
fare affari *m pl*	to do business

fare fallimento *m*, **fallire**	to go bankrupt
fare le ore straordinarie *f pl*	to work overtime
fare l'inventario *m*	to take stock
fare un assegno *m*	to make out/to issue a cheque
fare un tirocinio *m*	to serve an apprenticeship
fattura *f*	invoice
fattura *f* **commerciale**	commercial invoice
fattura *f* **consolare**	consular invoice
fattura *f* **proforma**	pro-forma invoice
fatturare, addebitare	to charge
fatturare, emettere una fattura *f*	to bill, to invoice
fatturazione *f*	invoicing
fidatezza *f*	reliability
fiera *f*	fair
fiera *f*, **mostra** *f*, **esposizione** *f*	exhibition
fiera *f* **commerciale**	trade fair
fiera *f* **industriale**	industrial fair
fiera *f* **specializzata**	specialized fair
file *f*	file
filiale *f*	branch
firma *f*	signature
foglio *m* **di istruzioni** *f pl*, **volantino** *m*	instruction leaflet
fondare	to establish, to found
fondere, fondersi	to merge
fondo *m* **pensioni** *f pl*	superannuation fund, pension fund
formare professionalmente, istruire	to train, to instruct
formazione *f* **per addetti** *m pl* **alla vendita** *f*	training courses for salespersons
formazione *f* **professionale**	vocational training
fornire un cliente *m* **con merci** *f pl* **consegnare**	to furnish a customer with goods, to supply
fornitore/fornitrice *m/f*	supplier
fornitura *f*, **consegna** *f*	delivery
fornitura *f* **di ricambio** *m*	replacement
forza *f* **di lavoro** *m*, **personale** *m*	personnel, workforce, staff
forzare	to compel

franco di spese *f pl*, **gratis,** **gratuito**	cost-free, free of charge
fusione *f*	merger
garanzia *f*, **mandato** *m*	guarantee, warrant
gerente *m*, **dirigente** *m*, **direttore/direttrice** *m/f*	manager(ess)
gestire un'impresa *f*	to run a business
giro *m* **d'affari** *m pl*, **fatturato** *m*	turnover
giroconto *m*	giro account
grado *m*, **categoria** *f*, **classe** *f*, **qualità** *f*	grade
gratis, franco di spesa *f*, **gratuito**	cost-free, free of charge
grossista *m*, **commerciante** *m* **all'ingrosso** *m*	wholesaler
gruppo *m*, **consorzio** *m*	group, concern, consortium
guasto *m*, **difetto** *m*	defect
holding/società madre *f*	holding/parent company
hostess della fiera *f*	hostess (fair)
identificativo *m* **utente** *m*	user identification
imballaggio *m*	packing, wrapping
imballaggio *m* **al prezzo** *m* **di** **costo** *m*	packing at cost
imballaggio *m* **per** **esportazione** *f*	export packing
imballaggio *m* **per trasporto** *m* **marittimo**	seaworthy packing
imballaggio *m* **speciale**	special packing
immagazzinare	to stock, to store
immediatamente	immediately
impiegato/a *m/f*, **dipendente** *m/f*	employee
impiegato/a commerciale *m/f*	clerk
importare	to import
importatore *m*	importer
importo *m* **in sofferenza** *f*	amount overdue
imposta *f*, **tassa** *f*	tax

imposta *f* di successione *f*	inheritance tax
imposta *f* patrimoniale	property tax
imposta *f* sui profitti *m pl*	tax on profits
imposta *f* sul consumo *m*	excise tax
imposta *f* sul patrimonio *m*	wealth tax
imposta *f* sul reddito *m*	income tax
imposta *f* sul valore *m* aggiunto (IVA)	VAT (Value-Added Tax)
imposta *f* sulla cifra *f* d'affari *m pl*	turnover tax
imposta *f* sulla plus valenze *f pl*	capital gains tax
imposta *f* sulla società *f*	corporation tax
impresa *f* individuale, unico proprietario *m*	sole proprietorship
impresa *f* industriale	industrial plant
imputazione *f* dei costi *m pl* comuni	overhead charges
in anticipo *m*	in advance
in base *f* alla Vs. ordinazione *f*	in accordance with your order
in sofferenza *f*, scaduto *m*	overdue
in transito *m*	in transit
inaugurare una fiera *f*	to open a fair
incluso, compreso	included
indagine *f* del mercato *m*	market survey
indebitamento *m*	indebtedness
indennità *f* accessoria addizionale	fringe benefits
indennizzare	to compensate
indennizzo *m*, risarcimento danni *m*	compensation
indirizzo *m*	address
indirizzo *m* d'avviso *m*	notification address
informare	to inform
informazioni *f pl* dettagliate su	detailed information about
ingiungere il pagamento *m*	to demand payment
ingresso *m*, entrata *f*, input	input
iniziare un'azione *f* legale	to bring an action against somebody
input, entrata *f*, ingresso *m*	input
inserzione *f*, annuncio *m*	advertisement
insolvenza *f*	insolvency

interesse *m*	interests
interesse *m* composto	compound interest
interesse *m* di mora *f*	interest for default
interfaccia *f*	interface
intermediario *m*, commissionario *m*	commission agent
intestazione *f* (di lettera *f*)	printed letterhead
inventario *m*	inventory
investigare	to investigate
investimento *m*	investment
inviare, spedire	to send off, to ship, to forward, to dispatch
invitare al pagamento *m*	to demand payment
ipoteca *f*	mortgage
istruire, formare professionalmente	to instruct, to train
istruzione *f*	education, training
istruzione *f* professionale	training on the job
istruzioni *f pl* di manutenzione *f*	service manual
istruzioni *f* per il funzionamento *m*	operating instructions
istruzioni *f* per il montaggio *m*	assembly instructions
IVA (imposta *f* sul valore *m* aggiunto)	VAT
joint venture, associazione *f* in partecipazione *f*	joint venture
lamentarsi di	to complain about
lavoro *m* a turno *m*	shift work
legale *m*, avvocato *m*	lawyer
legalmente protetto	legally protected
lettera commerciale *f*	business letter
lettera *f* d'intenti *m pl*	letter of intent
lettera *f* di credito *m* (irrevocabile e confermata)	letter of credit (irrevocable and confirmed)
lettera *f* di sollecitazione *f*	reminder, dunning letter
lettera *f* di vettura *f*	consignment note, waybill
lettera *f* di vettura *f* ferroviaria	railway consignment note
lettera *f* pubblicitaria	sales/promotional letter

lettera *f* **pubblicitaria susseguente**	follow-up letter
libro *m* **delle commissioni** *f pl*	order book
licenza *f* **d'importazione** *f*	import licence
licenza *f* **scolastica**	school leaving certificate
licenziamento *m*	dismissal
limite *m* **determinato per prestazioni** *f pl*	deadlines
linea *f* **di comunicazione** *f*	communication line
linguaggio *m* **di programmazione** *f*	programming language
liquidazione *f*	settlement
liquidazione *f*, **fallimento** *m*	bankruptcy, liquidation
liquidità *f*	liquidity
listino *m* **dei prezzi** *m pl*	price list
lite *f*, **causa** *f*	dispute
luogo *m* **di destinazione** *f*	place of destination
luogo *m* **di spedizione** *f*	place of dispatch
magazzinaggio *m*	storage
magazziniere *m*	stock clerk
magazzino *m*	warehouse
maggiorazione *f* **del prezzo** *m*	surcharge
malvolentieri	reluctantly
management, direttivo *m*	management
mandato *m*, **garanzia** *f*	guarantee, warrant
manodopera *f* **avventizia**	temporary staff
manodopera *f* **diretta**	direct labour
mantenimento *m* **del prezzo** *m* **di vendita** *f*	price freeze
manuale *m*	manual
marcatura *f* **di spedizione** *f*	shipping marks
marchio *m*	brand, trademark
marchio *m* **registrato**	registered trade mark
margherita *f* **di stampa** *f*	daisy wheel
margine *m* **commerciale**	trade mark-up
margine *m* **degli utili** *m pl*	profit margin
marketing, distribuzione *f*, **vendita** *f*	marketing
maschera *f*	mask, picture
mastro *m*	master

mastro *m*/libro mastro *m*	ledger
materiale *m* da esposizione *f*	display material
materiale *m* difettoso	faulty material
materiale *m* diretto	direct material
materie *f pl* prime	raw materials
membro *m* consiglio *m* di gestione *f*	works council member
memoria *f*	memory (computers)
memoria *f* a massa *f*	disk storage
memoria *f* a sola lettura *f* (ROM)	read-only memory (ROM)
memoria *f* ad accesso *m* casuale (RAM)	random-access memory (RAM)
memoria *f* di lavoro *m*	working storage (computers)
mercanteggiare	to bargain
mercanzia *f*, merce *f*, merci *f pl*	commodity, goods, merchandise
mercato *m*	market
mercato *m* altamente competitivo	highly competitive market
mercato *m* comune	common market
mercato *m* nazionale	domestic market
mercato *m* unico europeo	single European market
merce *f*, merci *f pl*, mercanzia *f*	commodity, goods, merchandise
merce *f* difettosa	defective goods
merci *f pl*, merce *f*, mercanzia *f*	commodity, goods, merchandise
merci *f pl* alla rinfusa *f*	bulk goods
mettersi in proprio	to set up a business
miscela *f*	blend
misura *f*	size
mittente *m*	consignor, shipper
modello, campione	model, specimen, sample
modificare un contratto *m*	to amend a contract
modulo *m* d'ordinazione *f*, cedola *f* commissione *f*	order form
montaggio *m*	assembly
montare lo stand *m*	to set up a stand
movimento *m* anno stimato *m*	estimated annual turnover

nastro *m* magnetico	magnetic tape
negoziare le condizioni *f pl* di un contratto *m*	to negotiate the conditions of a contract
noleggiare	to rent; to rent out
noleggiare un'area *f* dell'esposizione *f*	to book exhibition space
noleggio *m* stand *m*	stand rental
nolo *m*	forwarding/freight charges
nolo *m* assegnato	freight collect
nolo *m* incluso	freight included
non conformità *f* al campione *m*	non-conformity with sample
nota *f* d'accredito *m*	credit note
nota *f* d'addebito *m*	debit note
notificazione *f*	notification
numero *m* della fattura *f*	invoice number
numero *m* limitato di	number, a limited . . . of
obbligare	to compel
obbligarsi per contratto *m*	to become contractual
offerta *f*	offer, proposal
offerta *f* d'appalto *m*	tender
officina *f* meccanica	machine shop, workshop
offrire a minor prezzi *m pl*	to undercut
offrire a prezzo *m* e condizioni *f pl* fissi	to make a firm offer
offrire salvo approvazione *f*	to offer subject to confirmation
oggetto *m*, riguardo *m*	subject line (letter)
oggetto *m* d'esposizione *f*	exhibit
omaggio *m* di pubblicità *f*	advertising gift, gimmick
onesto/a	honest
operaio/a *m/f*, specializzato/a *m/f*	skilled worker
opporsi a	to object to something
opuscolo *m*	brochure, leaflet
orario *m* di lavoro *m* flessibile	flexible working hours, flexitime
orario *m* lavorativo	working hours
ordinazione *f*, ordine *m*	order
ordinazioni *f pl* a disposizione *f*	orders on hand
ordine *m*, ordinazione *f*	order

ordine *m* anticipato	advance order
ordine *m* del giorno *m*	agenda
ordine no. *m*	order number
ordine *m* permanente	standing order
ordini *m pl*, prevenuti acquisizioni *f pl* di ordini *m pl*	bookings
ordine *m* susseguente	repeat order
organizzare una fiera *f*	to organize a fair
organizzatore *m* della fiera *f*	organizer (of a fair)
output, rendimento *m*, produzione *f*	output
paese *m* di destinazione *f*	country of destination
paga *f*	wage(s)
pagamento *m*	payment, settlement
pagamento *m* a mezzo credito *m* documentario *m* confermato e irrevocabile	payment by irrevocable confirmed documentary L/C
pagamento *m* a mezzo tratta a vista *f*	payment by sight draft
pagamento *m* al recapito *m* della merce *f*	payment on receipt of goods (ROG)
pagamento *m* alla consegna *f*	cash on delivery (COD)
pagamento *m* all'ordinazione *f*	cash with order (CWO)
pagamento anticipato *m*	advance payment
pagamento *m* contro accettazione *f*	payment by acceptance
pagamento *m* contro documenti *m pl*	cash against documents (CAD)/ documents against payment (D/P)
pagamento *m* contro garanzia bancaria *f*	payment against bank guarantee
pagamento *m* mediante assegno *m*	payment by cheque
pagamento *m* parziale	part payment
pagamento *m* restante	payment of the balance
pagare	to pay
pallet	pallet
pareggiare un conto *m*	to balance an account
parola *f* d'ordine *m*, password	password

partecipare ad una conferenza *f*	to attend a conference
partecipare ad una fiera *f*	to participate in a fair
partecipazioni *f pl* commerciali	business partnerships
parti *f pl* contraenti	contracting parties
partita *f* di merci *f pl*	lot
passivo *m*	liabilities
patrimonio *m* netto	equity capital
pena *f* convenzionale	penalties
percentuale *f*	percentage
perdita *f*	loss
periodo *m* addizionale	additional period of time
periodo *m* di produzione *f*	production period
periodo *m* di prova *f*	probation period
personale *m*, forza *f* di lavoro *m*	personnel, workforce, staff
peso *m* lordo	gross weight
peso *m* netto	net weight
pianta *f*	floor plan
pianta *f* della sala *f*	hall plan
pignoramento *m*	attachment
plotter	plotter
polizza *f* di assicurazione *f*	insurance policy
polizza *f* di carico *m* marittima, Bill of Lading	Bill of Lading (B/L)
posizione *f*, posto di lavoro *m*	job, position
posizione *f* di monopolio *m*	monopoly
posta *f* elettronica	electronic mail/E-mail
posto *m* di lavoro *m* posizione *f*	job, position
posto *m* vacante	opening, vacancy
potenziale *m* di vendita *f*	sales potential
potere *m* d'acquisto *m*	purchasing power
prelevare denaro *m* da un conto *m*	to draw money from an account
premio *m*	premium
prendere in affitto, noleggiare	to rent
prendere una decisione *f*	to decide on a motion
prenotare	to book (tourism)
prenotare un'ordinazione *f*	to enter/to book an order
prescrizione contrattuale *f*	period of limitation
presentare istanza *f* di	to file for bankruptcy

presentare una mozione *f*	to bring forward a motion
presentare un'offerta *f*	to submit an offer
presentazione *f*	demonstration
presidente *m/f*	chairperson
presso, c/o	c/o (care of)
prestito *m*	loan
preventivo *m* di spesa *f*	estimate
prezzi *m pl*	prices
prezzo *m* al consumo *m*	consumer price
prezzo *m* al minuto *m*	retail price
prezzo *m* alla produzione *f*	factory gate price
prezzo *m* all'ingrosso *m*	wholesale price
prezzo *m* competitivo	competitive price
prezzo *m* complessivo	all-in price
prezzo *m* di acquisto *m*	purchase price
prezzo *m* di costo *m*	cost price
prezzo *m* di listino *m*	list price
prezzo *m* di sottoscrizione *f*	subscription cost
prezzo *m* di vendita *f*	selling price
prezzo *m* favorevole	favourable price
prezzo *m* fisso	fixed price
prezzo *m* ragionevole	fair price
prezzo *m* speciale	special price
prezzo *m* unitario	unit price
prima *f* ordinazione	initial order
procedimento *m* comune di spedizione *f*	Community Transport Procedure (CTP)
processo *m*, causa *f*	lawsuit, litigation
procuratore *m*	proxy
prodotti *m pl* finiti	finished goods
prodotti *m pl* in corso *m* di lavorazione *f*	work in progress
prodotti *m pl* semilavorati	semi-finished goods
produrre	to make, to produce, to manufacture
produzione *f*	production
produzione *f*, rendimento *m*, output	output
produzione *f* fuori serie *f*	special design
produzione *f* in serie *f*	series production
produzione *f* industriale	industrial production

produzione *f* **singola**	one-off production
profito *m* **lordo**	gross profit
profonda conoscenza *f* **del settore** *m*	in-depth knowledge of the trade
progettazioni *f* **tecniche**	engineering
programma *m* **di fabbricazione** *f*	production schedule
programma *m* **operativo**	operations programme
programma *m* **produttivo**	production programme
prolungare	to prolong, to extend
prolungare un contratto *m*	to extend a contract
promozione *f*	promotion of a (person)
promozione *f* **delle vendite**	sales promotion
proprietà *f*	property
proroga *f*	extension, prolongation
prospetto *m*	prospectus, catalogue
protezione *m* **da scittura** *f*/**del file** *m*	write-lock file
protezione *f* **degli archivi** *m pl*	file protection
protezione *f* **della memoria** *f*	memory protection
proventi *m pl*, **entrate** *f pl*	receipts
provvigione *f*	commission
provviste *f pl*, **stocks** *m pl*, **scorte** *f pl*	inventories
pubbliche relazioni *f pl*, **public relations**	public relations
pubblicità *f*	advertising, commercial
qualificazione *f* **qualifica** *f*	qualification
qualità *f*	quality
qualità *f*, **classe** *f*, **categoria** *f*, **grado** *m*	grade
qualità *f* **buona media**	fair average quality (faq)
qualità *f* **corrente**	standard quality
qualità *f* **d'uso commerciale** *m*	commercial quality
qualità *f* **eccellente/primissima**	outstanding quality
quantità *f*	quantity
quantità mancante *f*	shortage
questionario *m*	questionnaire
quotare prezzi *m pl*	to quote prices
quotazione *f* **prezzo** *m* **corrente**	quotation

raggiungere il quorum	to constitute a quorum
ragioniere *m*, **contabile** *m*	accountant, bookkeeper
ragioniere *m* **professionista** *m*	chartered accountant
rappresentante *m*, **agente** *m*	representative, agent
rappresentanza *f* **generale**	general agency
rata *f*	instalment
rata *f* **di nolo** *m*	freight rate
recapitare	to deliver
recipienti *m pl* **a rendere**	returnable container
reclamo *m*	complaint
reclamo *m* **fondato/giustificato**	well-founded complaint
redditività *f*, **rendita** *f*	return, yield
redditività *f*	profitability
redigere il verbale *m*	to take the minutes
referenze *f pl*	references
registrare	to book, to enter a booking
registrare in conformità *f*	to book in conformity
registrazione *f*	entry
regolamento *m* **della fiera** *f*	exhibition regulations
regolare il reclamo *m*, **equiparazione** *f*	adjustment
regolare un sinistro *m*	to settle a claim
regresso *m*	recourse
relazione *f* **annuale del bilancio** *m*	annual report
relazioni *f pl* **commerciali**	trade relations
rendiconto *m*	statement of earnings
rendimento *m*, **produzione** *f*, **output**	output
rendita *f*, **redditivitá** *f*	return, yield, profitability
reparto *m* **di cambio** *m* (sull'estero)	foreign exchange department
reparto *m* **spedizione** *f*	dispatch department
reputazione *f* **sul campo** *m* **affari** *m pl*	business reputation
responsabilità *f*	liability
responsabilità *f* **per il prodotto** *m*	product liability
rete *f* **di distribuzione** *f*	distribution network
revisione *f*	auditing
revisore *m* **dei conti** *m pl*	chartered accountant

revocare un'offerta f	to revoke an offer
ribasso m, **sconto** m	discount
ricavati m pl, **ricavi** m pl	revenues
ricerca f **di mercato** m	market research
ricevuta f	receipt
richiedere	to request
richiesta f, **domanda** f	inquiry
richiesta f **di informazioni commerciali** f pl	credit inquiry
richieste f pl, **fabbisogno** m	requirements
riconoscere un reclamo m	to allow a claim
ricordare a	to remind somebody of something
riduzione f **di prezzo** m	price reduction
riferimenti (Rif.) m pl	reference (business letter)
rifiutare un reclamo m	to refuse a claim
rifiutare una mozione f	to reject a motion
rifondere, rimborsare	to refund
riguardo m, **oggetto** m	subject line (letter)
riguardo a	concerning
riguardo a una mozione f	to decide on a motion
rimborsare, rifondere	to refund
rimborso m **di spese** f pl	refund
rimborso m **di spese** f pl	refund
rimessa f	remittance
rimettere	to remit
rimozione f	removal
rincrescere, essere spiacenti	to regret
riportare	to carry forward
riporto	brought forward, carry over
riprendere la merce f	to take the goods back
risarcimento m **dei danni** m pl, **indennizzo** m	compensation
risarcire	to compensate
riserva di proprietà f	reservation of title
riserve f pl **legali**	legal reserves
risultato m	result
risultato m **di gestione** f	trading result
ritardo m	delay
riunioni f pl, **sedute** f pl, **assemblee** f pl	meetings

rivolgersi a	to refer to
rotazione *f* **delle scorte** *f pl*	stock rotation
sacco *m*	bag, sack
sala *f* **d'esposizione** *f*	showroom
salario *m*, **stipendio** *m*	salary
saldare un conto *m*	to settle an account
saldo *m*, **bilancio** *m*	balance
sbaglio *m*, **errore** *m*	fault
scadente qualità *f*	poor quality
scadenza *f*, **data** *f* **di** **rimborso** *m*	due date
scadenza *f* **del contratto** *m*	maturity date of contract
scadere	to fall due
scanner *m*	scanner
scaricare	to unload
scatola *f*	can, metal container, case
scelta *f*, **una grande . . . di**	range, a wide . . . of
schermo *m*, **monitor** *m*	screen, monitor
sconto *m*, **ribasso** *m*	discount
sconto *m* **commerciale**	trade discount
sconto *m* **per contanti** *m/* **sconto** *m* **di cassa** *f*	cash discount
sconto *m* **speciale**	special discount
sconto *m* **sulla quantità** *f*	quantity discount
scorte *f pl*, **provviste** *f pl*, **stocks** *m pl*	inventories, stock
SE & O (salvo errori ed omissioni)	E & OE (errors and omissions excepted)
secondo diritto *m* **di** **brevetto** *m*	under patent law
secondo la Vs. ordinazione *f*	as per your order
sede *f* **legale**	registered office
sede *f* **principale/centrale**	head office
sedute *f pl*, **riunioni** *f pl*, **assemblee** *f pl*	meetings
segretaria *f* **di lingue** *f pl*	foreign language secretary
segretario/a *m/f* **(del capo** *m*)	personal secretary
segretario/a di . . . *m/f*	secretary (to XY)
sentenza *f* **iniziale di** **fallimento** *m*	receiving order

senza addebitamento *m*	without charge
senza impegno *m*	without obligation
servizio *m*	service
servizio *m* roll-on/roll-off	roll-on/roll-off service
sicurezza *f*	security
sicuro	sound
sindacato *m*	trade union
sistema *m* operativo	operating system (OS)
sistema *m* operativo (DOS)	disc operating system (DOS)
situazione *f* mercato *m*	market situation
situazione *f* economica	economic situation
slittamento *m*	skid (rollers)
slot *m*	slot (computers)
smistare, assortire	to sort
smontare lo stand *m*	to dismantle a stand
società *f*, dittà *f*, compagnia *f*	company, firm, business
società *f* affiliata/sussidiaria	subsidiary
società *f* madre *f*, holding *f*	parent/holding company
società *f* magazzini *m pl* generali	warehouse company
software *m*	software
soggetto a tasse *f pl*	liable for tax
solvenza *f*	solvency
somma *f*/importo *m* della fattura *f*	invoice amount
somma *f* forfettaria	lump sum
somma *f* totale per un ammontare *m* di £. . .	total (sum) amounting to £. . .
soprattassa *f*, tassa supplementare *f*	surtax
sotto indicato	undermentioned
sottomesso a diritti *m pl* di licenza *f*	subject to payment of royalties
sovvenzione *f*	subsidy
spazio *m*	blank, space
specializzato/a *m/f*, operaio/a *m/f*	skilled worker
specificare la via *f* di spedizione *f*	to specify delivery route
specificazione *f*, elenco *m* dettagliato	specification

spedire, inviare	to forward, to send off, to ship, to dispatch
spedizione *f*, consegna *f*	consignment, shipment
spedizione *f* postale cumulativa	mail circular, mail-shot
spedizioniere *m*	carrier, forwarder
spesa *f* extra	extras
spese *f pl*	expenses, expenditure
spese *f pl* da pagare	accruals
spese *f pl* di amministrazione *f pl*	administration expenses
spese *f pl* di nolo *m*	freight/forwarding charges
spese *f pl* di trasporto *m*	forwarding/freight charges
spese *f pl* di vendita *f*	selling expenses
spese *f pl* e proventi *m* di gestione *f*	operating expenses and income
spese *f pl* fisse	fixed costs
spese *f pl* pubblicitarie	publicity expenditure
spese *f pl* totali	all-in costs
stampo *m*	pattern
stand *m* della fiera *f*	booth
standard *m* industriale	industrial standard
statistica *f*	statistics
stato *m* patrimoniale	financial standing
stipendio *m*, salario *m*	salary
stipulare un contratto *m*	to contract, enter into a contract
stipulare un'assicurazione *f*	to take out insurance
stocks *m pl*, provviste *f pl*, scorte *f pl*	inventories
stornare	to cancel
stornare/disdire un contratto *m*	to cancel a contract, rescind a contract
strettamente confidenziale	strictly confidential
struttura *f* finanziaria	capital structure
subappaltatore *m*	subcontractor
superiore *m/f*	superior
svendere	to sell off
sviluppo *m* commerciale	business development
sviluppo *m* previsto	expected growth
svista *f*, errore *m*	error, oversight

take-over, fusione *f*	take-over, merger
tara *f*	tare
tassa *f*	charge, fee, tax
tassa *f* supplementare, soprattassa *f*	surtax
tasso *m* d'ammortamento *m*	amortization rate
tasso *m* d'interesse *m*	interest rate
tasso *m* della sconto *m*	discount rate
tasso *m* forfettario	flat rate
tastiera *f*	keyboard
termine *m* ultimo	deadline
tessera *f* d'espositore *m*	fair pass
testa *f* magnetica	magnetic head
testina *f* di stampa *f*	write-head
titolare *f/m* d'una polizza *f*, assicuratore *m*	policy holder
titoli *m pl* esigibili	receivables
traffico *m* combinato strada-rotaia *f*	piggyback (combined road and rail) traffic
traffico *m* merci *f pl* a breve distanza *f*	short hauls
traffico *m* merci *f pl* a lunga distanza *f*	long hauls
transito *m*, in . . .	transit, in . . .
trarre allo scoperto *m*	to overdraw on an account
trasbordo *m*	transshipment, reloading
trasferimento *m* dati *m pl*	data transfer
trasferire	to transfer
trasporti *m pl* ferroviari	rail transport
trasporto *m*	transport, freight, cargo, carriage
trasporto *m* aereo	air transport
trasporto *m* alla rinfusa *f*	bulk haulage
trasporto *m* fluviale/marittimo	water transport
trasporto *m* merci *m*, carreggio *m*,	carriage
trasporto *m* su strada *f*	road transport
tratta *f*	draft
trattare	to treat
trend *m*	trend

ufficio *m* di incasso *m*	collection agency
unanime	unanimous(ly)
unico proprietario *m*, impresa *f* individuale	sole proprietorship
unità *f* a nastro *m*, stazione *f*	tape drive unit
unità *f* centrale di elaborazione *f* CPU)	central processing unit (CPU)
uso *m* commerciale	trade custom, business use
d'uso *m* commerciale	accepted in the trade
utensile *m*, attrezzo *m*	tool
utile *m* tassabile	pre-tax profit
utile *m* tasse *f pl* detratte	net profit
utilità *f*	utility (program)
utilizzare un brevetto *m*	to exploit a patent
valido	valid
valore *m* contabile	book value
valuta *f* estera	foreign currency
valutazione *f*	valuation
vendere	to sell
vendere come rappresentante *m* esclusivo	to sell as sole agent
vendere merce *f* in commissione *f* vendita *f*	to sell goods on commission
vendita *f*	sale
vendita *f*, distribuzione *f*, marketing *m*	marketing
vendita *f* con patto *m* di riscatto *m*	sale or return
vendita *f* forzata	compulsory sale
vendita *f* su base *f* di commissione *f*	sales on commission
vendite *f pl*	sales
venditore *m*	seller
verbale *m*, redigere/stendere . . . di	minutes, to take the . . . of
versare	pay into an account
via . . .	via . . .
video *m*, schermo *m*	display, screen
vidimare/legalizzare un contratto *m*	to certify a contract

virgola *f* **mobile**	floating point
visitare una fiera *f*	to visit a fair
visitatore della fiera *f*	visitor at a fair
voce *m*, **articolo** *m*	item
volantino *m*, **foglio** *m* **di istruzioni** *f pl*	leaflet, instructions, handbill
votare per/contro	to vote for/against
zona *f* **di vendita** *f*	sales territory
zona *f* **tariffaria**	tariff zone

6

Index